Militarization and Demilitarization in Contemporary Japan

Militarization and Demilitarization in Contemporary Japan

Glenn D. Hook

London and New York

First published 1996
by Routledge
11 New Fetter Lane, London EC4P 4EE

Simultaneously published in the USA and Canada
by Routledge
29 West 35th Street, New York, NY 10001

Typeset in Times by Florencetype Ltd, Stoodleigh, Devon
Printed and bound in Great Britain by
T.J. Press (Padstow) Ltd, Padstow, Cornwall

British Library Cataloguing in Publication Data
A catalogue record for this book is available from the
British Library

Library of Congress Cataloging in Publication Data

ISBN 0-415-02274-6

To K

Contents

Figures

Series editor's preface

It remains unfortunately true, as the new century approaches, that Japan is an underreported country. Despite significant increases in the amount of information and analysis now available, it remains the case that few aspects of Japan are discussed in comparable depth, or with similar assumptions about familiarity, to discussions of the United States, Britain, or other major countries. Differences of language and culture of course constitute a barrier, though less so than in the past. As the patterns of our post cold-war world consolidate, it is more than ever clear that the regional and global importance of Japan is increasing, often in ways more subtle than blatant. We should, to borrow a phrase from Ronald Dore, start 'taking Japan seriously', but we should do so with the clearest possible perception of the directions in which Japan is heading.

The Nissan Institute/Routledge Japanese Studies Series seeks to foster an informed and balanced, but not uncritical, understanding of Japan. One aim of the series is to show the depth and variety of Japanese institutions, practices and ideas. A second is, by using comparison, to see what lessons, positive and negative, can be drawn for other countries, and a third is to incorporate Japanese experience into the construction of mainstream theory in a variety of fields.

Echoes of Japan's role during the Second World War continue to reverberate around Asia, in part because of Japanese official reluctance to admit responsibility for many atrocious acts committed during that bleak period. During the first half of the 1990s these matters became a matter of public discussion within Japan to a much greater extent than before. The coincidence of the death of the Showa Emperor (Hirohito) at the same time as political change in Japan and the ending of the cold war forms the background to this debate, which reached a peak in 1995 with the fiftieth anniversary of Japan's surrender.

Even though it is economic, not military, expansion by Japan that forms the essence of her regional and global influence, concern over the possibility of a revived Japanese militarism has for many years constituted a sub-theme of reactions to Japan in Asia and elsewhere. The dynamics of Japan's defence policy, torn between constitutional prohibitions, American pressure to rearm, domestic political rivalries and official obfuscation, has long been difficult to understand. The ending of the cold war and the changing political map of Asia adds a further perplexing dimension. In this book Professor Hook explores in detail and depth the clashing pressures to build up and to restrain military capacity in Japan. In doing so he penetrates to the core of the political system and throws light on some of the most sensitive areas in Japanese politics. He thus shows why the wartime legacy remains so divisive and why it has been so difficult to arrive at a new political consensus on defence issues.

J.A.A. Stockwin

Preface

This book's genesis is in the cold war era, although it was completed in the early 1990s, after the euphoria of the cold war's ending had been overshadowed by the Gulf War, the war in the former Yugoslavia, and Russia's internal war in Chechnya. During the intervening years the cold war framework of Japanese politics also had crumbled, and the old certainties of rule under the Liberal–Democratic Party had given way to a confusing array of new parties and coalition governments. Reflecting the change in both the international and domestic environments, the despatch of Japanese Self-Defence Forces (SDF) on peace-keeping operations (PKO) for the first time in 1992 was followed by an intense debate on Japan's place in the world. Such changes were the outcome of a major transition in the role of the SDF and popular responses to their new activities. To many, Japan was well on the way to becoming a 'normal' military power in the post cold-war era.

Nevertheless, despite these changes, mass opposition persisted against the use of the SDF as a military instrument of state policy. When asked in what ways Japan should contribute to international society in the new era, the overwhelming popular response continued to be 'by non-military means'. This did not mean a rejection of the SDF's role in peace-keeping operations, as is evident by their deployment in Cambodia, Mozambique and Zaire. But it did mean a continued resistance to the SDF becoming a regular military force. It meant, more than anything, a rejection of the Japanese military once again becoming an aggressor in international society.

These attitudes have grown out of the experience of the war, particularly the atomic bombings of Hiroshima and Nagasaki, and the 'indigenization' of an anti-militaristic Constitution introduced during the Occupation. The way in which this dual experience has constrained state power in the formulation of defence and security policies is at the heart of this study. It grows out of a fascination with the way that, despite the passage of fifty years, the twin experiences of the war and support for the Constitution continue as a source of legitimization for an anti-militaristic identity for Japan in the nuclear era. It is this, above all else, that challenges the use of the SDF as 'normal' military forces.

My interest has been stimulated over the years through discussions with Japanese friends and colleagues. I would like to thank in particular Sakamoto Yoshikazu, Hatsuse Ryūhei, Takahashi Susumu and Tanaka Hiroshi for insights and support over the years. In the preparation of this book I received valuable advice from David Swain and Aurelia George Mulgan. I am grateful to them for spending the time to comment on my work. Siegfried Kohlhammer has been a willing listener and critic for this and other projects. I take this opportunity to thank him for his intellectual companionship. A special note of thanks is due to Frank Langdon, who has been a source of encouragement for many years. His comments on early drafts were instrumental in clarifying my thinking, especially on Chapter 3. I am grateful to Arthur Stockwin for making this book possible. He kindly invited me to write down my thoughts as a volume in the Nissan/Routledge series, helped me clarify the purpose of my contribution and offered incisive commentary on the text.

Although I have benefited enormously from all of the above, I bear sole responsibility for mistakes in fact and interpretation.

My department at the University of Sheffield granted me the time to complete the writing of a number of chapters in the first semester of 1994/5. I thank Ian Gow, in particular, for making this possible.

The Daiwa Anglo-Japanese Foundation, the Japan Foundation Endowment Committee, the MacArthur Foundation and the Nuffield Foundation have provided financial support in carrying out this research. I thank them and the Faculty of Law, University of Tokyo, where most of my field work has been carried out.

Parts of Chapters 6 and 7 first appeared in earlier versions in the *Journal of Peace Research* (vol. 24, no. 3, 1984) and *Current Research on Peace and Violence* (vol. 7, no. 2/3, 1984 and vol. 10, no. 1, 1987). I thank the editors for permission to use the material in this book.

Finally, following Japanese convention, the names in the text and notes are given with the family name followed by the given name. In writings in English, however, the personal name is followed by the family name. Except for the place name Tokyo, all long vowels are indicated by a macron.

G.D.H.

Introduction

The end of the cold war and the start of coalition governments in the 1990s have brought to the forefront of domestic as well as international concern the recurring question of Japan's global role. Although half a century now has passed since the defeat of militarism in 1945, this question still continues to be raised, both inside and outside Japan. True, the spectacular economic development of the nation especially over the past forty years has lifted the vast majority of Japanese people out of the poverty experienced under militarism, at the same time as the government's export-oriented growth strategy has built up an awareness of the nation's economic role in the world, with ubiquitous made-in-Japans giving 'economic superpower' a concrete meaning to most of us. But the question of Japan's military role is different: fears of a 'revival of militarism', both at home and in other parts of Asia, and international concern over Japan's possible challenge to the United States as a military as well as an economic rival in the twenty-first century, highlight the continuing ambivalence. This suggests the need to investigate the impact of militarization and demilitarization on Japanese defence and security policies in the post-1945 era. For such an investigation will contribute to a deeper understanding of Japan's political and military roles in the world, which are not as well understood as its economic role.

The reason for this situation is complex, involving a curious mixture of popular attitudes, state structures and external pressures, and the way that they have interacted over time in shaping Japanese defence and security policies. For the question of Japan as a military power goes to the very heart of two intertwined issues: first, Japan's 'identity' in the world; second, the 'normality' of the world. The choice of this duo may appear odd as the starting point for a book concerned with military matters, as such studies usually focus on a state's defence policies, or the guns, bombs and tanks at their core.

Certainly, this is part of our concern, too, but the question of Japan's military role in the world cannot be understood fully without taking into account the complex interaction between the people, the state and international society in defining 'identity' and 'normality' in the process of determining defence and security policies.

In one respect, the problem goes back to the meaning of war and defeat to the people, with the aggressive excesses of Japanese militarists and the horrors epitomized by the atomic bombings of Hiroshima and Nagasaki providing the basis for an identity rooted in anti-militarism and anti-nuclearism at the mass level. Similarly, the defeat led to the introduction of an institutional framework for a state identity rooted in these ideals, with the Constitution, especially the Preface and Article 9, reinforcing the popular antipathy towards war, militarism and nuclear weapons.[1] In a mutually reinforcing way, the Constitution came to symbolize the quintessence of anti-militarism and anti-nuclearism as the core of a new identity for the state and society in the aftermath of the nation's physical and ideological defeat. In a sense, giving meaning to the war experience and normalizing the Constitution's ideals have been at the heart of the efforts made by political forces at the national and mass level to create a new identity for Japan in the post-1945 world. In terms of the established practices of international society, however, such an identity was 'abnormal', especially as manifest in concrete policy proposals giving life to constitutional principles, such as the opposition Japan Socialist Party's (JSP) security policy, which was rooted in the ideal of 'unarmed neutrality'.[2]

This brings us to the other crucial aspect of the war and Japan's defeat: the ability of the victors and their domestic collaborators to reinterpret these two meanings in the wake of the new sense of 'normality' emerging in international society. The intensification of the cold war in the late 1940s and early 1950s meant that the process of Japan's 'normalization' commenced during the Allied Occupation (1945–52). For another consequence of war and defeat was the ability of the Occupation forces to reinterpret constitutional principles, in line with the strategic goals of the United States, as well as certain political forces within Japan. So on the instigation of the Occupation Authorities the Japanese government in 1950 established fledgling military forces, the seeds for Japan to start to grow towards becoming a normal military state, and then in 1951 went on to sign a peace treaty and a security treaty centring on the United States. Such actions were viewed by many at the mass level as eroding the ideals and principles of the Constitution and constraining the creation of a new, anti-militaristic identity for Japan. In the intervening years, the security treaty between Japan and the United States has been strengthened, in line with the nation stepping further along the path to becoming a military power in international society. In this way, the process of the Japanese state starting to create a 'normal identity' was rooted in a reinterpretation of the Constitution, and the integration of Japan into the emerging cold war structures.

What the above brings to light is how the intertwining of the dual processes of the demilitarization of the state and society, on the one hand, and the remilitarization of the state within a bilateral alliance relationship, on the other, gave birth to a complex set of contradictions in terms of 'identity' and 'normality', with competitive attempts to legitimize rival concepts of the two unfolding as an integral part of the process of determining the nation's defence and security policies. At the core of this contradiction is the persistent influence of the demilitarization of society, as manifest in popular resistance to an identity as a normal military state. This suggests that the question of Japan's military role in the world needs to be understood by taking into account the normativity at the base of these definitions of identity and normality. Thus, in the broadest sense, the purpose of this book is to shed light on how the uneasy contradiction between the demilitarization of state and society, on the one hand, and the (re)militarization of the state within a bilateral alliance, on the other, has shaped defence and security policies, with the role of 'demilitarized society', as manifest at the mass level in terms of normative preferences, being of central concern.

Over the years, anti-nuclear attitudes rooted in the experiences of the atomic bombings and anti-militaristic attitudes based on support for Article 9 of the Constitution have remained salient at the mass level. These attitudes have influenced defence and security policies at the governmental level, at least to some extent. Nevertheless, during the 1980s and early 1990s the complex interactions between popular attitudes, state structures and external pressures led to the erosion of certain anti-militaristic constraints set in place earlier. Despite popular opposition to concrete policy choices, such as the scrapping in 1987 of the 1 per cent of gross national product (GNP) ceiling on military spending during the premiership of Nakasone Yasuhiro (1982–7), and the initial opposition to the despatch of the MSDF on minesweeping operations after the termination of the Gulf War in 1991, support for the Japanese military establishment and the security relationship with the United States has increased markedly over the past few years. What is the significance of this change?

Reflecting different conceptions of 'identity' and 'normality', two contradictory views of the 1980s build-up of the SDF, the increased commitments under US military strategy and the overseas despatch of forces as part of the nation's 'international contribution' in the post cold-war world have emerged in Japan in the early 1990s. One view holds that, as the anti-militarism of the Constitution remains at odds with the 'common sense' of both the cold war and post cold-war worlds, Japan's new military posture puts it on the road to a 'normal' identity. Namely, the nation at last has begun to shoulder the type of 'international responsibility' that fits its status as a 'big power'. Such a policy is congruent with the flow of history, for big powers are expected to possess military and political power commensurate with their economic power; and, in the contemporary world, where a state's security is constantly under threat, whether in the form of a nuclear attack or the instability of the post cold-war order, Japan's only real option is to maintain an alliance with the United States, share the 'defence burden' and make an 'international contribution' by using its military forces.

The other view holds that, in a world where many countries have already been sucked into the vortex of 'abnormal' militarization processes, the principles of the Constitution provide Japan with the ideals with which to strive towards an alternative identity in the nuclear yet post cold-war era. From this perspective, Japan's true international responsibility is to promote nuclear disarmament and to make an 'international contribution' by non-military means; such a policy, it is argued, is congruent with the Constitution, which embodies the principles of a democratic, non-aggressive state; and, even today, it is possible for Japan to pursue security without relying on an arms build-up or a nuclear alliance with the United States or any other nation.

Of the two views, most extant research has focused on the former.[3] Scholarship in English on the latter's influence on Japanese defence and security policies is rather scant.[4] In a narrow sense, this study aims to help fill this gap. More broadly, the purpose is to examine in what ways anti-militaristic ideas, attitudes and language have played a role in shaping defence and security policies in contemporary Japan. Given that, our aim is not to provide an array of data on the increase in the SDF's military hardware, its relationship to American nuclear strategy or the military role being played by Japanese forces in the post cold-war era, except in so far as is necessary in order to come to a deeper understanding of the role of militarization and demilitarization processes. Nor is it to address the economic aspects of militarization, as seen in the growth of the Japanese arms industry if not in the military–industrial complex; nor, again, is it to examine the claims of a 'Soviet threat' during the cold war 1980s, as manifest most conspicuously in the naval build-up in Asia–Pacific. Rather, the primary purpose of this study is to investigate the 'software' that supports militarization and demilitarization. This focus is a logical consequence of giving primacy to the political, not technical, implications of militarization in contemporary Japan. For it is ultimately mass political actions and attitudes that determine the government's defence and security policies.

More specifically, we are interested in how, and in what ways, the people have responded to demilitarization and militarization. What is the nature of these processes in the cold war and post cold-war era? In what ways have they affected persistence and change in mass attitudes? What political rhetoric has been used in order to legitimize the acceptance or rejection of specific defence and security policies? These questions are the essential ingredients in developing the arguments presented here.

STRUCTURE OF THE BOOK

Few social scientists now maintain that social science is 'value free', especially in the wake of the ending of the cold war. It is thus of foremost importance at the outset of this study to lay down the critical approach taken towards militarization, and to distinguish it from the 'mainstream'. Most studies in English on Japanese military matters accept or even encourage the increase in the Japanese military presence in the world, focus almost exclusively on the role of the state and its agencies, and tend to be driven by explicit or implicit policy concerns, especially as related to the United States. Despite the useful insights that such research has provided, the overwhelming tendency to adopt a top-down perspective centring on the state and the institutions of the state in the formulation of policy has led to a neglect of the link between the state and society, especially the way that ideas, attitudes and the political use of language help to shape state policies. In order to enhance understanding of these less studied aspects of militarization and demilitarization, we thus have tried to balance our investigation of the 'hard' side of Japanese militarization, as evident in the defence build-up during the 1980s and the despatch of troops in the early 1990s, with a more detailed study of the 'soft side', as seen in the values, attitudes, norms, and language used in legitimizing militarization and demilitarization processes.

Accordingly, we commence our study with a section on general approaches to militarism and militarization, on the one hand, and the Japanese approach to these phenonema adopted by intellectuals in the early cold war years, on the other. The two chapters that make up Part I introduce the critical approaches to militarization at the heart of the debate over 'normality' and 'identity'. The approach taken here is to regard militarization from a critical standpoint, where Japanese institutions and practices are examined not as 'a given' but in relation to the operation of underlying social forces. More specifically, Chapter 1 takes up the central concept employed in this study, 'militarization', not to try to provide a definition of militarization capable of encompassing the total scope and multifarious nature of these processes in the contemporary world, but to draw attention to a number of its important dimensions as the backdrop against which to study militarization processes in Japan during the cold war 1980s and beyond. Although in the literature the concept of militarization frequently is used interchangeably with 'militarism', a term employed by both Marxists and liberals, we draw a distinction between these two concepts – namely, that 'militarism' essentially refers to excess, both quantitatively and qualitatively, whereas 'militarization' refers to a dynamic process of increasing military influence. The concept of militarization thus can be employed to study a society where militarism has not yet taken root, as in the United States, where militarization has been most saliently identified in the growth of the military–industrial complex, as well as in Japan, where the erosion of the anti-militaristic structures, attitudes and norms constraining the use of the military as a legitimate instrument of state power are of greater concern.

Chapter 2 is a detailed analysis of three important statements issued in 1949–50 by the Peace Issues Discussion Group (Heiwa Mondai Danwakai), a group of leading intellectuals formed at the time with a view to influencing the policy choices of the Japanese government, particularly the security policy to be adopted after the end of the Occupation. The attempt that the Group made to influence the government's policy by appealing to the masses was rooted in the members' commitment to peace as a reflection on their wartime experiences. The statements that they issued provided the theoretical basis for peaceful coexistence between the two blocs at a time when the intensity of cold war antagonisms ruled out coexistence in the minds of many in the United States and Japan. The Group's proposal of 'unarmed neutrality' – more precisely, unarmed non-alignment – which was rooted in a trenchant analysis of the impact of Japan joining either the Western or the Eastern Bloc, exerted a powerful influence on the security debate at the time. In this sense, the ideas of the Group can be considered as the theoretical 'starting point' of thought on demilitarization as 'normal', for throughout the cold war they provided both the Opposition and the peace movement with a yardstick by which to judge the policies pursued by the Japanese government. Despite the passage of time, these statements still contain powerful insights into the fundamental problem of Japanese identity in the nuclear but post cold-war era. In this we can see the long-term influence of the Group's peace thought in Japanese society.

Part II focuses on the exact nature of militarization and demilitarization in terms of policies, activities and attitudes. Chapter 3 examines the militarization under way in Japan in the cold war 1980s, with particular emphasis on the Nakasone era. At this time, the indices of militarization most easily measured, the increase in military hardware and the boost in military spending, were only part of a much broader and deeper integration of Japanese forces into the US nuclear infrastructure in Asia–Pacific. Such actions led to the scrapping of the 1 per cent ceiling on military spending and the erosion of the restraint on 'self-defence' as understood in the framework of normative constitutional principles. The agreement to export weapons-related technology to the United States led to the weakening of another normative restraint on militarization – the ban on arms exports. The 'free-rider' argument, which was frequently employed as a means to legitimize these closer ties with the United States, is examined from both perspectives, those of Japan and the United States, to show how in many ways the United States is in fact the 'free-rider'. Another impediment to militarization, the piedge not to permit the introduction of nuclear weapons, was further eroded during the 1980s. To what extent these changes were a result of external pressure from the United States, or the autonomous decision of the Japanese government, is a particular point of focus in this chapter as in the next.

Chapter 4 takes up the increasingly active role that the Japanese military has been playing as an instrument of state policy in the post cold-war era. After the 1991 Gulf War this came to include the despatch of the SDF, first in minesweeping operations and then in PKO in Cambodia and elsewhere. In examining the erosion of the principle of not despatching the SDF overseas, we show how this was one part of a longer process of constitutional reinterpretation. Both internal and external pressures were exerted on the government to adopt a new military role at this time, and we again trace the balance between external and internal pressures on the policy-making process. Some of the changes were carried out without passing Diet legislation, as with the decision to despatch minesweepers to the Gulf. But the despatch of ground troops to Cambodia could not go ahead without appropriate legislation. This brought to light the change in the stance of the opposition parties towards a military role for Japan in the world, with the ruling party, a minority in the Upper House, cooperating with the Kōmei Party and the Democratic Socialist Party (DSP) in supporting legislation to deploy the SDF overseas as part of their normal role. This led the JSP to adopt radical tactics as a means to try to prevent the passage of the legislation, albeit without success. In what ways these domestic forces interacted in reshaping Japan's military role in line with a new identity for Japan as an increasingly 'normal' military power is a particular point of focus in this chapter.

Chapter 5 is an attempt to come to grips with the persistence and change in attitudes towards militarization and demilitarization as manifest in support or opposition for defence and security policies, especially during the 1980s and early 1990s. Our premise is that, in the struggle between different understandings of Japanese 'identity' and 'normality', mass attitudes have been of crucial significance in constraining the normalization of the military as a legitimate instrument of state power. We thus turn to examine public opinion polls in regard to revision of the Constitution, especially Article 9; the SDF's necessity, size and budget; the role of the SDF and Japan's international contribution in the post cold-war era; and finally the US–Japan security treaty and nuclear weapons. These polls demonstrate the persistent strength of anti-militaristic attitudes, which remain in areas such as support for Article 9 of the Constitution, resistance to a major build-up in the military, and opposition to Japan's possession of nuclear weapons. At the same time, changes emerge in terms of the greater popular willingness to support the despatch of the SDF in the post cold-war era, especially after the end of the Gulf War. Even so, this is within a framework of restraint, such as the United Nations, and does not necessarily represent popular support for Japan to play an independent military role in the world.

Part III focuses on a particularly neglected area of study: the political role of language and discourse. Thus, Chapter 6 addresses the role that discourse and political rhetoric played in legitimizing militarization during the cold-war era. On the popular level, militarization is largely experienced as part of the information environment. As such, the boundaries of the security discourse and the political rhetoric employed by political leaders in talking about a normal military identity for Japan is a crucial element in the formation of popular attitudes on defence and security issues. One of the tasks of those with vested interests in militarization has been to highlight, shade, or obfuscate certain aspects of reality at the expense of others in an attempt to undermine an essentially anti-militaristic macro-discourse. Euphemisms and metaphors have here proved efficacious. The use of 'advance' rather than 'invasion' in school textbooks illustrates how the government has tried to shape the next generation's attitudes towards Japan's military past. But euphemisms occasionally are replaced with a direct expression in order to highlight rather than obfuscate an aspect of reality, as in the case of the switch from 'partnership' to 'alliance' in referring to US–Japanese relations in the 1980s. At other times political leaders have employed metaphors in order to boost military spending, facilitate a military build-up or strengthen military ties with the United States – 'hedgehog', 'shield and spear', 'unsinkable aircraft carrier' and 'insurance' are examples of metaphors that Japanese prime ministers employed in order to facilitate acceptance of their policies at the mass level in the 1980s. In the 1960s Prime Minister Satō Eisaku had already discovered the political utility of metaphors when he called for the elimination of the people's 'nuclear allergy', a metaphor that we will analyse in detail.

Chapter 7 focuses on the evolution of the anti-nuclear discourse which Prime Minister Satō sought to undermine. This discourse, which centres on victims' perspectives of nuclear war, has served as a solid point of reference for those seeking an alternative to militarization. For the atomic bomb experiences of Hiroshima and Nagasaki have been integrated into an anti-nuclear discourse denying the validity of a purely military approach to security in the nuclear era. The role that activist *hibakusha* (atom-bomb victims) have played in undermining a pro-nuclear interpretation of the bombings as an unavoidable cost in ending the war is crucial here: they have striven to give meaning to their existence by challenging the user's perspective on the atomic bombings by a two-pronged attack, emphasizing America's strategic designs against the Soviet Union and the experimental nature of the air raids as of essence in explaining the decision to drop the bombs. It is against the background of the political challenges to the pro-nuclear discourse that the anti-nuclear discourse has evolved. In the early post-war years,

US censorship restricted the widespread distribution of information on the atomic damage. When information did become widely available, the initial reaction was one of shock at the bomb's cruelty, which led to anti-Americanism. But with the Bikini incident of 1954 the universal significance of the atomic bombings came to be recognized more widely. That the Japanese came to view themselves as victims of the bomb rather than of the Americans is seen by their rejection of a call in the early 1960s by Gensuikyō (Japan Council Against Atomic and Hydrogen Bombs) to oppose only 'capitalist bombs and tests'. By the post cold-war era the universal significance of the atom-bomb experience had been strengthened by expanding the boundaries of the definition of *hibakusha* to embrace other nuclear victims around the world.

The Conclusion ends the book by highlighting a number of points from the preceding chapters as a prelude to examining two of the wider societal influences on the defence and security policies pursued by the Japanese government: education and mass action. The role of education in inculcating pro- or anti-military attitudes in subsequent generations has led to political controversy over the content of education, especially as a result of the Ministry of Education's certification of textbooks. The difference between the pre- and post-inspection textbooks used in schools suggests that the system works to control educational contents, directly or indirectly, as seen in the general emphasis that the texts place on the government's approach to such controversial issues as the constitutionality of the SDF and the legacy of the war. The Japanese peace education movement has been active in protesting against this system as well as in taking the countervailing step of producing materials in order to teach youth about the atomic bombings, the life of the *hibakusha* and other peace–war issues. Many of those involved in the movement consider peace education as well as peace action to be essential ingredients in maintaining a peaceful regime. Peace action took place in response to a variety of issues during the cold-war era, with mass movements during the 1980s focusing on the issue of nuclear disarmament. In the early 1990s, however, the peace movement was dormant. Of significance at this time was the intellectual activity surrounding the publication of a wide array of proposals on Japanese security and Japan's place in the world in the post cold-war era. We end by examining one such proposal aimed at promoting demilitarization and a role for Japan in a regional collective security system.

Part I

1   Militarization: a critical approach

Two specialized agencies of the state, the police and the military, which are duty-bound to protect the lives and property of the citizens, continue to maintain the most significant control of the modern means of violence, despite the profileration of weapons to nationalist and terrorist groups. Certainly in modern industrial states, most threats to domestic peace are met by the police, those to international peace by the military. If we follow Max Weber in regarding the state as a human community claiming a monopoly on the legitimate use of violence,[1] then by definition the state's specialized agencies employ violence legitimately – that is, in the interests and with the sanction of the community – although occasions do arise when either the police or, more often, the military, pose a threat to the very citizens it is charged with protecting. This most saliently occurs as a result of trampling on the people's rights, forcing them to become aggressors or victims, or both. What is more, the indiscriminate aerial bombardment of civilian populations during the Second World War, the use of nuclear weapons and their further development in the post-1945 period suggest that, in a future nuclear war, the very survival of the community that the military is charged with protecting can be imperilled. Two questions thus arise: in what ways can the military be a threat to the citizens, even in carrying out its appointed duty? Second, can the use of nuclear and other indiscriminate weapons be considered the legitimate use of violence?

The critical study of this sort of deleterious impact by the military has traditionally been carried out by employing the concept of 'militarism'. The central thrust of such research is a concern with the military's 'excessive' impact on society and society's 'excessive' faith in military solutions to human problems. 'Militarism' thus arises once a certain normative, albeit sometimes legally defined, boundary between 'normal' and 'excessive' military influence has been crossed.

This understanding of a normatively based 'excess' can embrace the wider academic, societal or international community. The premise of this type of analysis of militarism is that, so long as a situation does not arise in which the military's impact is excessive – as a result of aggressive wars, input into the policy-making process, claim on societal resources, threat to the lives and property of the citizens, and such like – then it does not endanger the state and civil society. In this sense, the existence or influence of a 'normal' military establishment is not part of the problematique in critical studies of 'militarism'.

Especially after the advent of nuclear weapons, however, the question of whether the threat from the military arises solely from 'excess' has been subject to closer scrutiny. For these weapons cast into doubt the very *raison d'être* of the military establishment, even in the post cold-war but not yet post-nuclear world. More precisely, the speed, accuracy and destructive power of modern-day nuclear weapons mean that, once they have been used, the military can no longer perform its assigned task of protecting the state and civil society. Such weapons also pose a threat in terms of accidents, leakage and disposal, not to mention their proliferation to other states. These various threats, together with the continuing reliance of states on 'security-through-strength' type of security policies, mean that the need for critical studies of the military's influence exists even in societies where 'militarism' has not taken root.

The concept of 'militarization' offers a way to analyse the military in this context. By bringing within the purview of study the military's very existence and activities, the problem of the military can be approached critically. Thus, in research on militarization, the normative question of why states do not pursue a non-nuclear security policy, despite the contradiction between increasing weaponry and decreasing security, can be posed. In this sense, the concept provides a means of critically approaching the military in the nuclear era, where military influence not captured by the concept of 'militarism' can be addressed.

In this chapter we will introduce a number of critical approaches to militarization as seen in the West, and then as a prelude to a detailed study of peace thought in Chapter 2, go on to a brief overview of the critique of militarization in Japan, as it developed in the Occupation and early cold war years. Before discussing militarization in these two respects, however, we will first examine the concept of militarism as it has been employed by both Marxists and liberals, with emphasis on the latter. In so doing, we aim to provide an overview of the critical discourse on the military as seen in studies of militarism and militarization, rather than to search for an all-encompassing definition of either of these two concepts.

THE CONCEPT OF MILITARISM

The word 'militarism' was probably coined by Madame de Chastenay in 1816–18.[2] Subsequently, the word or concept has been used in a variety of ways, but common to all these usages is a *critical* approach to the military, most plainly seen in analyses of the military's 'excessive' influence on society.[3] More specifically, the vast majority of research on militarism has analysed critically the military's impact on one of three dimensions – the economic and social structure of capitalist societies, the legal and political system of the state, and the attitude of the citizens towards the ideology and values of the military. Two main approaches have been adopted: the Marxist and the liberal. The former focuses primarily on the first dimension; the latter, on the second and third dimensions.

First, the Marxist approach takes militarism to be a problem of the social and economic structure of capitalist society. More concretely, Marxists analyse how external expansion and internal repression are integral to the development of the capitalist mode of production and class system. With varying degrees of emphasis, the approach shares three distinctive features. To start with, militarism is viewed as a phenomenon peculiar to class societies. Thus Karl Liebknecht, who regards capitalist society as the final stage of the class society, argues that militarism inevitably appears at the pre-socialist stage of development. In other words, militarism is a scourge of capitalist, but not socialist, society.[4] Second, militarism is viewed as a tool of the ruling class, which makes use of the military to pursue its own interests. The work of Lenin, who regards the military as a means to suppress any movements on the part of the proletariat, and as an instrument for external expansion, is representative here.[5] Third, militarism is regarded as a means to facilitate the pursuit of profit, both internally and externally. It was Rosa Luxemburg who pointed to this dual structure of profit-making under militarism. By analysing the mode in which militarism appeared in the historical development of capitalism, Luxemburg demonstrates how imperialist powers employed the military in the grab for colonies in the late-nineteenth century and how, on the domestic front, increased investment in the military sector provided the ruling class with new opportunities for profits.[6]

Next, in focusing upon the legal and political system, liberals are concerned with the functional relationship which should be maintained between the military and the civilian branches of the state in order to guarantee healthy civil–military relations. For liberals view militarism as the product of the military's predominance over the civilians in state affairs. In short, militarism arises when the legal and political constraints on the military are not functioning in accordance with the dictates of civilian control, leading to an excess in the military's political influence. Moreover, in regard to the attitude of the people towards military ideology and values, liberals view the apotheosis of the military at the mass level as a clear-cut sign of militarism. The popularity of military service, uniforms, insignia and songs, as well as the strength of the martial spirit, are representative indicators of the extent to which militarism has taken root in civil society. The relationship between the military and civil society is thus crucial to the liberal discussion of militarism.

Historically, Alfred Vagts' *A History of Militarism* (1937) is a landmark in the study of militarism in the liberal tradition.[7] Theretofore, Anglo-Saxon researchers had tended to consider militarism as a functional problem of maintaining a healthy relationship between the military and the civilian – the problem of civilian control – whereas central European researchers had tended to consider it one of the attitudes of the citizens – the apotheosis of military ideology and values in civil society. It was with the publication of Vagts' work that these two strands of liberal scholarship were united in the 'liberal approach' to militarism.[8]

But 'militarism' has not been simply of academic concern: the defeat of Germany and Japan meant that the Allied Powers faced the practical question of how to deracinate the roots of militarism from the body politic of these two former enemies, at least in the early post-1945 years.[9] It involved not only legal and political reforms to prevent the military from again becoming politically powerful, but also educational reforms to prevent the schools from once again inculcating militaristic values in future generations. In this sense, the Allied forces aimed to prevent the resurgence of militarism by changing the structure of the political system as well as the attitudes of the citizens, in line with a belief that Japan's wartime military activities had been 'excessive'.

In the early post-war years, a lively debate developed in West Germany and Japan on the nature of 'militarism'. This debate, which revolved around how to interpret the 1930s, flourished in an international environment where militarism had been defeated, both physically and ideologically. In this sense, German and Japanese researchers started to study militarism against a background of critical international opinion,[10] quite different from that against which the discussion on militarization took place during the later, cold war years.

In Germany, the debate on militarism opened in 1953 at the XXII Congress of German Historians. At this time Gerhard Ritter, a leading historian, defined militarism as:

1) 'The onesided determination of political decisions by military–technical considerations replacing a comprehensive examination of what is required by *raison d'état*' – which comprised both the military aspect of state policy as well as the moral code. 2) 'The onesided predominance of militant and martial traits in a stateman's or nation's basic political outlook' to the extent that the most important task of a state is neglected, which is 'to create a durable order of law and peace among men, to promote general welfare and mediate continuously in the eternal struggle among divergent interests and claims in domestic affairs and between nations'.[11]

The predominance of the military in the Third Reich thus was not a historical product of the social and economic structure of Germany, but rather an anomaly, divorced from the past. In *The Sword and the Sceptre* he developed his ideas on the nature of German militarism more fully. It was in a critical review of this work by Ludwig Dehio that Ritter's definition of militarism came under attack.[12] For Dehio argued that a policy placing priority on '*raison d'état*' need not differ from a militaristic policy. The policy of the Prussian state from the eighteenth century onwards epitomized the problem for Dehio: the policy was clearly militaristic, despite being formulated in consider-ation of *raison d'état*. From this perspective, the Third Reich was not, as Ritter had tried to argue, an anomaly; it was an outcome of the very historical development of Germany's social and economic structures.

In the case of Japan, the kind of debate witnessed in Germany did not arise in liberal circles as, from the outset, researchers followed the same tack as Dehio in treating militarism as a historical product of the social and economic structure of society. This was the approach adopted by the leading political theorist, Maruyama Masao, who proved particularly influential.[13] Maruyama defined militarism as a condition where the political, economic, educational and cultural aspects of the people's life are subordinated to military considerations.[14] In this sense, militarism is a problem of civil society's subordination to the military, as manifest in the behaviour, attitude and ideology of the people. For Japanese researchers, the problem was not to disown their past, as Ritter seemed to imply, but to try to explain how social and economic structures supportive of militarism could take root in Japanese society.

In this way, the threat from the military has been dealt with in terms of the social and economic structure of society, the function of the legal and political system of the state, and the people's attitudes towards military ideology and values. There are nevertheless certain limitations in employing the concept of militarism to analyse the threat from the military in the contemporary world. In the first place, while militarism is a valuable concept for drawing critical attention to the harmful impact of the military due to excessive influence in affairs of state or in civil society, the latent threat of nuclear war, arms races, proliferation and so on indicate that the existence of the military, as such, requires critical investigation. Second, analysis of the excessive influence of the military tends to be from the static perspective of a system or condition; however, in analysing the threat from the military in the contemporary world, the increase or decrease in the influence of the military needs to be analysed as a dynamic process. Third, in research on militarism the problem of the military tends to be taken up within the boundaries of one state; however, the threat from the military crosses state boundaries, penetrating other societies and influencing the structure of the international system as a whole. Hence an international or transnational, not simply national, perspective is called for.

THE CONCEPT OF MILITARIZATION

The concept of militarization can be used to bring into critical focus the increase in the size, strength or influence of the military as a dynamic process with international or even transnational implications. In particular, the process of change occurring in a society where militarism has yet to sink firm roots – as in the United States and the Soviet Union during the cold war – can be analysed in terms of direct and indirect influences, nationally, internationally and transnationally. For in constructing the global nuclear threat system, the United States and the Soviet Union both experienced militarization processes, at least to some degree, and these processes are dynamically interrelated. Thus, we will next examine how the militarization processes that affected these states have been approached, and then go on to discuss the critique of militarization in early cold-war Japan.[15]

At the outset, we should note that Harold Lasswell warned against the growth of a 'garrison state' in the United States even before the end of the Second World War.[16] Lasswell's fear, which was based on a transnational perspective, grew out of an awareness of the military's burgeoning impact on politics: 'The simplest version of the garrison-state hypothesis is that the arena of world politics is moving toward the domination of specialists on violence.'[17] During the nuclear cold war the United States' 'specialists on violence' developed a threat system centring on the continuing production of nuclear weapons, with militarization processes exerting the most salient impact on the social and economic structures of US society. The concrete manifestation of this impact was the growth of the 'military–industrial complex', which still continues to exert an influence in the post cold-war world.

As we saw above, the liberal approach to the problem of militarism treats the military and the civilian as two separate, independent centres of power, where, in healthy civil–military relations, the civilians control the military. In contrast, the concept of the military–industrial complex is premised upon the *union* of interests between three centres of power – the military, the industrial and the civilian. The concept of the military–industrial complex is thus important for understanding the form that militarization took in post-1945 America.

The expression 'military–industrial complex' can be traced back to President Dwight D. Eisenhower's 1961 Farewell Address to the American people, when he put the nation on 'guard against the acquisition of unwarranted influence, whether sought or unsought, by the military–industrial complex'.[18] However, it was not until the end of the 1960s – that is, until the Vietnam War turned American eyes inwards on the structure of the American state – that the military–industrial complex began to attract widespread attention.[19] John Kenneth Galbraith's approach typifies the attempt that researchers made to come to grips with a phenomenon presumed at odds with America's identity as a democratic state. In this case, Galbraith tried to explain the emergence of the military–industrial complex by reference to the bureaucratization of American life, on the one hand, and the widespread fear of communism, on the other.[20] It was the dynamic interrelationship between these two factors, Galbraith argued, that created a situation where the military, together with a phalanx of industrial allies, could concentrate human and financial resources in their own hands, playing on the fear of the 'communist threat'.

Thenceforth, critical research was carried out on the military's increasing influence on the foreign policy decision-making process, the pressure from the military–industrial complex to boost military spending, the close ties between retired military officers and the arms industry, and so forth. In the 1970s, Dieter Senghaas made a full critique of the nature of the complex by arguing that, in order to fully understand a 'complex' centring on the military, the concept of the military–industrial complex needed to be expanded in scope to include politicians, ideological groups, scientists, engineers and others with vested interests in the military establishment.[21] Senghaas stressed the importance of this expanded definition of the military–industrial complex as a means to come to grips with the various sociopolitical groups supporting militarization processes.

The Soviet Union, too, was not free from the structural impact of militarization processes, indicating that militarization is not a phenomenon peculiar to capitalist societies. The question of whether the USSR's 'military–industrial complex' was similar if not the same as the 'complex' in the United States, has nevertheless been a point of contention. For instance, Vernon Aspaturian, in attempting to apply the concept of the military–industrial complex to Soviet society, implied that the Soviet Union was not much different from the United States.[22] This position was challenged by Egbert Jahn, who criticized the application of an American concept to Soviet society. For Jahn the problem was how to identify a Soviet-type 'complex'.[23] Hence he argued that, although the same kind of vested interests evident in the US arms industry's pursuit of profits did not exist in the Soviet Union, this is not to say that a complex did not exist at all. In fact, as with the United States, a complex with vested interests in militarization processes did exist, but one centring on the Soviet military and bureaucracy, not military and industry, as in the United States.[24] By analysing the structure of socialist society in this way, Jahn was able to highlight how militarization processes were common to both capitalist and socialist societies.

How did the growth of these complexes affect the weapons produced? Mary Kaldor has raised two important points: first, as a result of weapons technology having reached the 'baroque' stage, spin-offs from advances in military technology now rarely benefit the civilian sector.[25] Second, although in this process weapons became more elaborate, complex and expensive, this did not lead to a concomitant improvement in their military effectiveness; in fact, even the reverse was sometimes the case. This provided evidence for both an economic and a military critique of the growth of the military establishment: the existence of the military and the production of ever more sophisticated weaponry generated a negative impact on the socioeconomic structure of society, as epitomized in the US and Soviet complexes during the cold war, at the same time that improvements in weapon technology did not necessarily enhance the security of the state or civil society.

Finally, as mentioned above, the concept of militarization allows the threat arising from the military to be treated as an international or transnational phenomenon, not limited within the boundaries of one state. This is the case with arms transfers, which can produce a negative impact on the producer, the receiver and the international system as a whole.[26] For instance, arms transfers have been one of the ways that the militarily developed and developing countries have been linked together in international or transnational militarization processes. As Robin Luckham has shown,[27] these linkages have exerted a malign influence on developing countries: arms transfers have not only taken resources away from economic development, but they have served also to create a dependent relationship between certain of the developed and developing countries. For along with the transfer of military hardware, which helps to put in place technological dependence, came the transfer of strategic software – that is, the transfer of an ideology, despite differences between the sociopolitical circumstances in the militarily developed and developing worlds. In the cold war, for instance, this revolved around the 'communist as enemy' in the capitalist world, and the 'imperialist as enemy' in the socialist world. In this way, the path of economic development pursued by developing countries often was distorted by militarization processes.

CRITICAL APPROACHES TO MILITARIZATION IN JAPAN

The radical demilitarization of state and society during the early years of the Allied Occupation meant that, in contrast to the situation in the United States and the Soviet Union during the cold war, where militarization processes became rooted firmly in the socioeconomic structures of society, Japan remained relatively free from militarization processes in this respect. Like many developing countries, however, it was linked to international militarization processes as a result of the bilateral relationship with a militarily more developed country, the United States. As we will see in detail in Chapter 3, militarization in post-Occupation Japan, especially in the 1980s, was mainly a process of eroding the normative impediments to a revival of militarism established during the Occupation and intervening years, in line with the strategic interests of the United States. These impediments have functioned to limit the existence and scope of military activities, such that what is considered 'normal' by Japan's allies is considered sufficient or 'excessive' by many at the mass level in Japan. Although numerous political attacks on militarization have unfolded against this background of international linkages, especially within a critique of 'American imperialism', the central arguments can be grouped around three poles, reflecting different, though often overlapping, approaches to the problem of militarization in Japan: (1) the politico–military, (2) the humanist–legal, and (3) the economic. These three discourses on militarization or, more precisely, 'remilitarization', have played a significant role in sustaining a demilitarized identity for Japan.

The politico–military critique, which has perhaps exerted the profoundest influence, is based on a clear-sighted analysis of the fundamental meaning of the atomic attacks on Hiroshima and Nagasaki for the future of Japanese security; that is, the out-and-out vulnerability of state and society in the nuclear era. Recognizing the lasting impact that the development of nuclear weapons and their means of delivery has had on security, Japanese intellectuals in the early cold war years opposed militarization on military grounds: building a strong military establishment or joining an alliance with a military big power cannot, they argued, protect Japan in the event of a nuclear attack. As we will see in Chapter 2, even during the Occupation remilitarization and a security treaty with the United States were opposed on the grounds that, against the background of the emerging cold war, such measures would heighten international tensions between the East and West and might even embroil Japan in a war of American making. Instead of following this well-worn path to try to achieve security, the Heiwa Mondai Danwakai (Peace Issues Discussion Group) proposed promoting peaceful coexistence and unarmed neutrality as an alternative policy. This proposal was based on the understanding that, in the nuclear era, militarizing Japan and tying it into a nuclear security network with the United States or the Soviet Union would not add to the security of the Japanese state and society. Nor would it add to the peace of the region: Japanese troops might once again become aggressors against other Asian nations, perhaps as the 'mercenaries' of the United

States. The fear of Japan again becoming an aggressive military power, expressed both at home and abroad, supported this critique of militarization.

Second, the humanist–legal critique, which is based on a view of human nature and international relations enshrined in the new Constitution, has provided an alternative to the 'strong-eat-weak' logic supporting militarization. The preamble of the Constitution states:

> We, the Japanese people, desire peace for all time and are deeply conscious of the high ideals controlling human relationship, and we have determined to preserve our security and existence, trusting in the justice and faith of the peace-loving peoples of the world.

Therefore, Japanese security is not to be sought in building up conventional or nuclear forces, employing them politically as deterrents or militarily by actual use, but by trusting in the 'peace-loving peoples of the world'. Article 9 of the Constitution, renouncing the right of belligerency and the maintenance of military forces, has been understood as calling for an alternative to dependence on the military as a means to preserve peace. We thus find Kuno Osamu, one of Japan's leading philosophers and anti-war activists, advocating the use of non-violent means – non-violent action, civil disobedience and non-cooperation – as an alternative to a military establishment in preserving security.[28] Others have insisted that the Constitution can serve as a model for human society in the nuclear age, as with the Kyōto Scientists Conference, which was formed in 1962, at a time of rising fear over the danger of nuclear war.[29] Still others have pointed to the right of the individual to resist military service on the grounds of conscience.[30] Whatever the area of concern – delegitimizing the military establishment, pursuing an alternative form of security in the nuclear era, opposing the revival of the conscription system – the humanist–legal approach provided a normative platform from which to launch a critique of militarization during the cold-war era.

Third, the economic critique, which exerted a powerful influence especially in the 1950s, incorporates two kinds of criticism of militarization: militarization as a negative factor in the growth of the Japanese economy, on the one hand, and militarization as a pernicious influence on the improvement of the people's life, on the other. This dual attack on militarization suggests why, even among some of the conservative politicians, support was voiced for constraining the growth of the SDF during the cold-war era. One of the reasons that former Prime Minister Yoshida Shigeru gave for opposing early American requests for Japan's rearmament, for instance, was its weak economic power.[31] From this perspective, the security treaty with the United States offered a way for the conservative governments to maintain a low level of military expenditures. The fear of a pernicious influence on the people's standard of living, on the other hand, was one of the reasons for the labour unions' opposition to remilitarization, particularly during the early post-Occupation years. 'Tax thief!' (*zeikin dorobō*), 'waste!' (*mudazukai*), and so on were common cries when the worker's precious yen was squandered on 'guns' instead of being used for 'butter'. Critics pointed out that, even if remilitarization of the economy did expand employment opportunities, wages would remain stagnant and the conditions of employment poor.[32] Intellectuals, too, criticized Japan's military ties with the United States partly on economic grounds. One of the points emphasized by opponents of the revision of the security treaty in 1960, for instance, was that the new treaty would stimulate the growth of an arms industry and limit the budgetary allocation for education, social welfare and so forth, thereby impinging on the people's everyday lives.[33] It is for this very reason that, with the improvement of employment conditions particularly in the high growth period of the 1960s, the labour unions' opposition to militarization became less strident and the economic criticism of militarization was turned on its head by those supportive of militarization: Japan could have 'guns' as well as 'butter'.

CONCLUSION

In the same way that the concept of militarism is useful for directing a critical eye towards military excess, so the concept of militarization serves to direct attention to the threats arising from the existence and increasing influence of the military. In the case of the United States and the Soviet Union, much of the analysis has focused on the military's impact on the socioeconomic structures of society, as seen in the growth of the military–industrial (bureaucratic) complexes. The proliferation of weaponry after the end of the cold war, and the intense competition to export weapons, particularly to the successful East Asian economies, points to how the military–industrial (bureaucratic) complexes continue to exert a profound influence in the post cold-war world. In this we can see a continued need for further research to be conducted on militarization.[34]

In Japan, the dominant critiques of militarization have highlighted the fundamental incompatibility between achieving security and the existence, not simply excess, of nuclear weapons in the contemporary world, the possibility for cooperation, not only conflict, between different peoples, and the negative influence that militarization can exert on the economy and the people's everyday lives, even if 'guns' and 'butter' are both possible. The three main arguments against militarization – the politico-military, the humanist–legal, the economic – have served to create critical anti-militaristic discourses in Japan, challenging the *raison d'être* of the military as a legitimate instrument of state power and providing the intellectual foundation for a demilitarized Japanese identity. What is more, as the first victims of nuclear war, a number of leading intellectuals took the initiative in the early years of the Occupation to address the problem of Japanese security in the nuclear era. This critique also was bolstered by the humanistic and anti-militaristic principles of the Constitution, as well as by concern with the people's daily lives. It became central to what we will discuss in more detail in Chapter 2 as Japanese 'peace thought'.

At the same time, the anti-militaristic discourses and peace thought developed during the cold-war era, although successful in helping to constrain the government's flexibility on defence and security policies, have lost much of their effectiveness in the wake of changes, both at home and abroad, affecting the Japanese state and society. In the first place, during the 1980s Japan became locked into militarization processes in the Asia–Pacific region. This went hand in hand with more open political support by Japanese leaders for the nation's role in the strategic framework of the United States. The result was the erosion of certain of the normative anti-militaristic principles at the base of the post-war critique of militarization. Likewise, with the end of the cold war, Japan has come to play a more important military role in East Asia and elsewhere. This has gone hand in hand with an increase in political support for Japan becoming a 'normal' military state, especially following the outbreak of the Gulf crisis in 1990 and the first deployment of Japanese forces on PKO in 1992. These are issues to which we will turn in chapters 3 and 4.

2 Demilitarization: the impact of peace thought

Innumerable books and articles have been published in Japan on issues related to the military, security and peace following the defeat of 1945. Although it is difficult to select from among these any one piece of writing as the most influential in shaping Japanese peace thought during the cold war era, any discussion of the topic could not justifiably ignore the work of the Peace Issues Discussion Group (Heiwa Mondai Danwakai, hereafter Danwakai or Group). Three statements that the Group issued between 1949 and 1950 proved particularly influential: 'Statement on war and peace by Japanese scientists', 'Statement on the peace treaty problem by the Peace Issues Discussion Group', and 'On peace, for the third time'.[1] These statements represent an innovative attempt to come to grips with the problem of security in the nuclear era. All three contain prescient insights into cold war militarization processes. This chapter identifies the specific characteristics of the peace thought and values expressed in these statements. In the process, we hope to shed light on the significance of the Group's thought in trying to create a demilitarized Japanese identity in the emerging cold war situation.

The Danwakai was formed in 1948 after a statement, 'Social scientists appeal for peace', was issued by a group of scholars who met in Paris in the summer of 1948 in response to a request by UNESCO to study the causes of tensions leading to war.[2] The group consisted of Gordon W. Allport, Georges Gurvitch and six other distinguished social scientists, including one Eastern Bloc scholar, Alexander Szalia. The Civil Information and Education Section of the Supreme Commander for the Allied Powers (SCAP) passed the UNESCO statement resulting from this meeting to Yoshino Genzaburō, the editor-in-chief of *Sekai*, an influential liberal monthly magazine which had started publication after the defeat.[3] With the help of one of Japan's future leading sociologists and activists, Shimizu Ikutarō,

Yoshino brought together a broad spectrum of Japan's most respected intellectuals from the physical sciences and humanities as well as the social sciences, in order to discuss the issues of war and peace raised by the UNESCO statement.[4] Included among the ranks of the more than fifty intellectuals who came to form the Danwakai were such intellectual giants as Abe Yoshinori, Tanaka Kōtarō, Yanaihara Tadao, Watsuji Tetsurō, Rōyama Masamichi, Nakano Fumio, Kuwabara Takeo, Tsuru Shigeto, Maruyama Masao and Kuno Osamu, to mention some of the more influential senior and younger members. The Group came into formal existence with the signing of the first statement, 'Statement on war and peace by Japanese scientists', which appeared in the March 1949 issue of *Sekai*. The statements to follow, 'Statement on the peace treaty problem by the Peace Issues Discussion Group' (*Sekai*, March 1950) and 'On peace, for the third time' (*Sekai*, December 1950), exerted a tremendous impact on how the debate on the upcoming peace treaty and the security treaty developed, inspiring the radical political parties, the unions and the peace movement.[5] The Danwakai continued to hold meetings throughout the 1950s but, with the publication of 'Statement on the problem of revising the security treaty' (*Sekai*, February 1960), for all intents and purpose its activities came to an end.[6]

There are two major reasons why these statements are worth re-examining at this time. First, they take up the problems of peace and security at the most fundamental level – the level of thought and values – so often omitted in current discussions. More specifically, by examining a number of fundamental questions – what view of reality to adopt in regard to the international situation, what kind of security policy to pursue in the face of the destructive power of atomic weapons, how to think about the relationship between peace and other values in the nuclear era – the Group offered a number of prescient insights into the problems of peace and security. Many of those who now are striving to reshape Japanese identity, with the state becoming a military as well as an economic and political big power, fail to address precisely these kinds of fundamental questions.

Second, in the years immediately following the end of the war Japan was all but completely demilitarized by the Occupation forces. The statements issued by the Group epitomize the independent and creative role that Japanese intellectuals played at this time in proposing security policies based on affirming a future identity for Japan as a demilitarized state. In this sense, the Danwakai's statements can be viewed as a focal point of post-war peace thought on demilitarization, for they were issued in opposition to the practical start of remilitarization at the behest of the United States. Clarifying the strengths and weaknesses of that thought should thus help us to understand the intellectual challenge that Japanese intellectuals mounted against militarization in the early cold war years. The history of the statements themselves strongly suggests that their relevance to the problem of peace and security continued much beyond the debate of the late 1940s and early 1950s: after their debut in *Sekai* at this time, they appeared again appended to the September 1962 issue of the monthly, and once again as part of a special July issue of the fortieth anniversary *Sekai* (July 1985), which was devoted to a discussion of the Group.

In order to draw attention to the relevant aspects of the Danwakai's peace thought, it will help to clarify first the meaning of the Japanese term *shisō*, by introducing a distinction between 'thought' and 'idea'. Then follows an analysis of the Group's statements on peace and security in light of this distinction. Finally, a number of comments on the significance of its ideas are presented.

'THOUGHT' AND 'IDEA'

In elucidating the meaning of 'thought' (*shisō*, in Japanese), we bear in mind the warning of Aoki Shoten's *Tetsugaku Jiten* that 'the content of this term is complex and ambiguous. No precise definition of the term exists, despite frequent use.'[7] Given this lack of an acceptable definition, Heibonsha's *Tetsugaku Jiten* suggests that the meaning of the English words 'thought' and 'idea' are embraced by the Japanese word *shisō*: 'We should note that the meaning of the Japanese term *shisō* extends across these two meanings. Put simply, the former (thought) has a strongly individualistic sense, whereas the latter (idea) gives a strong sense of something objectifiable.'[8]

These two different strands of meaning can be found in the use of 'peace thought' (*heiwa shisō* or *heiwa no shisō*). If we understand the strongly individualistic sense of 'thought' to include subjective and emotional elements, then Tsurumi Shunsuke's 'peace thought' is an apt illustration of the word's usage in this sense. For Tsurumi, 'peace thought' is not simply made up of scholarly and objective analysis of the present situation.[9] It is based on an individual's firm stand against war or their hatred of war:

> What can be relied upon as peace thought is a plan to carry out action (or inaction) against war (or to express hatred of war) based

on one's own understanding of the situation. This understanding, which starts from a determination to oppose war, comes from an analysis of what one sees and hears. This is the sequence for the formation of thought. Although it is not necessary to adopt the same sequence for the expression of thought, peace theory (*heiwaron*) without such subjective involvement cannot be expected to contribute to peace.[10]

Tsurumi is here attacking highly abstract peace theory which fails to pay attention to subjective factors – the individual's commitment to peace.[11] In his view, 'peace thought' must be rooted in an individual's strong antipathy towards war or his or her hatred of war. The members of the Danwakai, who shared with other Japanese the wartime experience of being placed in the position of either 'aggressor' or 'victim', shared such antipathy.

In contrast, the strong sense of an objectifiable element at the heart of 'peace idea' differs fundamentally from the 'peace thought' emphasized by Tsurumi. Two points bear mention: first, an 'objectifiable peace idea' is on a higher plane of abstraction than is 'subjective peace thought', as in the Constitution of Japan, which renounces the state's right of belligerency and the maintenance of land, sea and air forces. Second, 'peace idea' exists irrespective of the 'subjective involvement' of the individual. This does not mean, however, that these two strands of *heiwa shisō* are incompatible; rather, they are complementary. In this sense, 'peace thought' and 'peace idea' are both important in order to understand the characteristics of the Danwakai's *heiwa shisō*.

CHARACTERISTICS OF THE GROUP'S PEACE THOUGHT

The two strands of *heiwa shisō* discussed above are intertwined in the Danwakai's statements on peace and security. Three characteristics of the Group's thinking warrant our atttention: (1) subjective commitment; (2) the necessity and possibility of 'peaceful coexistence' and 'unarmed neutrality'; (3) prioritizing peace as a value.

Subjective commitment

In its first statement, 'Statement on war and peace by Japanese scientists', the Group emphasized that, in order to prevent war, the members should maintain a close and trustful relationship with the people: 'We scientists can achieve something only when we place our trust in the people and walk in step with them.'[12] This commitment to 'walk in step' with the people sprang from a sense of guilt and self-recrimination at failing to devote themselves wholeheartedly to the prevention of Japan's aggressive war:

> Looking back upon ourselves, we Japanese scientists are shamefully aware of the fact that, despite being sufficiently acquainted with the kind of ideas contained in the UNESCO statement, we as a whole succeeded little in serving as a brake upon the country's march into the war of aggression and certainly showed ourselves lacking in both courage and effort in actively attempting to prevent such a war.[13]

This keen sense of responsibility, which was manifest as a strong individual commitment to oppose all war,[14] is in stark contrast to the attitude of the UNESCO social scientists, who comment: 'The scientists whose research has been used in the development of atomic and biological warfare are not themselves responsible for launching a curse upon the world. The situation reflects the forces now determining the uses to which science can be put.'[15] Clearly, the UNESCO social scientists felt no need to impugn the scientists directly involved in the production of the atomic bombs dropped on Hiroshima and Nagasaki. The use of the atomic bomb to end the war against militarism suggests that the UNESCO social scientists were not swayed by the same moral imperative as the Japanese scientists, who were keenly aware of their own responsibility in failing to stop their country's aggressive war. The defeat of Japan, both physically and ideologically, led the Group to raise fundamental questions about the very meaning of war and the role that intellectuals should play in society.

The members of the Danwakai shared with other Japanese the concrete, personal experience of war. Although members of the Group did not actively collaborate with the government in prosecuting the war, as did some intellectuals, they nevertheless felt a sense of individual responsibility for having lacked the courage and effort to try to prevent the implementation of the military regime's policies. Through their own experience, the members knew the difficulty of resistance *after* war breaks out. For this reason, even during the Occupation, they tried to fulfil their responsibility as intellectuals by resisting government policies viewed as likely to heighten the danger of Japan becoming embroiled in another war. In short, the Danwakai brought its 'courage' and 'effort' to bear on preventing the adoption of any policy judged inimical to peace in the nuclear era.

The commitment to 'walk in step' with the people meant that the Group opposed any government policies viewed as likely to exacerbate the danger of the people once again being forced into a situation of becoming either 'aggressors' or 'victims'.[16] This commitment was concretely manifest in efforts to galvanize opinion against the signing of a peace treaty or a security treaty with either one of the two camps, capitalist or communist, and in opposition to the remilitarization of Japan. Instead of becoming locked into one camp in the cold war confrontation between East and West, as implied by the government's preparations to sign what was known at the time as the 'one-sided peace treaty' with the West as well as the US–Japan security treaty, the Group proposed peaceful coexistence, unarmed neutrality and peace treaties with all, i.e. with all former adversaries, including the Soviet Union and the People's Republic of China. This was put forward as the most appropriate security policy for Japan to pursue.

Peaceful coexistence and unarmed neutrality

The Group's proposal of 'peaceful coexistence' and 'unarmed neutrality', which represents 'objectifiable peace ideas', is closely tied to the view of reality that it adopted. This view was given substance through the contributions of Maruyama Masao, one of the Danwakai's leading political thinkers.[17] It can be elucidated in connection with two 'ideal type' views of reality, the 'competitive' and the 'cooperative'. For among those in favour of a 'one-sided peace treaty' with the West and a security treaty with the United States, the competitive view predominated,[18] whereas in the writings of the Danwakai, the cooperative view prevailed.[19] Simply put, the former view gives central place to the Hobbesian analogy of international society as a war of 'all-against-all', where security must be based on military preparations for the 'worst-case scenario', alert to the threat of an enemy's attack. Hence the support for a nuclear alliance. The latter view instead gives central place to the possibility of cooperation between states, where security can be based on trust, with nuclear war as the 'worst-case scenario'. Hence the call for peaceful coexistence. The crucial point is that, for the Danwakai, the latter view is a result of subjective choice in the form of autonomous action, not 'objective reality' in the form of the communist threat. The Group's adoption of the 'cooperative' view thus should not be taken as a sign that the members embraced an optimistic evaluation of the world situation. Quite the reverse. In fact, it was precisely because of their realistic appraisal of the destructiveness of modern warfare that they proposed peaceful coexistence as the normal situation to be strived for between the 'two worlds'. That is why the Group appealed for a change in the perception of reality held by the political leaders of Japan, the United States and the Soviet Union, and a change in behaviour based upon this changed perception. In this the members recognized the crucial role that perception can play in making peaceful coexistence possible. In other words, the Group did not view reality as an objective 'given', but instead as the product of the subjective value judgements and actions of autonomous individuals, who could change reality by pursuing their values. This idea has exerted a profound influence on the development of the critique of militarization in post-Occupation Japan.

The logic of the Danwakai was as follows: if one side acts to promote cooperation, this could encourage the other side to initiate similar action; alternatively, if both sides stick to the same view of reality, believing cooperation between East and West to be impossible, then this assessment will be self-fulfilling. In this sense, the problem of whether or not to adopt the cooperative or competitive view of reality is not merely one of the choice of objective perception; it includes the opportunity for subjective choice, too. Thus, action based on either the 'competitive' or 'cooperative' view of reality can influence the transformation or maintenance of reality – namely, the shape of the international order. The Group believed in the positive significance of the perception of reality adopted, and emphasized the need to adopt a view that affirmed, rather than denied, the possibility of peaceful coexistence between East and West. This is a dynamic, not a static, view of reality,[20] with choice viewed as a tool of rationality as well as a vehicle of intentionality.

With this view of reality as the backdrop, the Danwakai proposed that the government play an active role in promoting cooperation and peaceful coexistence between the 'two worlds' as part of a new Japanese identity. Simply put, Japan should make no enemies on either side, cooperate with both, and work for the peaceful resolution of East–West conflicts. The 'one-sided peace treaty' with the West and the signing of the US–Japan security treaty was diametrically opposed to the policy preferences of the Group. Instead, as detailed in the 'Statement on the peace treaty problem by the Peace Issues Discussion Group', which was issued as a response to news of

Allied efforts to bring about a peace settlement, the Danwakai called for the conclusion of a peace treaty with all former adversaries, economic and political independence, inviolable neutralism, admission to the United Nations and opposition to Japan's provision of bases to a third power.[21]

These proposals resulted from the Group's evaluation of the international impact of signing the 'one-sided peace treaty' and the US–Japan security treaty as serving to heighten international tension. So far from enhancing the security of the Japanese nation, the Group saw that the government's policies would in fact threaten it. For with the advent of nuclear weapons, reducing international tensions that might lead to war, not pursuing policies bound to reinforce bipolarity, was of highest priority. The Danwakai reached this conclusion on the basis of its understanding of the nature of nuclear weapons: nuclear weapons had made war 'outmoded'. As spelled out in 'Statement on war and peace by Japanese scientists': 'Inasmuch as any future war is bound to be atomic and/or biological, humanity literally faces the danger of extinction once war breaks out. It must be said that war has already become an outmoded means completely behind the times.'[22] It was precisely because the Danwakai adopted this perception of reality that it proposed peaceful coexistence and unarmed neutrality.

Although the security policy proposed stemmed from the members' antipathy towards war and their perception of the world situation, particularly as influenced by the advent of nuclear weapons, it was at the same time a concrete expression of the Constitution's anti-militaristic principles.[23] The clause renouncing the right of belligerency and the maintenance of military forces, it should be recalled, was at least partly motivated by the desire of the Allies to punish Japan for the aggressive war. In this sense, the Japanese nation was almost bound to accept the principles of the Constitution, as the Group recognized:

> It is clear enough that, inasmuch as our Constitution stipulates the renunciation of the right to resort to war, and inasmuch as our very existence depends on the goodwill of those powers which brought our wartime leaders to justice in the name of peace and civilisation, the problems of peace and war are of special concern to us ... Although we are deeply disturbed by the present state of the world, we ... at the same time bear the great and difficult responsibility to realise the reconstruction of Japan by peaceful means.[24]

The anti-militaristic principles of the Constitution were none the less not simply accepted as a 'punishment' or a 'gift' of the Allies. The Group rejected such a narrow interpretation of these principles in favour of one meant to transcend their specific historical origins. What it strove to do was to impute a *positive* meaning to these principles as the core of a new identity for Japan in the nuclear era. As asserted in the 'Statement on the peace treaty problem' by the Peace Issues Discussion Group, this meant to promote coexistence between East and West:

> If we are to abide faithfully by the pacifist spirit of our Con-
> stitution, we are required to take a positive attitude in attempting
> to bring about harmony between the two worlds, instead of
> passively adopting our attitude on the peace settlement problem
> in line with the vicissitudes of international politics.[25]

In this way, the Group grappled with the problem of how to give life to the normative principles of the Constitution as the basis for a new identity in tune with the realities of the nuclear era.

Peace as supreme value

By the time the Danwakai published its third statement, 'On peace, for the third time', the confrontation between the 'two worlds' had grown more hostile. In response, the members set down in greater detail their thoughts on the problem of war and peace in the nuclear era. What was called for in the face of the worsen-ing international situation, the Group argued, was to prioritize peace over military means, for 'at present, war has without doubt become the *absolute evil* on earth ... For the people of the world, the preserving and exalting of peace has become a primary objective, without which no other values can be realised.'[26] It follows that

> The idealistic position holding peace to be the supreme value
> and war to be the absolute evil has become, as a result of war
> reaching the nuclear stage, at the same time highly realistic. It is
> appropriate to note the comments made by the American inter-
> national relations specialist, Frederick Schuman, in this regard:
> '*All wars occur because men value certain other things more than
> they value peace.*'[27]

This prioritizing of peace as a value followed from the Group's understanding of how the advent of atomic weapons had radically altered warfare. For it reasoned that, as a result of the tremendous increase in the destructive power of weapons, as witnessed in the atomic bombings of Hiroshima and Nagasaki, no legitimate political objective could be achieved by their use. This led the Group to conclude:

> No ideal on earth is worth pursuing at the cost of world peace. This is so because, as the final outcome of going to war to achieve that ideal, the ideal itself will be destroyed by the unfolding of war's own logic.[28]

In this sense, war could not be used 'as a means' to solve the concrete issue of immediate concern to the Group – the confrontation between the 'two worlds'.[29]

The Danwakai believed that the leaders of the United States and the Soviet Union were aware of the perils posed by war between the 'two worlds'. Any such war, it concluded, would produce 'not one Rome but two Carthages', i.e. not one winner but two losers.[30] In this situation, the 'most appropriate' security policy for Japan to pursue in order to 'maintain independence and autonomy' was one based on 'spiritual and cultural or political and legal methods'.[31] The most realistic course to chart was one designed to uphold peace as the supreme value and peaceful means as the method to solve conflicts. In proposing this course, the value and method were congruent with the normative principles of the Constitution, as the Group recognized: 'Couldn't it be said that the attitude we express naturally arises from the principles of the renunciation of war and demilitarization, as we Japanese firmly pledged to the world in our new Constitution?'[32]

This prioritizing of peace as the supreme value has none the less come in for sharp criticism. In a 1965 discussion between Miyazawa Ki'ichi, later prime minister of Japan, and Sakamoto Yoshikazu, a leading scholar of international politics who follows in the tradition of the Group, Miyazawa had the following to say on the problem of peace as the supreme value:

> Peace itself is not a value to be placed in the supreme position in a value system. The real 'values' are surely freedom and independence ... Peace itself is not a value. If you ask what values should be protected, then wouldn't the answer be freedom and independence? It is preferable to achieve these values in a condition of peace, but this surely does not mean that peace is preferable to everything else.[33]

Miyazawa here touches on two essentially different problems – the problem of the position of peace in a value system and the problem of whether peace is a value or not. Sakamoto's response takes up the latter point, arguing in favour of treating peace as a value:

> I think it is odd not to regard peace as a value. So far as the *individual* is concerned, peace is a condition where his or her life is not in danger. For human beings, life itself is a value, so we cannot simply say that peace is a condition for other values. In war, for instance, when people are placed in a life–death situation, there is the problem of whether they would themselves choose to be in that position. In this sense, I would like the premise of our discussion to be that peace, itself, is a core value.[34]

Depending on the perception of reality adopted, peace as the 'supreme value' or peace as a 'core value', as suggested by the Danwakai and Sakamoto, can be accepted or rejected. The decision centres on the following questions. Is the value of individual human life to be subordinated to some other value? And, if so, can that value be protected or realized without inviting its destruction in war? For Miyazawa, peace is a situation or condition; the values to be protected or realized are 'freedom' and 'independence'. Basic to this ranking of values is the 'better-dead-than-red logic' of the cold war era: it is better to die fighting for 'freedom' and 'independence' than to live under 'slavery'. For Sakamoto, in contrast, war or peace is an individual's problem – whether or not his or her life is imperilled – and involves individual choice. In this sense, the fundamental problem for Sakamoto is whether or not an individual can *choose* to sacrifice his or her individual value (life) for a general value (freedom or independence).

Prioritizing peace as an individual value can thus be seen as part of democratic control over the decision of whether or not to resort to the force of arms, and in case of choosing to do so, whether or not to go nuclear.[35] The fear of the Danwakai was that, even in the new Japan, political leaders who exalted a value at the expense of peace again may lead the nation into war in the name of the pursuit of that value, as had already happened. As a result, the people would be forced into the position of being either aggressors or victims. Alternatively, if peace were prioritized over other values, then, in the name of pursuing the value of peace, the people would be able to reject the political leaders' decision to go to war, and thus take action to protect their own life (value). By making peace the supreme value, therefore, the Group placed highest priority on the citizen's freedom of choice, thereby enhancing their possibility of democratically participating in decisions relating to war and peace – something that they had been deprived of prior to the defeat.

In the modern nation-state the dominant mode of thinking has permitted political leaders, with a modicum of popular control, to protect or pursue the values of their choice, even at the expense of the citizens' lives. In concrete situations, moreover, the power to decide on whether or not to go to war in order to protect or pursue these values lies in the hands of the political leaders, not the citizens. The resulting contradiction, as poignantly described by the Danwakai, is that in protecting or pursuing these values the risk to an individual's life (value) is not distributed equally between the political leaders and citizens:

> In modern wars, despite the fact that the belligerents of both sides constantly emphasise that their only aim is to put an end to the enemy government and a handful of evildoers connected with it, and do not regard the peace-loving citizens as enemies, in reality, as best illustrated in urban air raids, government leaders and agencies are the first to be evacuated to safe areas, while the most terrible suffering is inflicted upon the innocent masses, who wander about with their homes destroyed and their kin lost. This is the irony, or rather the tragedy, of modern war.[36]

From this perspective, prioritizing the peace value was thus a necessary step in order to prevent this unequal exposure to the risk of death, as seen most graphically in war. And, as touched on earlier, by individuals exercising their right to reject war, the Danwakai sought to enhance democratic participation in decisions affecting this risk. With their eyes on the perils of a future nuclear war, the Group did not tackle the thorny question of whether or not 'violence for equality or justice' in wars of independence and such like should be regarded as legitimate. Nor did they address the question of whether or not the use of force against an aggressor who has flagrantly violated international laws and norms should be countenanced. These are major limitations of the Danwakai's peace thought, especially in the context of the post cold-war era. But its position that 'the unfolding logic of war destroys the original ideal' not only applies to nuclear war, but to many wars of independence, which, in the unfolding logic of 'violence for equality or justice', often destroy the very ideals being fought for. In this sense, the Group was able to highlight an issue of perennial concern.

THE SIGNIFICANCE OF THE STATEMENTS

The conclusion of the 'one-sided peace treaty' with the West, the signing of the US–Japan security treaty and the remilitarization of Japan are all concrete evidence of the Danwakai's failure to influence the Japanese government's ultimate choice of security policy. Such a short-term political defeat should none the less not be taken to mean the long-term defeat of the Group's thought. The possibility to promote democratic change, as suggested in its statements, should be noted. As the philosopher Kuno Osamu later argued:

> Even if we accept political defeat, this is not the immediate defeat of thought (*shisō*). Political 'victory' is in fact no more than victory outside the arena of thought, although this may over time result in its defeat. By truly learning from political 'defeat', and improving the principles of thought, political victory may be achieved in the future.[37]

Certainly, the security scheme outlined by the Danwakai did not become the policy of the Japanese government. But this did not mean the death of the Group's peace thought. For the ideas that it proposed can be said to have played a significant role in shaping mass attitudes and promoting mass action on security issues in the cold war era, not to mention the impact on the security policy of the Japan Socialist Party.[38] If we follow Albert Camus in regarding ideas at odds with reality as 'utopian', then the Group's peace thought was indeed 'utopian'.[39] For instead of simply accepting the choice of joining either one of the eastern or western camps, it proposed maintaining autonomy and independence from both under a policy of unarmed neutrality. This approach to security was of dual significance: it allowed Japan to pursue an independent path between the two camps, and it offered a positive alternative to the militarist path that Japan had trodden in the years prior to defeat. In other words, it provided the pillars for a new identity for Japan in the nuclear era which was firmly rooted in the experience of the war and the anti-militarism of the Constitution.

Although the policy of unarmed neutrality was not adopted by the Japanese government, the *idea* of unarmed neutrality was embraced by the socialists and other progressive opposition parties and citizens' groups – as a goal towards which they could strive as well as a standard by which they could criticize the present order. However, as the idea of unarmed neutrality is rooted in the Constitution as well as in the Danwakai's thought, the basis for criticizing the present order was an integral part of that order. In this sense, the effort to realize 'utopia' meant to try to normalize constitutional principles in the face of a ruling party set on fulfilling its obligations as a 'normal' member of international society, as we will discuss in Chapters 3 and 4.

If the 'utopian' principles of the Constitution had been realized, then 'utopia' would have become a normal aspect of Japan's new identity, and Japan would have trodden a quite different political path to the one taken. At this point in time, however, little will come of wondering how Japan could have influenced the international order had the Danwakai's security policy, not that of the conservative elite, been adopted. But one simple fact does bear mentioning: only one security policy can be pursued at one time.[40] In this sense, the 'one-sided peace treaty' with the West and the security treaty with the United States cannot be said to have been the 'best' option. For in any situation more than one option is available. It can, of course, be countered that only plausible options should be considered. From this point of view Japan's only option superficially appeared to have been to accept an early treaty with the West (and the security treaty with the United States). What the Danwakai's statements highlight, however, is how the definition of 'plausible option' differs depending on the perception of reality adopted. In this sense, even though at the time the Group's ideas were not regarded as plausible as the government's policy, with the thaw of the cold war a few years later and the neutralization of Austria, the policy of neutrality became a much more acceptable option in the newly emerging situation than at the height of the Korean War in 1951–2. Even though the Group's policy was not acceptable in 1951, therefore, this may have been different in 1954–5. Irrespective, many Japanese came to regard the ideas of the Danwakai as plausible yardsticks against which to measure security policies in the cold war years and goals towards which to strive.

We can see this by examining the significance of the Danwakai's thought, which embraced both practical and normative elements, on the following three levels: the international level, which entailed the issue of the 'two worlds'; the national level, with the proposal for 'unarmed neutrality'; and the individual level, where the problem of becoming neither 'aggressor' nor 'victim' was of central concern.[41] First, on the international level, the Group was clearly correct in suggesting the possibility of peaceful coexistence between the 'two worlds'. The 'two worlds' coexisted, despite cold war antagonisms, and in the post cold-war era the basis of their antagonisms has largely disappeared. The ideological confrontation between the United States and the Soviet Union did not, as many had argued at the time, preclude cooperation. Throughout the cold war era a majority of Japanese people tended to support peaceful coexistence and a relaxation of tensions between East and West. The government, at least to some extent, also adopted a stance favouring coexistence within the constraints of the security treaty system. In this we can see the longer-term impact of the peace thought articulated by the Group and widely supported at the mass level.

At the national level, the Danwakai's proposal of 'unarmed-neutrality' did not become government policy. Instead, the National Police Reserve and later the Self-Defence Forces were established, the peace treaty with the West was signed and, under the US–Japan security treaty, bases were provided for the exclusive use of the United States. Nevertheless, 'unarmed neutralism' did become the basis for the security policy proposed by the socialist opposition and the peace movement. It should also be noted that, throughout the cold war era, the demilitarized state remained a reference point in discussions on peace and security issues. As a result, fundamental questions seldom asked in 'normal' military states were frequently at the heart of mass-based attitudes. Why a military build-up? For what purpose? For whose benefit? Such questions were raised and continue to be raised in the post cold-war era in Japan. The government's adoption of restrictions on military spending cannot be understood without taking into account the popular attitude at the base of these questions.

At the individual level, the Danwakai put forward the idea that the individual has the right to choose not to become either an 'aggressor' or a 'victim'. This linked democracy and peace as essential to the creation of a new identity for the Japanese people. This line of reasoning provided a theoretical point of departure for the peace movement, which has opposed the security policies pursued by the governments of both Japan and the United States by non-violent means. The few radical elements that eschew the non-violent preference have quickly lost popular support. What this has meant is that, in resisting government policies viewed as likely to endanger peace, both parliamentary and extra-parliamentary tactics have been seen as legitimate. The quintessential point has been to act to promote the realization of a peaceful regime. As Maruyama has stated: 'the people's power of control over the government in order to prevent war' is at the heart of democratic control.[42]

CONCLUSION

From the above discussion it should be clear that, even though the Danwakai's peace thought did not exert enough impact to shape directly the policies adopted by the Japanese government in determining the path to chart in the early cold war years, it still provided a basis for a critical discourse on the military, security policy and Japan's identity in the world. What is most striking about the sort of defence and security policies adopted in the intervening years is how constraints have been placed on the use of the military as a legitimate instrument of state power. The enduring influence of anti-militaristic thought during the cold war is evident in the preservation of Article 9, the ban on the despatch of military forces, the imposition of a ceiling on defence spending, and so on. True, the government has managed to build up one of the most powerful militaries in the world, and gradually erode these constraints. Nevertheless, the military use of the SDF in order to realize state goals still does not enjoy popular legitimacy, even after the end of the cold war. This is a point to which we will turn in Chapter 5. Before discussing persistence and change in mass attitudes, however, let us first address how militarization processes advanced in the 1980s, and then go on to examine the role of the SDF in the post cold-war era.

Part II

3 Militarization in the cold war 1980s

The militarization processes affecting Japan in the 1980s arose in a sociopolitical environment still strongly influenced by the policies of demilitarization and democratization implemented by the Allied Occupation Forces immediately after the defeat. In Chapter 2 we saw how the Danwakai sought to lay an intellectual foundation for the Japanese government's pursuit of a demilitarized policy as part of a new identity for Japan in the emerging cold war, giving life to these twin goals. The war-weary masses supported them overwhelmingly. Under the leadership of the United States, demilitarization had been pushed forward in the immediate years after defeat in four different dimensions: (1) the military, as the armed forces were physically abolished; (2) the political, as the military was banned in the new Constitution and military influence on the policy-making process was eliminated; (3) the economic, as the great arms industry of the *zaibatsu* (business combines) were dismantled; and (4) the social, as the military and all it stood for were rejected by most at the mass level. The attempts that the Allies made to deracinate militarism thoroughly from Japanese soil were bolstered by the implementation of legal, political, economic, social and other reforms, which also enjoyed popular support. Thereafter, these institutionalized impediments to militarism implanted during the Occupation, along with 'peace thought', anti-militaristic mass attitudes and political activities seeking to give life to these ideals, interacted in such a way as to create a mutually reinforcing environment of constraint on the military and its activities. For those forces supportive of an identity for Japan as a 'normal' military big power, therefore, breaking out of these constraints and restoring legitimacy to the military as an instrument of state policy has been the task *sine qua non*.

Militarization in the 1980s thus can be examined in the context of the government's attempt to restore legitimacy to the military in the face of established norms of constraint. What are these constraints? In the first place, during the 1950s the conservative government successfully undermined the anti-militaristic intent of Article 9 by establishing and then, in the ensuing decades, building up the power of the Self-Defence Forces (SDF). Nevertheless, these forces have had to be placed under constraints in terms of budget, weaponry and roles. For as the euphemism implies, the SDF are to be limited to 'self-defence', and are not to take part in 'collective defence' activities. The most important of these constraints have been the ban on the overseas despatch of the SDF, established in 1954; the three non-nuclear principles of not to possess, produce or introduce nuclear weapons into Japan, established in 1967 under the Satō Eisaku administration; and the 1 per cent ceiling on the percentage of the gross national product (GNP) to be spent on defence, established in 1976 under the Miki Takeo administration. What is more, in line with the ideal of Japan as a demilitarized state, other constraints have been imposed in order to restrict the activities of Japanese arms manufacturers, as seen in the tripartite ban on arms exports established in 1967, which prohibited arms exports to communist countries (already covered by Japan's membership in the Co-ordinating Committee of Export Control, or COCOM), countries presently involved in international conflicts and countries bordering on involvement. These principles were reinforced by Miki in 1976, when the scope of the ban was expanded to all other countries and a prohibition on the export of weapon-related technology was added. It is the process of eroding some of these normative principles that symbolizes the nature of militarization in Japan in the cold war 1980s.

First, Japanese militarization was linked more widely to the militarization processes under way in the Asia–Pacific region, themselves only one aspect of the global process of militarization. These international or even transnational linkages were manifest in concrete US demands for Japan to bolster its 'defensive strength' in line with US strategic imperatives in the region, as part of the global strategy against the Soviet Union. The dynamic linkages between these different levels of militarization helped to shape the nature of militarization processes in Japan. Second, the influence of the military in Japanese politics and society was not particularly salient in the 1980s, and the rate of military spending, officially at around 1 per cent of GNP, remained lower than other industrially advanced countries as a percentage of the GNP. It is in this sense difficult to say, as some did both at home and in neighbouring East Asia, that Japan experienced a revival of 'militarism' in the 1980s. Nevertheless, as detailed

below, a marked tendency can be noted at this time for the government to place priority on military policies, as evidenced in the rapid
improvement in both the quantity and quality of the SDF's weaponry,
and the growth in the political power of those supportive of a militarily strong Japan, as symbolized by the election of Nakasone
Yasuhiro in 1982, the first LDP prime minister to have served a term
as the director-general of the Defence Agency. This suggests that,
even though 'militarism' as such did not recrudesce, the existence
and growth of the military and its influence at this time did start to
go beyond popularly accepted normative boundaries. Third, as we
will discuss in Chapter 5, from the mid-1950s onwards a majority of
Japanese people had come to accept, and a minority had struggled
to maintain, the anti-militarism of the 1947 Constitution. In spite of
this, the Nakasone government sought to take a number of initia-
tives aimed at breaking out of the normative constraints imposed
on the military as a legitimate instrument of state policy. In order to
investigate the significance of this dynamic process of change – i.e.
from near zero military establishment after the defeat to an emerging
normal military big power in the 1980s – the policies of the Nakasone
government need to be examined.

THE MILITARY BUILD-UP AND US–JAPAN MILITARY COOPERATION

From the beginning of the 1980s, the militarization of policy, particularly the defence policies pursued by the Nakasone Cabinets
(1982–7), which followed an earlier tendency to increase Japan's
military might and integrate its forces with those of the United States
in the region, was one of the most salient features of militarization
during these years. The defence policies adopted during the interval
direct our attention to how, in the 1980s, the government had begun
to place priority on making Japan into a conventional military big
power, linked into the global strategy of the United States.

Of crucial significance in understanding the exogenous pressures
to strengthen bilateral cooperation between the two Pacific allies is
the formal standing given to the developing military relationship
through the implementation of what are known as the 'Guidelines
for Japan–US defence cooperation', drawn up in November 1978.[1]
As a result of the Guidelines' implementation, Japan not only continued to contribute to US strategy indirectly through the provision
of bases and increased support for US forces deployed on Japanese
soil, but also became much more deeply committed to making a

direct military contribution to the implementation of US strategy in Asia–Pacific. Indeed, the Guidelines can be said to have brought about nearly as much change in the nature of the military relationship between Japan and the United States as would a revision of the security treaty.[2] For instead of limiting US–Japan military cooperation to cases where Japan was exposed directly to military attack, as heretofore, the Guidelines expanded the range of cooperation to include (1) preemptive defence against attack, (2) cases of possible military attack against Japan, and (3) situations in the Far East judged to exert a serious influence on the security of Japan.

Despite these enormous changes, the Guidelines were exposed neither to political debate nor ratified by the Diet, simply being passed by the Cabinet. Avoiding public debate and Diet ratification of a controversial measure related to military cooperation between Japan and the United States has a long history, going back to the Occupation. At that time, the debate over the San Francisco peace treaty and the security treaty was fierce, as we have noted in Chapter 2, but the Administrative Agreement, stipulating the exact form that the US military presence in Japan would take, was kept secret until after it was signed, and never subject to Diet ratification. In this sense, the Guidelines can be seen as a further challenge to democratic control, as the newly emerging military relationship with the United States, which gained legitimacy through the Japanese Cabinet, took precedence over the anti-militaristic Constitution, which ultimately gains legitimacy through the Japanese people. As we shall see below, the new Status of Force Agreement, signed on the basis of Article VI of the revised security treaty, and similarly not subject to Diet ratification or popular discussion, was given new meaning in the 1980s as a way to deal with the US demand for the government to cooperate financially in maintaining the US presence in Japan.

The changes in the nature of Japan's military commitment to this newly emerging relationship are clear from the qualitative and quantitative improvement in the SDF's weaponry as well as in the increased military cooperation between the two countries. In the first place, the qualitative and quantitative improvement in the armed forces is evident from the acquisitions made by the Maritime Self-Defence Forces (MSDF) and Air Self-Defence Forces (ASDF) of modern, highly sophisticated military equipment.[3] In order to provide the MSDF with submarine detection capability, for instance, a large number of P-3C Orion anti-submarine patrol planes were acquired during the 1980s, starting with five in 1982, five in 1983, five in 1984, seven in 1985, ten in 1986 and nine in 1987, for a total number of ninety-four by 1993. This build-up of P-3Cs followed a visit to the United States in May 1981 by Prime Minister Nakasone's predecessor, Suzuki Zenkō, who pledged to protect the sea lines of communication (SLOC). At the time, the government justified this major change in the SDF's force structure in terms of protecting merchant shipping bringing oil from the Middle East, and carrying Japanese finished goods to other parts of the world. But this emphasis on the protection of Japan's own economic interests was only part of the reason for these acquisitions. It was a discourse that sought to ameliorate criticism when the MSDF began to engage actively in patrolling the SLOC up to one thousand nautical miles from Japan, bringing within range Vietnam, the Philippines and other Asian nations. For the strength of the popular opposition to Japan becoming more deeply involved in the cold war nuclear confrontation between the United States and the Soviet Union created a need to obfuscate the more immediate reason. This was the deployment of these weapons against the Soviet Union as part of US global strategy.[4] The P-3Cs gave the MSDF the ability to track Soviet submarines in the Pacific Ocean, East China Sea, Sea of Japan and Sea of Okhotsk, and, in an emergency, cooperate with US forces in blockading the three straits of Tsugaru, Sōya and Tsushima.[5] This integration of Japan into US strategy challenged directly the interpretation of the Constitution as only permitting the SDF a role in 'self defence', not 'collective defence', and subverted the original intent of the revised security treaty, which limited joint defence to the protection of 'territories under the administration of Japan' (Article V; see Appendix 3). At the same time, this change in the SDF's role began to erode one of the most important normative premises of the commitment not to become a normal military big power, namely, to refrain from despatching the SDF overseas. As we will see in Chapter 4, after the end of the cold war the government was able to despatch the Ground Self Defence Forces (GSDF) too.

Likewise, the ASDF purchased the E-2C Hawkeye early warning plane in order to acquire the capability to detect low-flying aircraft as well as direct friendly air operations in defence and attack missions, starting with two in 1982, two in 1983, two in 1984 and two in 1985, for a total of 11 by 1993. The E-2C could be used in an emergency to direct air operations for the 50 or so US F-16 nuclear-capable Falcons deployed at the Misawa Air Base between 1985 and 1987. The ASDF also purchased the F-15 Eagle, starting with 13 in 1982, 17 in 1983, 17 in 1984, 23 in 1985, 12 in 1986, 12 in 1987 for a total of 116 by 1993. The role of this plane was seen to be in possible air-to-air fighter attacks against Soviet T-26 Backfire bombers in the event of war. These acquisitions, too, suggested how the build-up during the cold war 1980s tied Japan ever more tightly into US strategy, undermining the scope of its own military forces to act independently of the United States in the protection of Japan's own security interests.

The extent to which Japan was by the mid-1980s already well on the way to becoming a conventional military big power in terms of weaponry is suggested by the comments of the then head of the US Defense Information Center, former Rear-Admiral Gene La-Rocque, who in 1984 pointed out that Japan's total military force capability compared favourably with that of the NATO allies. For instance, only four NATO allies had more submarines than Japan, and only three had a greater tonnage in destroyers and frigates.[6] Similarly, the Department of Defense 1987 *Report on Allied Contributions to the Common Defense* indicated that, in the Pacific, the Japanese military had over twice the number of destroyers and three times as many anti-submarine patrol planes as the Seventh Fleet, and about the same number of fighters to protect the archipelago as the US military deployed to protect the continental United States.[7]

Military cooperation

Japan's weapons build-up in the cold war 1980s takes on even greater significance when considered along with the heightened level of military cooperation between the Pacific allies. The concrete forms that this military cooperation took were, most importantly, (1) cooperation in military planning, (2) combined military exercises and (3) technology transfer.[8] Most importantly, the Guidelines provided the basis for strengthening cooperation between the two militaries for actual war-fighting.

Military planning

The Guidelines are the basis for research on a number of military contingencies likely to involve joint action by US and Japanese forces.[9] First, research on the type of joint action to be taken should Japan be attacked was started in January 1979, completed in December 1984 and signed by Japan's Chairman of the Joint Chiefs of Staff and the Commander of the American Forces in Japan on 26 December 1984. The results of this research have been classified 'top secret' (*kimitsu*). This is the highest level of classification in Japan (the other two levels being 'secret', *gokuhi*, and 'confidential', *hi*), and even the Diet was not informed of the content. Second, research on the Japanese military's role in a crisis in the Far East, which was started in January 1982, is still continuing. Third, even though not part of the Guidelines, joint research on the defence of the SLOC was started on the initiative of the Defence Agency in March 1983, and completed in December 1986.

Access to information on the type of military planning is almost impossible to obtain, reflecting the increase in the amount of secrecy surrounding military affairs during the 1980s.[10] What has become available, however, indicates the nature of the relationship between the two militaries established at this time. Information on the joint research on the SLOC, which was leaked to a national daily in January 1987, provides insight into the implications for Japanese security of the type of war-fighting jointly envisioned.[11] For part of the scenario is where, as a result of US–Soviet confrontation in the Middle East spreading to the Far East, some 30 per cent of shipping to Japan is destroyed within one to six months of the opening of hostilities, and Japan suffers heavy military losses and the Soviet occupation of Hokkaidō, all by conventional means. The conclusion seems to be that, so long as Japan can hold on, then the United States at some time will be able to launch a counter-attack against the Soviet Union. Irrespective of how realistic such a scenario is, particularly after the end of the cold war, it is important for clearly exposing Japan's position as a forward base in US strategy. Or, as one US official frankly admitted at the time, Japan is a 'picket line' against the Soviet Union.[12] In this sense, Japan continued to contribute to the defence of the US mainland as envisioned by US planners at the time that the original security treaty was signed.

Combined exercises

During the 1980s combined exercises gradually became a routine form of cooperation between the military forces of both countries.[13] The ASDF and the US Air Force started combined exercises – combat training with fighters – in November 1978, just after the Guidelines were introduced, and thenceforth began to conduct exercises on an approximately monthly basis. In the 1985 fiscal year, for instance, the ASDF conducted thirteen and in 1986 twelve exercises, including fighter combat training, air defence combat training, rescue training and a command post exercise.

The MSDF had cooperated with the US navy from 1955 onwards in small-scale anti-submarine and mine-sweeping operations, but more active, large-scale cooperation followed in April 1978, when the aircraft carrier *Midway* participated in combined naval exercises. But it was in 1980 that naval cooperation took a major leap forward, with the MSDF for the first time taking part in the biennial Rim of the Pacific (RIMPAC) exercise. At the time this involved the United States, Canada, New Zealand and Australia, and was expanded to include South Korea in 1990 (New Zealand no longer took part after 1986, following the adoption of an anti-nuclear policy).[14] The MSDF participated in these exercises throughout the 1980s and continues to do so in the 1990s. The size of the Japanese contingent has grown – for instance, the number of personnel increased from 690 in 1980 to 2,140 in 1986, naval vessels from two to nine, and the quality of the eight aircraft improved, with P-2J taking part in 1980 and P-3C in 1986.[15] By the time of the 1994 RIMPAC exercise the Japanese contingent for the first time included the MSDF's Aegis, and the increased cooperation now meant that for the first time two senior MSDF officers were able to take part in command operations aboard the US aircraft carrier *Enterprise*. In line with the Japanese mission of blockading the three straits, combined mine-sweeping exercises were started again in February 1984 after a 13-year lapse, and have since been conducted on a regular basis.

The first time that the Ground Self-Defence Forces (GSDF) participated in combined exercises was in July 1980 at Camp Zama, when a command post exercise was carried out with the US army, although officially the Defence Agency lists a communication exercise between the GSDF and the Marines in October 1981 as the first combined exercise.[16] Of most importance, however, was the start of field exercises in February 1982, when the Yama-Sakura series got under way. Taking part in this type of war games marked the closer integration of Japanese and US ground forces. In a November 1982 exercise, for instance, 500 Japanese and 200 American troops were involved. The scope of the exercises expanded, with the GSDF starting to carry out annual exercises with the American Marines from October 1984. By October 1986 a total of 13,000 Japanese and American military personnel participated in the combined exercise 'Keen Edge 87'. The Yama-Sakura V exercise in November 1983, although not listed as such by the Defence Agency, can also be regarded as the first combined operation involving tri-service representatives from the two nations.[17] Finally, in February 1986 the central command post of the Defence Agency and the military headquarters of American forces in Yokota, Zama and Yokosuka conducted the first combined exercise involving the central command posts.

Technology transfer

Historically speaking, the development of weapons under the US–Japan security system had gone ahead with Japan relying on the transfer of high levels of technology and information from the United States. Such transfers were based on the Mutual Defence Assistance Programme of 1954, the Data Exchange Agreement of 1962 and the Memorandum on Joint Research and Development of 1966. Despite the use of the terms 'mutual', 'exchange' and 'joint', however, the flows of technology and information were only one way, with no transfers from Japan to the United States. This changed in the wake of the adoption of the Guidelines. What with the improvement in the level of Japanese technology, together with the changing needs of US weapons systems, the demand to gain access to advanced Japanese technology led to the signing of a number of administrative-level agreements to increase technological cooperation between the two countries.

By 1983 the Japanese and US governments had signed an agreement on the exchange of technology which officially opened the way for the United States to gain access to Japanese technology with military application.[18] A protocol giving details of the procedures for transferring technology was signed in 1985.[19] These agreements provided the formal gateway for the United States to gain access to Japanese technology in both the public and private sectors: (1) technology in the actual possession of the government (e.g. Defence Agency); (2) technology originally provided by the United States under the licence and technology assistance agreement, which had been improved by either the Japanese government or the private sector; and (3) technology developed independently by the private sector. The Pentagon was interested especially in gaining access to dual-use technology such as very high speed integrated circuits and optical fibres, which could be used in future weapons developments. Japan was seen to have a lead in these high technology sectors. Such technology is essential for the United States in order to improve the speed, accuracy and reliability of the guidance mechanism for missiles and other high precision weapons as well as to improve the computer technology used as part of many sophisticated weapons systems today.[20]

In this way, the ban on the export of arms and weapon-related technology was undermined by making an exception of the United States. True, a number of loopholes in the ban already meant that Japan was involved to a limited extent in the export of weapons and weapon-related technology.[21] This decision is thus of most importance in signalling the formal erosion of a normative principle established as a constraint on militarization processes. What is more, after agreeing in 1986 to permit participation in the Strategic Defence Initiative (SDI), in 1987 the Japanese ambassador to the United States and the US Secretary of Defense signed an agreement setting the conditions for the participation of Japanese companies in SDI research, thereby linking Japanese technology with SDI research too.[22] This symbolized Japan's commitment to closer involvement in next-generation defence systems, as seen in the case of the decision to make an allocation in the 1995 defence budget to carry out research on Theatre Missile Defence (TMT), a sort of scaled-down version of the SDI.[23]

MILITARY EXPENDITURES AND EROSION OF THE 1 PER CENT CEILING

The exogenous pressures for Japan to build up the SDF and develop closer military relations with the United States went hand in hand with a major boost in defence expenditures. As we will discuss below, pressure from the United States, which dubbed Japan a 'free-rider', cannot be ignored in explaining the increase in the defence budget during the 1980s. As this pressure was nothing new, however, the endogenous sources of militarization also need to be examined. More specifically, we need to take into account the role that Prime Minister Nakasone played in actively pushing forward with policies aimed at 'settling the post-war accounts' (*sengo seiji no sōkessan*), a euphemism for undoing many of the reforms introduced during the Occupation, including anti-militarism, and their embodiment in government policy.[24] As prime minister, Nakasone failed in many of his efforts to jettison the normative constraints on the Japanese military and establish Japan as a 'normal state' (*zairaigata kokka*).[25] This is true of his failed attempts to introduce a war measures act, pass a state secrets law[26] and despatch minesweepers to the Gulf, not to mention his renunciation of the cherished goal of revising the Constitution. Nevertheless, despite intra-party voices raised against Nakasone by party elders such as former prime ministers Miki Takeo, Fukuda Takeo and Suzuki Zenkō, and his weak factional position, as well as those of the political opposition and public opinion, he did forge ahead with an increase in military spending, going so far as to breach the 1 per cent ceiling in his last year in office.

The 1 per cent ceiling

The 1 per cent ceiling had been established in November 1976 by the Miki Cabinet in the wake of his administration's earlier decision to adopt the National Defence Programme Outline.[27] As military spending for the preceding decade had been below 1 per cent of GNP (0.9 per cent in 1976), and as a healthy rate of economic growth was predicted for the future (though not in fact achieved), the ceiling was both an indication of the extent to which the budget could still be expanded as well as an expression of the low level of popular support for higher military expenditures. At the same time, the introduction of the ceiling marked the government's success in reshaping the discourse on security to focus on fiscal matters. Although pressure from the Defence Agency had led to the addition of the wording 'for the time being' and 'aim at', thereby weakening the significance of '1 per cent',[28] the figure nevertheless came to embody symbolic significance both at home and abroad. For the Japanese public, '1 per cent' was the figure as close to the 'zero-point perspective' as practicable.[29] In other words, the '1 per cent ceiling' was a symbol of the ideal, demilitarized state as Japan's identity. For those overseas, especially in East Asia, the ceiling was perceived as a symbol of Japan's commitment to eschew becoming a normal military big power.

After a steady decline in the real GNP growth rate (down from around 5 per cent in the late 1970s to around 3 per cent in the 1980s), along with a steady rise in the military budget, Nakasone scrapped the ceiling in the 1987 budget. With a proposed wage increase affecting the SDF in 1985, the percentage spent on the military was expected to exceed 1 per cent in that year, but a five-year periodic review of the basis for calculating the GNP carried out by the Economic Planning Agency, which added to the GNP growth rate, meant that spending remained below 1 per cent in 1985 and 1986.[30] Nevertheless, despite the drop in oil prices and the appreciation in the value of the yen, which in principle allowed the government to keep military outlays below 1 per cent, the Nakasone government pushed through the ceiling, following steady increases from 1980 onwards, with 0.9 per cent in 1980, 0.93 per cent in 1982, 0.99 per cent in 1984, 0.993 per cent in 1986, and finally 1.004 per cent in 1987. As seen thereafter, the 'qualitative limit' established by the government in January 1987, which was based on the Mid Term Defence Plan (1986–90), did not constrain increases in Japanese military spending as did the previous quantitative ceiling, with the 1988 (1.013 per cent) and 1989 (1.006 per cent) budgets both being over 1 per cent.[31] The scrapping of the 1 per cent ceiling thus can be said to have arisen from the political priorities of the Nakasone government.

Likewise, the percentage of the general account devoted to defence-related items steadily increased during the 1980s, despite tight budgetary restrictions after 1981, suggesting that the Ministry of Finance does not necessarily act as a constraint on defence spending in the face of the prime minister's political will.[32] The percentage increased steadily from 5.2 per cent in 1982, through 5.8 per cent in 1984 and 6.2 per cent in 1986, to 6.5 per cent in 1987. Or, to put this into historical perspective, 1982 marked the end of a long-term decline in the percentage spent on the military going back over twenty years. The increase is even more pronounced as a percentage of the government's annual expenditure, with a rise of more than 3 per cent, from 7.3 per cent in 1980, through 7.9 per cent in 1982, 9.0 per cent in 1984 and 10.3 per cent in 1986, to 10.8 per cent in 1987.[33] What is more, this percentage leaves out certain disbursements included in NATO military expenditures, such as the cost of the coast guard, military pensions and base subsidies under the jurisdiction of local authorities. If strategic aid,[34] which often serves the same purpose as NATO military aid, were included along with these other expenditures as in NATO calculations, then Japan's military spending would have already been well over 1 per cent before 1987.[35] Furthermore, the appreciation of the yen after the 1985 Plaza Accord meant that, at least on a dollar-base calculation, Japan could now be talked about in the media as the third-ranked military spender in the world.[36] The increase in the value of the yen made procurement of US weaponry particularly attractive now. Japan's overall spending was higher than that of nuclear powers such as the United Kingdom and France, which at the time spent about one-third of their budgets on nuclear weaponry, and the former West Germany, which spent about one-quarter on financial assistance to Berlin.[37]

Thus, although the annual percentage of the GNP spent on the military was less than members of the North Atlantic Treaty Organisation (NATO), which ran at an average of 3 or 4 per cent for major European allies, the total amount, and the rate of increase, made Japan one of the world's military big spenders. The pace of this change is clear from the fact that, during the previous decade, the increase in the military budget had run at about twice the NATO average of 3 per cent, and from 1971 to 1985 increased 127 per cent, the second highest in the world, and much higher than the NATO average of 39 per cent for the same period.[38]

Finally, as a result of the practice known as 'deferred payments' (*saimu futan koi*), where only a small percentage of the total cost of major items of expenditure is paid at the outset, military expenditures as a matter of course were set to rise in certain categories.[39] The percentage of the total cost of weapons procurements paid in the first year decreased in the 1980s precisely because of the heavy burden of deferred payments: in contrast to the late 1970s, when approximately 4 per cent of the contract price for new weapons was paid, in the 1980s the amount fell to approximately 2 per cent, and less than 1 per cent for major capital items.[40] In the 1987 financial year 55 per cent of the budget was taken up with such deferred payments.[41] Taking into consideration the equipment ordered in 1987, including some for which no outlays were made, then two-thirds of 1987 expenditures were to be paid in the future.[42] The advantage to the Defence Agency of this method of payment is threefold: first, it allows the purchase of new weapons that could not be paid for out of a single year's budget; second, the expenditure for weaponry appears smaller than it actually is; and third, it places an obstacle in the way of any new administration set on reducing this category of expenditure. As the Ministry of Finance allowed the Defence Agency to adopt this deferred payment system from 1976 onwards, we again see that the ministry need not constrain military spending.

The Nakasone government's preferential treatment of military expenditures was in marked contrast to the way that expenditures for social welfare and education were held back. The budget is the concrete manifestation of a government's priorities. As such, the increase in the defence budget at the expense of these other budgetary items symbolizes Nakasone's priority. Spending on social welfare was reduced as a percentage of the general account, from 19.3 per cent in 1980, through 18.3 per cent in 1982 and 18.4 per cent in 1984, to 18.2 per cent in 1986, with a slight rise to 18.6 per cent in 1987. More markedly, spending on science and education was cut back from 10.6 per cent in 1980, through 9.8 per cent in 1982 and 9.6 per cent in 1984, to 9.0 per cent in 1986 and 9.0 per cent in 1987. The priority given to military expenses in contrast to welfare and education can be seen from the fact that, taking 1980 as the base line of one hundred, defence-related expenditures by 1987 had jumped to 157.7, whereas welfare only had increased to 122.9, and science and education had nudged forward to 107.3.[43] It is clear from these figures that, in line with the goal of settling the post-war account, the Nakasone government placed high priority on military spending.

The purpose of prioritizing defence is evident from the proportion of the general account spent on hardware, much of which is of US origin and paid for in dollars. This is especially so after the National Defence Programme Outline was established in 1976 – the year that deferred payments commenced, it should be recalled. Hardware expenditures grew by over 10 per cent in the following decade, with 16.4 per cent in 1976, 17.1 per cent in 1978, 20.7 per cent in 1980, 22.4 per cent in 1982, 26.3 per cent in 1984, 26.9 per cent in 1986, and 27.5 per cent in 1987. This brought Japan's capital expenditures (expenditures on military hardware, research and development, as well as equipment) up to the level of the United Kingdom and then West Germany.[44] This contrasts with expenditures on personnel and provisions, which were cut back by over 10 per cent, from 56 per cent in 1976, through 54.4 per cent in 1978, 49.3 per cent in 1980, 46.6 per cent in 1982, 44.6 per cent in 1984 and 45.1 per cent in 1986, to 43.9 per cent in 1987. This breakdown of expenditures within the military budget illustrates how, under the Nakasone government, the hardware capability of the SDF was built up at the expense of the budgetary allocation for military personnel.

FREE-RIDERS

The quantitative and qualitative improvements in the Japanese military, and the amount and increase in the defence budget, both in comparison with the historical pattern of spending as well as with that of the NATO allies, are eloquent testimony to the contribution that the Japanese government could be said to be making as a 'normal' alliance partner during the cold war 1980s. Despite this, Japan continued to be charged with taking a 'free ride' on the security treaty, with the focus placed on the small percentage of GNP spent on defence in comparison with other US allies. On the other hand, the United States continued to deploy troops on Japanese soil, with the archipelago acting as a 'picket line' in defence of mainland United States. Despite this, the security treaty continued to be strengthened as the central plank of the government's security policy. In order to answer the criticism of Japan as a 'free-rider', therefore, we need to examine the free-rider argument within the logic of the security treaty system. This should shed light on the ideological role played by the 'free-rider' argument as a means to legitimize militarization processes during the cold war 1980s.[45]

Japan as free-rider?

The free-rider argument of the cold war 1980s ran something like this.[46] As a result of signing the US–Japan security treaty in 1951, and going ahead with the revision of the treaty in 1960, Japan gained the protection of the US 'nuclear umbrella'. The United States, as the hegemon in international society, not only guarantees Japan's security, but also contributes to the peace and security of the Far East, which is threatened by the Soviet Union. Thus, Japan has been a double beneficiary of this situation: first, under the alliance with the United States, it has been able to devote a much lower percentage of its GNP to defence spending than would otherwise have been possible. Second, as a result of the United States' contribution to the peace and security of the world, it has been able to import raw materials and export finished products safely and thereby become one of the world's major trading nations. In this way, Japan has been able to develop its economy and enjoy prosperity at the expense of the United States. Therefore, in order to 'share the burden' and contribute to the peace and security of the world as a normal ally, Japan should devote more resources to the military, certainly beyond any normative limit, such as 1 per cent.

The first point to note about the 'free-rider' argument is the interpretation of the security treaty as a one-sided obligation on the part of the United States. This is an issue to which we shall return below. Here let us start by querying the premise of the argument: is Japan indeed protected by the United States? The 'competitive view' of reality, as discussed in Chapter 2, would suggest the use of the nuclear deterrent to protect a state's security. From the Japanese perspective, however, there are two problems. First, as is evident from the Korean and Vietnam wars, nuclear deterrence is ineffective against conventional conflicts and other wars at the regional level. In case of such wars in the Far East, however, the burden to defend the archipelago lies not with US forces, but overwhelmingly with the SDF. This is precisely the reason that Japan is obligated under Article III of the 1960 security treaty to build up defensive strength. Second, in the case of the nuclear threat from the Soviet Union, if the US deterrent failed and Japan did suffer a preemptive strike, whether or not the United States retaliated would be of no major consequence in the aftermath of nuclear devastation. What is more, a retaliatory US strike would mean a preemptive strike so far as the Soviet Union is concerned, casting doubt on the United States' willingness to take such action. None other than Admiral Noel Gayler, former Commander-in-Chief Pacific (CINCPAC) asserts bluntly: 'Anyone who thinks that the Americans are going to start a nuclear war in defense of them is deluded.'[47] The nuclear deterrent's effectiveness, if at all, is thus in deterring all-out war between the nuclear powers, not an attack against Japan.[48]

The second problem is with the premise that the US–Japan security treaty has allowed Japan to maintain low military spending. Two questions need to be addressed in this regard: (1) Specifically, did US military assistance keep spending down? (2) Generally, did the security treaty help in doing so? First, military assistance commenced in 1950 and ended in 1969, with over 80 per cent of the total occurring in the period up to the revision of the security treaty in 1960.[49] The grand total of assistance and sales calculated by the two sides differs considerably, with a Japanese total of 823.1 billion yen against a US total of 476.2 billion yen, brought about in part by Japanese calculation of equipment costs at replacement value, even though the US weapons were surplus. As a percentage of US total foreign military construction, sales and assistance, however, a Pentagon review of the period 1950–71 clearly demonstrates that Japan was only a minor recipient compared with other countries, accounting for 2.3 per cent of weapons sales, 3.4 per cent of surplus weapons sales, 12.9 per cent of licence production, 2 per cent of military assistance and 2.8 per cent of military training. The amount of military assistance at 2 per cent is slightly lower than West Germany (2.1 per cent), and the lowest in East Asia and the Pacific, far behind South Vietnam (17.2 per cent) and South Korea (9.5 per cent). These figures hardly suggest that Japan was a major beneficiary of US military assistance, thereby freeing the nation from the burden of military expenditures and allowing national energies to be poured into economic development. Second, neither did the security treaty prevent an increase in military expenditures. In fact, the reverse is true: the security treaty system has served to increase, not decrease, military spending. For except in the possible case of the Kennedy administration,[50] the treaty has acted as a lever for respective US administrations to pressurize Japan into strengthening the military and boosting the defence budget. On their part, Japanese administrations have often been somewhat reluctant, with the conspicuous exceptions of the Kishi Nobusuke administration in the 1950s and the Nakasone administration in the 1980s, to follow the path of a military build-up. What has kept military spending low, therefore, is not the security treaty but anti-militaristic attitudes at the mass level, supported by the following combination of factors, both external and internal.

Externally, fear of a revival of militarism on the part of Japan's Asian neighbours, and criticism of such signs, particularly by China, has been most significant in helping to put a brake on Japanese military expansion. This has played an internal role, too, for it is not only the anti-militaristic public that has lent an ear, but also part of the ruling conservative party and business elite: the former, out of a commitment to stop Japan once again becoming a military big power with aggressive intents against Asia; the latter, out of fear that a conspicuous military build-up would hinder economic penetration of the Asian mainland. Likewise, the anti-militaristic Constitution, the opposition parties, especially the Japan Socialist Party and the Japan Communist Party, and a variety of peace, anti-war and other social movements, as well as popular opinion, have all served to limit military spending. We could go so far as to say that, for the most part, the US and pro-military forces in the Japanese government, supported by their respective political forces with a vested interest in restoring legitimacy to the military establishment and expanding the SDF, have collaborated in eroding anti-militaristic political structures and attitudes.

Finally, although Japan's economic success has partly resulted from low military expenditures, this is not the whole story. For irrespective of the amount of spending on the military, other factors would still have contributed to this success, such as the development of a new industrial base after the war, the availability of cheap resources from, especially, East Asia, worker attitudes, development of an export-oriented growth strategy, and so on. So then why did the 'free-rider' criticism play such an important role in the military build-up of the 1980s? At heart lies the economic success of Japan in developing an export-oriented strategy premised on penetrating the US market. For the threat to security during the 1980s was not so much perceived by the Japanese to be the military threat of an attack by the Soviet Union as the economic threat of protectionist measures implemented by the United States. So the strengthening of a security treaty system not necessarily in the military security interests of Japan was accepted as part of the cost of maintaining its economic security interests. For those who accepted the 'Soviet threat', of course, the treaty was a cost in maintaining Japan's military security interests as well. In either case, the 'free-rider' argument could play a role in legitimizing the military build-up of Japan as part of Nakasone's efforts to make Japan a 'normal state'.

The United States as 'free-rider'?

The above would seem to suggest that, so far as the logic of the security treaty system is concerned, the US military presence in Japan is dictated by the security interests of the United States, and these were nuclear from the outset. As a 1951 Joint Chiefs of Staff memo states, the 'acquisition by the United States of its foreign bases has been dictated largely by atomic weapons considerations'.[51] It follows that 'the US nuclear umbrella, which does protect Japan, would not be any smaller or any different if Japanese security were not one of its functions'.[52] We have already shown how the treaty need not function in so far as Japanese security is concerned. What is therefore left is Japan's role as a 'picket line' against the Soviet Union. This is not to deny the obligation of the United States under the revised 1960 treaty to cooperate in joint defence of 'territories under the administration of Japan' (Article V). In reality, however, the performance of this task is in the hands of the SDF.[53]

It is for the above reasons that the primary concern of the United States has been to ensure the exclusive right to use bases in Japan for the preparation (deterrence) and prosecution of both nuclear and conventional wars in the security interests of the United States. The United States was guaranteed a free hand under the 1951 security treaty. Superficially, the revised 1960 treaty imposed restrictions on the freedom of US operations in the form of a need for 'prior consultation', but the 'introduction' of nuclear weapons into Japan in preparation for nuclear war, as discussed below, and the full use of US bases in the prosecution of the Vietnam War, illustrates its ineffectiveness in restricting US operations. What is more, as is clear from the case of the United States' unrestricted use of bases in Japan at the time of the 1991 Gulf War, the logic of Article VI of the treaty, 'contributing to the security of Japan and the maintenance of international peace and security in the Far East', has been expanded at will in terms of geographic scope.

The deployment of US military forces in Japan is thus of enormous value to the United States in pursuing its own regional and global interests. Yet the costs of maintaining this presence have been shifted increasingly to Japan, especially from the 1980s onwards. This follows the decline in US hegemonic power, epitomized in the realm of economics by the budget deficit and the trade deficit (the so-called 'double deficit').[54] The intertwining of political economy is evident in the pressures brought to bear on Japan to break out of the framework of financial obligations established at the time that the security treaty was revised. Then, under the Status of Force Agreement of January 1961, which was signed on the basis of Article VI of the revised treaty, Japan took on the obligation to provide the United States with land for military, communication and other installations. The cost of constructing these facilities, barracks and other buildings, wages for Japanese workers (which includes skilled technical staff) and expenses associated generally with the US presence in Japan, were to be borne by the United States. In principle, therefore, the Japanese government is not obliged under the Status of Force Agreement to pay the expenses incurred by the United States in deploying and maintaining military forces in Japan.

Bases for the exclusive use of the United States were in 1987 worth 36,000 billion yen at average residential land prices.[55] As obliged under the Agreement, the Japanese government paid the rent for this land. The annual amount during the 1980s increased from 40 billion yen in 1980, through 56.2 billion in 1984 and 59.2 billion in 1986, to 61.7 billion in 1987.[56] It had grown to 95.9 billion yen in 1990. Beyond this, from 1978 onwards the government started to contribute towards payment for Japanese workers at US installations. In this year, due to the appreciation in the value of the yen, the government accepted responsibility for their social security payments to a total sum of 62 billion yen. In light of the yen's rise these informal payments were dubbed by the head of the Defence Agency, Kanemaru Shin, 'sympathy' (*omoiyari*) payments. From 1979 onwards the government also agreed to pay that portion of workers' wages over and above the amount paid to public employees in Japan, and to contribute towards the payment for constructing barracks, schools and other amenities for the everyday life of American military personnel as well as runways, ammunition magazines and other facilities for upgrading the military capabilities of US forces.[57] Including the cost of rental payments for land, the Japanese government paid more than 2,000 billion yen towards the cost of the US presence in Japan during 1980–9, nearly three times the amount of the earlier decade.

The example of the 1987 fiscal year illustrates the way that the informal, *omoiyari* payments became an institutionalized part of the cost of the alliance in the face of Japan's global economic ascendance. In this year, following the Plaza Accord of 1985, another sharp rise in the value of the yen increased the dollar cost of payments to

Japanese workers and other Japan-side expenses. In this sense, the US-engineered revaluation of the yen at Plaza 'boomeranged' as higher costs in maintaining a military presence in Japan. The answer was to shift even more of the US financial burden onto Japan. Thus, under US pressure the government agreed to increase the payments for Japanese workers, including half of their severance pay and bonuses, with the total amount almost doubling compared to 1986, from 19.1 billion to 36.1 billion yen. What is more, Japan formally recognized *omoiyari* payments with the signing of a five-year-term Special Agreement between the two governments in January 1987. Excluding the cost of wages and suchlike for US personnel, and the budget for countermeasures around US facilities (e.g. measures against noise pollution), the Japanese goverment contributed nearly 40 per cent of the costs associated with US deployments in Japan in 1987. The trend was set to continue, with the signing of a Special Agreement in 1991 obliging Japan to bear all costs associated with the US presence in Japan by 1995 (except US salaries and removal expenses), and from 1995 onwards to commence payment of Japanese workers' salaries and utility expenses. Despite the ending of the cold war, therefore, the Japanese contribution to a defence burden they have not defined seems set to continue.

THE THREE NON-NUCLEAR PRINCIPLES

The erosion of the above normative constraints on Japan's conventional military role and its deeper financial integration into the US–Japan security system went hand in hand with the further erosion of the third of the three non-nuclear principles of not to possess, produce or introduce nuclear weapons. These principles, established in December 1967 by the then Satō government, have played a political role in restricting, at least to some extent, both the US and Japanese governments' flexibility in regard to nuclear policy. Over the years, however, evidence has accumulated to demonstrate that, irrespective of the Japanese government's denials, the principle of 'not to introduce' (*mochikomasezu*) nuclear weapons has not been honoured.[58] In other words, the government appears to have adopted a policy of deceit in denying that US planes and vessels are nuclear-loaded within Japanese territory. Indeed, 'confidential arrangements' between the American and Japanese governments suggest that the third of the non-nuclear principles was a deadletter from the start.[59]

Part of the problem revolves around the interpretation of *mochiko-masezu*: on the one hand, the US government does not seem to regard the transit of nuclear weapons through Japanese territory as 'introduction'; it is only their temporary off-loading, storage or deployment that counts as such.[60] On the other hand, the Japanese government includes transit in its official interpretation of *mochiko-masezu*. Nevertheless, as the United States, not Japan, possesses nuclear weapons, then the US interpretation, not the Japanese, is bound to take precedence unless the Japanese government insists otherwise, which it does not. So long as Japan respects the US policy of to 'neither confirm nor deny' the presence of nuclear weapons and permits entry to nuclear-capable US planes, ships and submarines without determining their nuclear status, then any potential enemy is unlikely to consider the archipelago nuclear-weapon free. Integration into US nuclear infrastructure in the Asia–Pacific region as a result of hosting communication facilities as well as the stationing of nuclear-capable forces in and about Japan ensures that the nation will be a higher priority target in any nuclear confrontation than would otherwise be the case, not to mention the risks arising out of a possibile nuclear accident occuring near densely populated metro-politan areas.

At the time that the US–Japan security treaty was revised in 1960 the Kishi–Herter Exchanges of Notes and the Kishi–Eisenhower Joint Communiqué implicitly provided for 'prior consultation' on any 'major changes' in American weapon and force deployments in Japan.[61] The meaning of 'major changes' has never been clarified, but this is understood to include Japanese approval of stationing nuclear weapons after 'prior consultation'.[62] The Japanese government has taken the stand that, should the United States wish to introduce nuclear weapons into Japan, it will seek to hold consultations with the US government prior to this 'major change'. As this prior consul-tation formula has never been invoked by the American side, then nuclear weapons have never been introduced into Japan, the Japanese government's argument runs.

In the 1950s, before the revision of the security treaty and the promulgation of the three non-nuclear principles, the United States had already made Japan into a nuclear-weapon store-house, as Peter Hayes, Lyuba Zarsky and Walden Bello revealed in 1986 on the basis of the first publicly available piece of official documentary evidence, the *Standard Operating Procedure for Atomic Operations in the Far East*: '[The Commander-in-Chief, Strategic Air Command, Far East's] *atomic weapons and components are stored in storage sites under the operational control of the component commands of the FEC* [Far East Command].'[63] In addition to being a store-house, Japan has been developed as a nerve centre of the United States' nuclear command and communication system, an integral part of the nuclear weapon infrastructure:

> the documents demonstrate conclusively that the United States, despite repeated refusals to confirm or deny the presence of nuclear weapons, routinely stored nuclear weapons in Japan and the Far East in the 1950s. They also show that Japan was the hub for nuclear command and communications and that nuclear bombers intended for attack on China and Korea were to have been launched from and 'recovered' to Japan.[64]

Even after the revision of the security treaty and the agreement on 'prior consultation', Japan's role as the nuclear-attack platform of the Far East continued. The Marines, for instance, stored nuclear weapons on the USS *San Joaquin County*, a Marine craft moored offshore at Iwakuni, in order to 'beat the air force to the nuclear draw', as discovered by Daniel Ellsberg, whose protest to Washington went unheeded.[65] It was moored at Iwakuni until at least 1966, when US Ambassador to Japan, Edwin O. Reischauer, called for its removal: 'I was furious because that was not according to the treaty at all. They were fudging it as the barge was not in transit.'[66] Or, as he phrased it in his memoirs: 'I erupted in outrage, because I felt this was an entirely different case from the transit of nuclear-armed ships through Japanese waters and was a violation of our understanding with the Japanese government.'[67]

A 1987 revelation of a secret telegram from the US Secretary of State, Dean Rusk, to the American Embassy in Tokyo on 24 February 1966, when Reischauer was ambassador, clearly exposes the duplicity of the Japanese government, for the telegram explicitly states that there are 'confidential *arrangements* with US on introduction of nuclear weapons under 1960 Security Treaty'.[68] The telegram, which noted the importance of these arrangements to the United States, also separately mentions 'that the confidential 1960 *agreement* affords US right to seek GOJ [Government of Japan] consent to introduction of nuclear weapons into Japan'.[69] In an interview with a Japanese reporter after the uncovering of this telegram Reischauer reiterated his own understanding that the transit of nuclear weapons aboard US planes and vessels is not subject to 'prior consultation' and that this interpretation was accepted by the Japanese government at the time of the revision of the security treaty.[70] The telegram, it should be noted, does not distinguish between transit and introduction and seems to imply the possibility of more than one 'arrangement'.

In any case, the full scope of the 'arrangements' or of the 1960 'agreement' may not have been fully known to Reischauer, as he was kept in the dark on more than the Marines' nuclear 'quick draw': 'a top secret plan for SAC [Strategic Air Command] aircraft to use two U.S. bases in Japan for recovery of Guam-based nuclear bombers and SAC "post-strike operations"' was also unknown to him.[71]

As is clear from the above, Reischauer's interpretation is that transit was permitted even after the revision of the security treaty. This is a point that he made in an interview with a Japanese reporter in May 1981, which caused an uproar in Japan.[72] The Japanese government has continued to deny transit, despite Reischauer's hopes to the contrary: 'After the affair had calmed down, I came to the conclusion that I had inadvertently gotten rid of a bothersome gray spot in Japanese–American relations.'[73] The implication is that, irrespective of anti-nuclear popular attitudes and the government's at least declaratory non-nuclear policy, the US–Japan security treaty should take precedence. This is the self-same logic of the Japanese government, as we shall see below.

The US response to the Soviet naval build-up in the 1980s signalled the end of the third non-nuclear principle in a practical sense. In the first place, the deployment of the sea-launched Tomahawk cruise missiles from 1984 onwards was bound to breach this principle.[74] Although technically nuclear weapons can be 'cross-decked' – that is, transferred between launch platforms, such as ships – every nuclear-certified aircraft or vessel entering Japanese territory cannot be expected to have transferred any nuclear-capable Tomahawk or other nuclear weapon prior to arrival. Already in 1974 Admiral LaRocque had testified before Congress that nuclear-weapon-capable US vessels did not unload their weapons prior to port calls to Japan.[75] The deployment of the Tomahawk missiles implied their presence aboard US vessels.

Second, the deployment of the Tomahawk went hand in hand with a tremendous increase in the number of port calls made by US submarines, a further manifestation of the US naval build-up in the 1980s.[76] After a decline in port calls to less than ten between 1974 and 1981, in 1982 a total of more than twenty submarines entered the ports of Yokosuka, Sasebo and White Beach. In 1986 US submarines made forty-one visits: thirty-one to Yokosuka, seven to Sasebo and three to White Beach. A Tomahawk-capable Sturgeon-class submarine, the *Tunny*, made a port call to Yokosuka in 1984. In 1986 the *Tunny* made three calls at Yokosuka, and one each at Sasebo and White Beach. The main port of call for submarines remained Yokosuka, with the number entering port jumping from less than ten in 1981 to over thirty in the mid-1980s. Submarine port calls at Sasebo were revived in 1981 to about ten a year after a brief spell of port calls from 1972 to 1974. Port calls to White Beach in the period after the reversion of Okinawa in 1972 continued at less than five a year (except for an absence in 1974–5), with a larger number after 1984. All in all the deployment of the Tomahawk and this increase in the number of port calls by nuclear-capable US submarines in the 1980s points to the demise of the third non-nuclear principle.

So why did the Japanese government not trot out the 'Soviet threat' as a means to legitimize port entries by nuclear-capable US vessels, thereby abandoning the pretence of maintaining the third principle? Of course, governments often lie and keep secrets – the flip side of the same coin – in order to mislead an enemy, deceive the public or both. But in the case of the denial of the introduction of nuclear weapons the Soviet Union was not misled. Nor was popular opinion, as we will discuss in Chapter 5. What this behaviour thus seems to signify is the fact that, even though popular opinion was not deceived, the government still calculated the political cost of admitting the erosion of an anti-militaristic principle to be greater than the political cost of the erosion of trust in the government resulting from continuing to lie. For to admit the introduction of nuclear weapons would be to admit the role of the security treaty in institutionalizing this sort of political behaviour. In this sense, the denial of the introduction of nuclear weapons signifies that the government feared an erosion of faith in the US–Japan security system more than an erosion of democracy. The militarization of the 1980s epitomizes how the security treaty came to take precedence over democratic and normative principles. The majority of the people's acceptance of the LDP's governance in the 1980s, despite the erosion of the third non-nuclear principle, highlights how the government's policy of giving precedence to the security treaty at the expense of the third non-nuclear principle was not viewed generally as a threat to Japan's military security interests through increased risk of nuclear accident or war, but rather as the cost of maintaining the economic security interests embedded in the US–Japan security system, from which the majority believed that they were benefiting.

EXTERNAL AND INTERNAL PRESSURES

The efficacy of the appeal to the US–Japan relationship is not to be ignored, for in this way both increases in military spending and the United States' transit of nuclear weapons could be made more acceptable at the mass level. There are thus both external and internal reasons why the US–Japan security system is pivotal to understanding the militarization of Japan during the 1980s. At the time, however, a popular argument often heard in Japan was that the rise in military expenditures, the build-up of the military and the closer military ties between the two nations were not a result of an autonomous decision on the part of Japanese government leaders, but rather a result of pressure from the United States. There is certainly some evidence to support this view, as we have seen above. What is more, concrete examples abound of how the Reagan administration, the Congress and the Senate all put pressure on Japan to boost its defence spending. A resolution adopted by the Senate in June and the House in July 1985, for instance, called upon Japan to make efforts to defend the SLOCs up to one thousand nautical miles by the end of the 1980s, and to improve sustained fighting capability, supplies of ammunition, logistics and so on.[77] Likewise, in June 1987 an amendment to the 1988 defence budget, which was passed by the US House of Representatives, called on Japan to boost defence spending to at least 3 per cent of GNP or pay the difference between current military expenditures and 3 per cent to the United States.[78] As the backdrop against which these kinds of resolutions were adopted was the popular feeling among politicians that Japan was taking a 'free ride' on US defence, and the feeling among opinion leaders and the general public that Japan should improve its defence capability. For instance, a 1981 survey taken of 100 members of the House and Senate shows that 53 think that Japan is taking a 'free ride' (24 think not).[79] A 1985 Gallup Poll of opinion leaders shows that 66 per cent think that Japan should increase its defence capability (23 per cent think not).[80] Among the general public 46 per cent favoured such an increase (27 per cent did not).[81]

Even though there were thus numerous US demands in the cold war 1980s for Japan to build up its military, the priority that the Nakasone administration placed on military affairs cannot simply be regarded as a result of such external pressure. For prior to the advent of the Nakasone administration, successive Japanese administrations had been able to use domestic political factors, such as the

Constitution or popular opposition to increased defence expenditures, as a means to resist pressure from the United States. This suggests that, despite external pressure, the Japanese government has the ability, if it has the political will, to exercise a degree of independence from the United States – at least more than was exhibited by Nakasone, who committed himself to the alliance as a way to facilitate the normalization of the Japanese military and the creation of a new national identity.

In this way, Prime Minister Nakasone strove to boost the nation's military might, accepting a greater 'defence burden' as demanded by the United States. This contribution to the 'common defence' was seen as important on both sides of the Pacific as a means to shore up America's declining hegemonic power. At the same time, however, the goal of strengthening Japan militarily was at one with Nakasone's own nationalistic goal of making Japan an 'international state', with a strong executive as in a presidential system of government.[82] At the most fundamental level this meant to restructure the state so as to enable Japan to play a political role in the world commensurate with its economic power, where the military could be employed as a legitimate instrument of state power. His calls to revise the Constitution, though abandoned, symbolize his linking of military powerism with political power. This big-power consciousness, which to some extent seeped down among the people during the Nakasone era, must also be taken into account when discussing Japanese militarization in the 1980s, as must changes within the ruling party, with Nakasone breaking out of the consensus mould of conservative politics characteristic of the 1970s.

This was the way forward for Nakasone to reshape Japanese national identity, redefining the idealized demilitarized state as an 'international state', with the war against Asia taking its natural place as an integral part of the new Japan. Thus, in 1985 Nakasone became the first prime minister after the defeat to visit Yasukuni Shrine in the official capacity of prime minister. In a sense, this was simply a political response to war veteran and other LDP support groups, which by the end of the 1970s had abandoned their attempt to pass a Yasukuni Bill in favour of the official visit of Cabinet ministers to the shrine. At heart, however, this represented an attempt to reshape Japanese national identity by legitimizing Japan's war in Asia as part of 'settling the postwar accounts'. As we will go on to discuss in Chapter 7, Yasukuni Shrine is the symbolic fountainhead of pre-war militarism, which 'has functioned as the fulcrum point for the maintenance of the spirit of militarism in Japanese society'.[83]

The resurgence of nationalism and big-power consciousness under the guise of 'internationalization' clearly demonstrates that, apart from external pressure, pressure to bolster Japan's military came from within the government and governing party, too. In this sense, Nakasone skilfully exploited American pressure as a means to legitimize the military build-up, despite opposition at the popular level.

The response of the former victims of Japanese militarism, however, epitomizes Nakasone's dilemma in trying to restore legitimacy to the Japanese military as an instrument of state policy. The 'Soviet threat' and 'free-rider' could, of course, ideologically function to legitimize the military build-up, but the visit to Yasukuni stirred East Asian memories of the activities of the military when it was last used as an instrument of Japanese state policy. Interred in the shrine, as China pointed out, are the spirits of war criminals such as Tōjō Hideki. The outcry from China and the two Koreas, in particular, of a 'revival of Japanese militarism' exposed the contradiction between the still-to-be-resolved question of Japan's war-time responsibilities and Japan taking up a role as a 'normal' military big power. In the wake of the 'Yasukuni problem', however, criticism from Asia became more subdued.[84] As we will see in Chapter 4, a much greater willingness to accept a Japanese military role in the wake of the ending of the cold war was to lead within a few years to wider support for an SDF presence in Cambodia.

The opposition parties during the 1980s abandoned many of their anti-military policies and gradually came to adopt a more accommodative stance towards the government's defence and security policies, except for the increasingly isolated Japan Communist Party.[85] Their change during this period, reflecting a waxing desire to taste the fruits of political power as part of a coalition government, can be seen now as a precursor to the changes in the political landscape of the early 1990s. In 1980, before the formation of the first Nakasone Cabinet, the DSP demonstrated a change to a pro-military stance in supporting the government's legislation to revise the Defence Agency Establishment Law, the Self-Defence Forces Law and the Defence Agency Employee Salary Law. Likewise, in the party's action programme for 1983 and in the 1983 Outline of Important Policy Points, the DSP called on the public to support greater defence expenditures and accepted a role for Japan in securing the SLOCs as a 'member of the West'. In 1981, at its nineteenth party convention, the Kōmei Party came out in support of the US–Japan security treaty, and by declaring support for forces capable of preserving Japan's territorial integrity, expressed conditional acceptance of the constitutionality of the SDF. Morever, like the DSP, the Kōmei Party accepted Japan's role as a 'member of the West', and accepted as 'unavoidable' the continued maintenance of the security treaty with the United States, which the party approved. The JSP, in contrast, continued to oppose the security treaty, at least formally until the formation of the socialist-led Murayama Cabinet in 1994. During the 1980s the party retreated from outright opposition to the existence of the SDF, declaring that, although the forces could not be regarded as 'constitutional', they could be regarded as 'legal', as the SDF had been created by the passage of Diet legislation. In this way, the gap between the major opposition parties and the ruling party grew narrower during the 1980s. As a consequence, the effectiveness of the opposition in putting the brakes on militarization processes was markedly reduced. To what extent this is true at the mass level will be addressed in Chapter 5.

CONCLUSION

It should be clear from the above discussion how, in the 1980s, the normative principles impeding the militarization of Japan were gradually eaten away as a result of both external and internal pressures, while certain elements of structural restraint, such as Article 9 of the Constitution, remained intact. Concretely, there was an erosion of the constraint on the growth of the military as symbolized by the commitment not to take part in collective defence; the third of the three non-nuclear principles; the ban on exports of weapons-related technology; and the 1 per cent limit on military spending. This was a consequence both of the US strategic design of making Japan a smoothly functioning cog in the US military machine, and the domestic political support for the bigger military establishment that this strategy implied, on the one hand, and the greater acceptance or at least diminished criticism of the Japanese military voiced at home and in other East Asian countries, on the other. The quantitative and qualitative build-up of Japanese forces, and the Japanese government's commitment to defend the SLOCs, to participate in blocking the three straits and in general to cooperate with the US military, demonstrate how the SDF became an integral part of a collective war-fighting strategy during the 1980s. For all practical purposes the third of the three non-nuclear principles never has functioned in so far as the transit of US nuclear weapons is concerned. The ban on arms exports was undermined by making an exception of military-related technology exports to the United States. And the 1 per cent ceiling came tumbling down in early 1987.

While it is true that, as with the scrapping of the 1 per cent ceiling, epiphenomenal factors do help to explain the inability of domestic forces to stop the growth of the Japanese military establishment, of more importance is the widespread acceptance of the fundamental reason for the speeding up of militarization processes: the SDF and the US–Japan security treaty. These are the two military pillars supporting the US–Japan security system. We have seen how in the 1980s the role of Prime Minister Nakasone was crucial to the reshaping of this system, with the aim of redefining Japanese identity in the world as a normal military big power. The task, however, was not completed. In particular, the government had been unable to despatch minesweepers to clear mines in the Gulf in 1987, not to mention the despatch of ground troops. With the end of the cold war, however, both these tasks were accomplished. It is to these changes that we turn in Chapter 4.

4 The Gulf War and 'international contribution' in the post cold war 1990s

We have seen in the previous chapter how Prime Minister Nakasone took the initiative in articulating Japanese national identity within a discourse establishing a role for Japan as a 'normal state' (*zairaigata kokka*). The fear of Nakasone's critics that, under the new, less stringent limitation on defence spending, the 1 per cent limit would continue to be broken, was not realized, owing to the economic downturn at home and the ending of the cold war internationally. In fact, military spending only broke through the barrier in 1987 and the following two years, before again dipping below 1 per cent.[1] In place of such increased rates of military expenditures in the 1980s, in the early 1990s the changing role of Japanese military forces came to symbolize militarization for many Japanese. True, militarization continued in terms of the quantitative and especially qualitative improvement of Self-Defence Forces (SDF) equipment, as seen in the deployment of the *Aegis*, and growing military cooperation between Japan and the United States, as evident in the 1994 RIMPAC exercises. Of far greater importance, however, were the political and legislative activities surrounding the task of eroding the constraints on the SDF's activities, and restoring legitimacy to the military as an instrument of state policy. Indeed, for the first time in the post-1945 era, militarization crystallized around the issue of the actual deployment of Japanese military forces. As we have seen in earlier chapters, this quest to establish Japan's position in the world as a 'normal' military power is at the heart of the contradiction between 'identity' and 'normality' in the 'militarization' versus 'demilitarization' debate.

In retrospect, the scrapping of the 1 per cent ceiling was of greater symbolic than practical importance in opening the way for the erosion of other anti-militaristic principles. In the early 1990s, the government sought to push forward with a policy aimed at eroding the central principle introduced at the time that the SDF were established – the ban on the overseas despatch of troops. The end of the cold war and the outbreak of the Gulf crisis offered a 'window of opportunity' for those political forces seeking to restore legitimacy to the military as an instrument of state policy. In this sense, the ultimate despatch of the SDF for peace-keeping operations (PKO) in Cambodia can be regarded as the LDP's last significant contribution to redefining Japanese national identity as a 'normal state' before the collapse of one-party rule in 1993, and the onset of coalition politics.

The ending of the cold war and the international calls for Japan to make an 'international contribution' acted as a catalyst for a renewed debate on Japanese security, the role of the SDF, the meaning of anti-militarism and Japan's role in the world. Although the ending of the cold war is obviously an important factor in explaining the burgeoning debate on Japan's future role, the crucial catalyst was the more specific process leading up to the passage of legislation and the despatch of the SDF in 1992, which started with the Gulf crisis in 1990. In this sense, the Gulf crisis was a watershed in reconfiguring the key questions of 'identity' and 'normality' at the heart of the post-1945 debate over Japan's role in the world. It is for this reason that, in this chapter, we will examine the process leading up to the passage of legislation to enable the SDF to be despatched overseas. How was this constraint eroded? What role did external and internal pressures play in bringing about this major change in Japanese security policy? In what ways did the new legislation restrict the scope of the SDF's activities? These are some of the questions that we will address. Before doing so, however, as a prelude let us briefly touch on the effect of the ending of the cold war on Japan.

JAPAN AND THE ENDING OF THE COLD WAR

The close military links developed between Japan and the United States during the 1980s were an integral part of the US response to the Soviet threat in Asia–Pacific, which was one aspect of the bipolar global cold war confrontation. In comparison with the situation in Europe, where the physical symbols of the cold war, like the Berlin wall, were destroyed, the end of the cold war in this region was not so clear-cut: the continued division of the Korean peninsula, the Chinese claim to Taiwan and the outstanding territorial issue between Japan and Russia remained as bleak reminders of the cold war – indeed, hot war – in the region.[2] What is more, whereas the cold war's ending in Europe involved the people's active participation, in Asia–Pacific the process was less clear-cut, more drawn out and experienced by the Japanese as spectators. Similarly, in stark contrast to the success of Premier Kohl's government, which played an active role in bringing the cold war to an end and reuniting the eastern and the western parts of Germany, the LDP government remained as a passive actor, an observer on the sidelines of the unfolding drama leading to the end of the bipolar division of the globe. In short, for Europeans the cold war structures were dismantled; for the Japanese, they collapsed. The failure of the LDP to break out of the syndrome of dependence on the cold war structures eventually led to the breakdown of the internal cold war structures, as symbolized by the '1955 system',[3] with Japan still divided as a result of the outstanding dispute with Russia over the 'Northern Territories'. The seeds for the breakdown of the ideological division over defence and security took root at this time in Japanese domestic politics.

As the ending of the international bipolar cold war system was accompanied by the revival of the United Nations, especially the role of the Security Council, and the unipolar military ascendance of the United States, the government, opposition parties and society took up the question of Japan's defence and security policies within the context of these new external conditions. Such reorientation thus was not pushed forward in response to new external threat perceptions, as could have arisen from the military build-up in China and the arms modernization programmes in Southeast Asia,[4] but rather as a response to external and internal pressures surrounding Japan's future role in the world. The leitmotif of the discourse was 'international contribution'.

The pressure to make an 'international contribution' in the early 1990s was a strong motivation for the ruling party to reconsider Japan's role in the post cold war era. From the outset, the debate evolved in terms of a military versus a non-military 'international contribution', both in the Diet as well as in society at large. This division over what was at heart the question of the nature of Japan's contribution to international society became salient at the time of the 1990–1 Gulf crisis, when the United States sought to gain legitimacy for military actions against Iraq through the United Nations.[5] In sharp contrast to the ending of the cold war, however, the Japanese government could now not remain as a mere spectator to the unfolding international crisis resulting from Iraq's invasion of Kuwait in August 1990. Both international and domestic pressures were exerted on the government to join the multinational forces incorporated under US hegemony, or to make a contribution in some other way, especially after the start of the Gulf War in January 1991. In another major issue of the early post cold-war era, the government was shortly thereafter faced with the question of how to respond to the need for PKO in Cambodia. In both these cases, the constitutional and other restraints placed on the SDF during the cold war era increasingly were challenged by forces in favour of Japan becoming a 'normal' military big power. In what ways were the constraints on the SDF eroded in order to make this possible?

EROSION OF CONSTRAINTS ON THE SDF'S DESPATCH

As we have seen earlier, the existence of the Preamble and Article 9 of the Constitution has meant that, ever since their establishment in 1954, the SDF's legitimacy has been contested. Despite the declared aim of the ruling LDP to *revise* the Constitution, thereby clearly establishing their constitutionality, the party's failure to gain the two-thirds majority of Diet seats required to implement this agenda created the need to deal with the problem in another way.[6] This was to expand by reinterpretation the scope of SDF activities permitted under the Constitution. On the other hand, the Opposition, particularly the socialists, sought to impose restraints on the scope of SDF activities by challenging such reinterpretations. What gives meaning to constitutional and other restraints on the SDF, therefore, is not so much the Constitution *per se* but how the political activities of the Opposition in the Diet, and more generally the actions and attitudes of the citizens, have served to constrain the ruling party in pushing ahead with a flexible interpretation of the Constitution which permits the growth and widening scope of SDF activities.

At the same time, it is important to note the existence of LDP politicians who have not necessarily supported a burgeoning role for the SDF. Of course, in so far as the LDP's party platform calls for a revision of the Constitution in order to establish their constitution-ality, all LDP Diet members can be said to support the existence of the SDF. But this does not mean that all have been in favour of expanding the scope of SDF activities to include the overseas despatch of troops. As surfaced at the time of the Gulf crisis, and as has become clearer in the context of the restructuring of the party system in the early 1990s,[7] intra-party opposition to an expanded role for the SDF also acted as a restraint within the ruling party. In this sense, our discussion of the political activities leading up to the despatch of the SDF at the time of the Gulf crisis helps to shed light on the emerging debate over a new security policy for Japan in the post cold-war era.

At the heart of the problem of deploying the SDF as part of the American-led multinational forces lined up against Iraq was the government's interpretation of what restrictions the Constitution placed on the SDF and Japan's role in the US–Japan security system. There are four main interpretations of the extent of the constitutional restraint imposed by Article 9:

> First, the LDP government's interpretation that, as the first clause of Article 9 does not go so far as to deny the right of self-defence, necessary minimum defence can be maintained based on the second clause. Second, the Ashida interpretation that, although the first clause of Article 9 does deny aggressive wars, as it does not deny wars of self-defence, war potential for self-defence can be maintained. Third, the dominant interpretation of constitutional scholars that, as the first clause of Article 9 renounces all wars, the second clause prohibits the possession of all forms of war potential. Fourth, the Naganuma court decision that, although the first clause of Article 9 does not deny wars of self-defence, as the second clause prohibits all forms of war potential, the result is that wars of self-defence also are prohibited.[8]

As the proliferation of these different interpretations of Article 9 highlights, the exact scope of the constitutional restraint imposed on the possession and use of military forces remains a major point of controversy in Japan, even in the post cold war era. What clearly should be noted, however, is that none of these four interpretations leaves the government a free hand in utilizing the SDF as 'normal' military forces. Hence the position of respective LDP governments was that, as the possession of necessary minimum force for self-defence is not the same as 'war potential', the SDF are constitutional for 'self-defence'.

More fundamentally, the constitutional interpretation of respective LDP governments rested upon a distinction between the right to individual self-defence (*kobetsuteki jieiken*), and the right to collective self-defence (*shūdanteki jieiken*). The government holds that, as in the case of any other sovereign member of the international community, Japan enjoys the right of individual self-defence as well as the right of collective self-defence under international law. The provisions of the Constitution, however, have been interpreted as precluding that latter right of participating in 'collective self-defence'. In other words, the Constitution permits only the right of 'individual self-defence', and then only within the limits set by the requirements of 'necessary minimum defence'. The flexibility of the boundaries of this interpretation is illustrated by the fact that both prime ministers Kishi Nobusuke in 1957 and Fukuda Takeo in 1978 declared nuclear weapons to be constitutional.[9] In essence, these prime ministers followed the logic that nuclear arms simply represent a difference in the quality rather than kind of weapons, and are thus in keeping with 'individual self-defence'.

Given that, and the history of militarism, as evident in military aggression abroad and harsh repression at home, the opposition both inside and outside the Diet has never been content to rely on Article 9 as the sole means of constraining the LDP's struggle to restore legitimacy to the military. Thus in 1954, at the time that the Defence Laws establishing the SDF and the Defence Agency went before the Diet, the opposition parties succeeded in imposing a ban on the over-seas despatch of the SDF. The socialists were then a powerful force in the House of Councillors. Indeed, the ruling Liberal Party, which in 1955 joined forces with the Democratic Party to form the LDP, was forced to swallow the ban as a condition for the passage of the Defence Laws.[10] Thereafter, Prime Minister Satō Eisaku in 1970 confirmed the principle of not deploying troops abroad in line with the government's interpretation of the Constitution.[11]

What constitutes the 'despatch of forces', however, has been less than clear-cut. We will discuss in Chapter 6 a number of different metaphors and euphemisms which have been used to facilitate mili-tarization, but here we should note how the government in 1966 employed a euphemism in order to draw a distinction between the SDF as an organization and the function of that organization. More specifically, in deliberations in the House of Councillors the then Foreign Minister, Shīna Etsusaburō, and Matsuno Raizō, Director General of the Defence Agency, drew a distinction between *kaigai hahei* (i.e. the overseas despatch of the SDF for the purpose of using force, in this case using the Chinese characters for the despatch of troops) and *kagai haken* (i.e. the overseas despatch of the SDF for purposes other than the use of force, such as monitoring ceasefires, in this case using the same characters as for the despatch of, for example, business employees).[12] The argument was that, so long as the SDF were not despatched for the purpose of using force, as denied by the government's interpretation of the Constitution, the despatch of SDF personnel was constitutional.

The constitutionality of despatching the SDF for purposes other than the exercise of force was the position taken in 1980 by the

Suzuki administration, although it was made clear that the SDF Law precluded this from taking place – in other words, the Law would need to be revised before the SDF could be despatched overseas in force.[13] The controversy surrounding the overseas despatch of the SDF meant that, on the one hand, SDF personnel have been posted abroad as attachés in Japanese embassies, on fact-finding missions to other countries and occasionally as monitors in UN-sponsored elections, with little domestic opposition. The despatch of minesweepers, although carried out secretly at the time of the Korean War,[14] had been regarded as too controversial to be included as a 'peaceful' despatch of the SDF, as was evident in the failure of Prime Minister Nakasone to despatch minesweepers to the Persian Gulf at the time of the Iran–Iraq war in 1987. As we saw in Chapter 3, however, the interpretation of 'individual self-defence' and Article V of the US–Japan security treaty was expanded in the 1980s beyond the defence of 'territories under the administration of Japan' (Article V). At this time, the right of 'individual self-defence' was widened to embrace the possibility of the Maritime SDF protecting US warships, even if the vessels were outside Japan's territorial waters, and to patrolling the SLOCs up to one thousand nautical miles from Japan.

This is illustrative of the erosion of the constraints imposed by the Constitution on taking part in 'collective self-defence'. For instance, in 1969 the Director of the Legislative Bureau announced before the House of Councillors' Budget Committee that participation in 'any form of collective defence organization would be, for Japan, unconstitutional'.[15] Insofar as the US–Japan security treaty is concerned, therefore, the government's interpretation has been that the SDF can take part in joint defence with the United States in repelling an armed attack in accordance with Article V of the treaty, but cannot take part in the 'maintenance of international peace and security in the Far East' (Article VI), except by indirect provision of bases and other facilities, as this would form part of 'collective defence'. In other words, Japan is reliant on the US military in this latter regard.

Nevertheless, in practice the boundaries of this interpretation have been expanded over the years. What started out as a regional treaty focusing on the 'Far East', with the area of the 'Far East' in 1960 being defined by the government as 'the North of the Philippines, Japan and the environs, including South Korea and Taiwan', was at the end of the 1960s expanded to include Vietnam, with the Gulf coming within the scope of the 'Far East' by 1990–1; that is, over the years the security treaty has been transformed from an essentially regional treaty into a near global treaty.[16] This has taken place without any change in the treaty's wording or legal basis since its revision in 1960. Despite 'prior consultation' under the revised treaty, moreover, the US government does not appear to have consulted the Japanese government prior to despatching American troops deployed in Japan to the Gulf.[17] In this sense, the treaty system continued to function in line with the strategic goals of the United States, both regionally and globally, as seen in the Japanese support of the US policy in the Gulf crisis.

THE GOVERNMENT'S RESPONSE TO THE GULF CRISIS: EXTERNAL AND INTERNAL PRESSURES

Thus, on one level, the Japanese government responded to the Gulf crisis within the framework established during the cold war era, the US–Japan security system. At the same time, however, the framing of post cold war issues like the Gulf crisis in terms of a more universally acceptable 'international contribution', rather than the particularistic, cold war 'Soviet threat', strengthened the framework of legitimacy for Japan to make a military contribution. Still, the domestic political debate unfolded in terms of making a 'military' versus a 'non-military' contribution, even though the United States was in a stronger position to exert pressure on Japan in the post cold-war era in terms of ostensibly universalistic criteria. As we have seen in Chapter 3, in the cold war era the Japanese government built up its military forces in support of the leadership role of the United States, especially regionally, provided bases free of charge, and from the 1980s onwards made ever larger contributions towards the cost of US deployments in Japan. In the post cold-war era, the government increasingly is being called upon to play an ever more important financial role in supporting the United States globally. In other words, although Japan's contribution at the time of the Gulf crisis was characterized in terms of 'international contribution' and 'contribution to international society', as we touch on below, critics charged that the core issue remained how to contribute to the United States, this time as the world's unrivalled military hegemon.

The centrality of the United States to the LDP leadership is nicely illustrated by a comment made by the then LDP secretary general, Ozawa Ichirō. In November 1990 he declared in a television programme interview: 'As the United States has the greatest influence on Japan, reference to international society can be replaced with reference to the United States. US–Japan cooperation is crucial.'[18]

In the wake of the Gulf crisis, such 'US–Japan cooperation' increasingly took precedence over the Constitution and other restraints on the role of the SDF. Indeed, given the close economic, political and military ties between Japan and the United States, along with a strongly felt sense of vulnerability on the part of LDP leaders, American pressure played the catalytic role in determining the Japanese government's response to the Gulf crisis.[19] Thus, after the Iraqi invasion of Kuwait in August 1990, a major challenge to then President George Bush's vision of creating a 'new world order', the Japanese government was put under mounting pressure to breach the restraints imposed on the SDF by making a 'human contribution' to the resolution of the Gulf crisis. At the time, the opposition parties and public opinion were strongly opposed to any contribution involving the despatch of Japanese troops overseas. In this sense, the government was sandwiched between both external and internal pressures, as in the cold war 1980s.

Nevertheless, against the background of constitutional restraints on the SDF, the US and wider international pressure on the Japanese government began to erode the consensus on the SDF not being despatched abroad in force. The US pressure took a variety of forms. In the first place, the president exerted direct pressure on Prime Minister Kaifu Toshiki. In August 1990, for instance, President Bush telephoned the prime minister on several occasions to ask for Japanese assistance against Iraq.[20] The prime minister, who had been elected as a compromise candidate from the small, dovish Komoto faction, lacked a strong base of support within the party, with his susceptibility to US pressure leading to charges that he was a member of the 'Bush faction'.[21] Second, the US Ambassador to Japan, Michael H. Armacost, sought to influence Japan's response to the Gulf crisis by holding meetings with Ozawa Ichirō, the 'power behind the throne', as well as by making public statements calling on Japan to do more in support of the multinational forces.[22] Third, pressure was exerted more generally by members of the American Congress and Senate. In a Senate statement on 10 September, for instance, John McKayne was critical of Japanese 'aid without substance [which] will only invite the world's contempt and America's anger'.[23] That McKayne, who had in the past defended Japan against its severer American critics, made such a statement, pointed to the widespread frustration with the Japanese response. In the House, this was symbolized by a letter sent to Prime Minister Kaifu by then Democratic Leader Richard Gephardt and a number of other members of Congress calling for 'meaningful voluntary restraints' on

Japanese exports of automobiles to the United States, if Japan failed to make a satisfactory contribution to the Gulf effort.[24] In December 1990 a threat was also made to withdraw American troops from Japan unless the government increased its contribution.[25] Fourth, as seen in the case of Lee Iacocca, chairman of Chrysler, the business community joined the chorus in calling on Japan to make a greater contribution to the resolution of the Gulf crisis. In this case, he called for a reduction in output of Japanese transplants in the United States, as there were 'sacrifices [America] may soon be called on to make in an area of the world that supplies most of Japan's oil'.[26] Finally, as seen in the case of *Newsweek*, the media launched a barrage of criticism against Japan, making the link between oil and American lives even more explicit: 'Japan, which is far more reliant on the Gulf than any other rich country, buys its energy security with the lives of young Americans'.[27] The toing and froing of the government under overseas pressure was such as to suggest to the foreign minister that, if it did not make a 'human contribution', Japan would be isolated internationally.[28] As we have seen, the overwhelming pressure was exerted by the United States.

At the same time, however, this external pressure was congruent with the aims of, and could be used by, Japanese political forces set on normalising the military, with the SDF playing a key role in redefining Japan's identity in the post cold-war world. More specifically, Ozawa Ichirō took the lead in seeking to reshape Japan's relations with the outside world by seizing upon the Gulf crisis as an opportunity for the government to reinterpret the scope of SDF activities permitted under the Constitution. He was supported by Nishioka Takeo, chairman of the LDP Executive Council, and other hawks in the LDP, especially members of the 'defence tribe'.[29] In a sense, he strove to push forward with the creation of what he called a 'normal state' (*futsū no kuni*), as did Nakasone, albeit as the 'power behind the throne' rather than as the prime minister.[30]

Immediately after the outbreak of the crisis Ozawa visited Prime Minister Kaifu in order to persuade him to change the government's interpretation of the Constitution. In essence, Ozawa sought to draw a distinction between 'collective security', as envisioned in the UN Charter, and 'collective self-defence', as prohibited by the Constitution. From this point of view, even without revising the Constitution or amending the SDF Law, Japanese troops could participate in UN military actions on the basis of decisions made in the UN Security Council, paving the way for Japan to participate in a UN army, as envisioned in Article 42 and Article 43 of the UN

Charter. This was in contrast to the 1980 position of the Suzuki Cabinet, and is a logic based on 'international contribution', not 'individual self-defence'. In other words, the constraint imposed by reference to 'individual self-defence' is totally absent in determining Japan's military role based on making an 'international contribution'. Precisely for this reason, the opposition parties strove to impose new restraints on the activities of the SDF.

The government's initial response

The Kaifu government at first responded to the Iraqi invasion by implementing non-controversial measures in support of the multi-national forces, on the one hand, and proposing new legislation to the Diet in order to permit the SDF to be despatched overseas, on the other. The first step that the government took was to announce a policy of economic sanctions against Iraq, and the freezing of Kuwaiti assets, trade credits, economic cooperation, and so on.[31] In this, Japan was following the lead already taken by the United States and the European countries, but did so quickly. Thereafter, the government came in for severe criticism for doing 'too little, too late', although in response to both domestic and US pressure, it made a variety of non-military contributions. At the end of August, for instance, the government agreed to provide transportation by civilian planes and vessels of food, water, medical supplies and other non-military goods, and the despatch of a medical team.

Even before the start of the Gulf War in January 1991, therefore, the Japanese government had already pledged to provide financial support to the multinational forces as well as aid to affected countries. At the end of August the government pledged $1 billion in support of the multinational forces. Next, after a visit to Japan by Secretary of State Brady, the government on 14 September pledged a further $1 billion, together with $2 billion in economic assistance to Egypt, Turkey and Jordan. Thereafter, as Japan's contribution towards the cost of the war, Finance Minister Hashimoto Ryūtarō agreed to a further $9 billion in support of the multinational forces at the time of the G7 meeting of finance ministers in New York in January 1991. Finally, as a result of fluctuations in exchange rates, the United States called upon the Japanese government to make up the difference between the yen and dollar amounts of the Japanese commitment, with the government thereafter transferring another half a billion dollars. In the end, Japan contributed $13 billion towards the war and associated costs. As it only reportedly took

Finance Minister Hashimoto 'fifteen minutes' to agree to the additional $9 billion dollars,[32] the Ministry of Finance again was not able to act as a major restraint on defence spending, as in the previous cases we mentioned in Chapter 3.

The enormous size of the Japanese financial contribution points to how the United States was in a sense raising an international tax on Japan at the time of the Gulf crisis, a tactic to be repeated in 1994, when the United States this time called upon the Japanese government to help pay for the construction of a light water nuclear reactor in North Korea.[33] As the resolution of the Gulf crisis and the nuclear issue on the Korean peninsula were in the security interest of Japan, the American demands generally were regarded as legitimate. In neither case, however, was the Japanese government a party to the decision-making process, simply being pressurized to contribute to the realization of goals determined by the United States.

The US pressure on Japan to make a 'human contribution' towards the resolution of the Gulf crisis was used by Ozawa Ichirō to put similar pressure on the prime minister to forge ahead with a new interpretation of the Constitution allowing the overseas despatch of the SDF. Later, Prime Minister Kaifu's comments suggest that originally he had no intention of despatching the SDF, preferring instead to establish a separate organization: 'At the time I first thought of the United Nations Peace Corps Cooperation Bill, the image I had in mind was the Japan Overseas Cooperation Volunteers.'[34] This would not, however, have facilitated the normalization of the military as envisioned by Ozawa and other nationalists. In the wake of his pressure, further support was garnered for their deployment, with the uniformed services and the LDP 'defence tribe' pressuring the Defence Agency to support this option. Likewise, the Foreign Ministry, which had initially favoured the idea of a separate organization, came to back the SDF's deployment, as with the Finance Ministry, which opposed the additional expense associated with setting up a separate organization, as implied by Kaifu's 'image'.[35] The pressure from the United States at the US–Japan summit in September 1990 finally convinced Prime Minister Kaifu to abandon the idea of a separate organization, with his government putting a UN Peace Cooperation Corps Bill before the Diet in that October. Once modified as a result of Diet debate, this legislation would have permitted the government to despatch up to one thousand SDF personnel in order to provide logistic support for the multinational forces.[36]

From the perspective of American tactics in the Gulf, of course, the SDF's contribution was always going to be of less importance than the amount of financial contribution made by the Japanese government, particularly in light of the United States' 'double deficit'. Within Japanese domestic politics, however, the key issue was the role of the SDF: financial contributions, especially when given in the name of logistic rather than front-line support, did not call into question a demilitarized identity for Japan at the mass level. Clearly, the government's attempt to pass the United Nations Peace Cooperation Corps Bill was a challenge to the domestic consensus on the role of the SDF. With a growing ambition within certain quarters of the LDP and the Ministry of Foreign Affairs to become a permanent member of the UN Security Council, however, the overseas despatch of the SDF offered a way to enhance the government's credibility to obtain a permanent seat, as in the later case of participating in Cambodian peace-keeping operations, as well as to demonstrate Japan's willingness to cooperate with US global strategy.[37] Thus, the Bill was a way to open a legislative path to despatch the SDF, despite the government's previous interpretation of constitutional restrictions, in line with trying to gain a permanent seat on the Security Council as part of a redefined 'big power' identity for Japan, as well as maintaining close political and military ties with the United States. Notwithstanding, due to the division of opinion within the ruling party, between the government and opposition, and within society at large, the government was unable to pass the legislation at this time. Much of the debate in the Diet grew technical in detail, with the socialist opposition striving to demonstrate how the Bill was a break from previous government commitments. At heart, however, was the despatch of the SDF *per se*. In other words, the government faced a split in politics and society over the role that the Japanese military should play in the post cold-war era precisely because the Bill brought to the surface the question of 'identity' and 'normality' at the heart of the debate.

OPPOSITION TO UN PEACE COOPERATION CORPS BILL

The government's introduction of the Bill was crucial in bringing to the surface of politics the underlying differences in the perceived identity for Japan in the post cold war era. As the break up of the LDP and the establishment of coalition governments have demonstrated, differences over the future role of the SDF existed within as well as among the then political parties. Crucially, within the LDP the Ozawa line of trying to clear the constitutional and other hurdles to the SDF's overseas despatch was opposed by a range of powerful politicians. This is the case, for instance, with Gotōda Masaharu, the Chief Cabinet Secretary in the Nakasone Cabinet, who did not support Ozawa, taking a cautious attitude towards any break from the status quo.[38] Similarly, Kanemaru Shin, another powerful party boss and deputy prime minister, was opposed to the Bill. The same is true of former prime ministers Fukuda Takeo and Suzuki Zenkō, as well as dovish Diet members such as Kujiraoka Hyōsuke. The intensity of the divisions within the LDP led party headquarters to distribute a document cautioning Diet members to be prudent in responding to media questions on the party's response to the Gulf crisis.[39]

As the Bill clearly sought to erode the constraints imposed on the SDF, the socialists were able to take the lead in expressing public opposition to the Bill by linking the despatch to symbols of Japan's anti-militaristic identity. In her opening attack Doi Takako, the leader of the JSP, stated:

Why must pacifist Japan take the same actions as military big powers, going so far as to oppose the ideal of the Constitution? The UN Peace Cooperation Corps is the overseas despatch of the military [*kaigai hahei*], with the SDF dressed in beautiful clothing, which even contradicts the government's own position of regarding this as prohibited by the first clause of Article 9.[40]

Despite unprecedented cooperation between the ruling and opposition parties during the earlier 118th Diet, with an unprecedented 94.3 per cent of bills passed, the highest percentage since the formation of the LDP in 1955, the socialists on this occasion refused to enter into negotiations with the LDP.[41] Rather than informal negotiations, therefore, the Diet became the focus of attention. Given the anti-militaristic position of the socialists, the debate at the time revolved not so much around oil; nor, for that matter, the ethical, legal or political implications of the Iraqi transgression of Kuwaiti sovereignty. Rather, the question of the SDF's future role and their place in Japanese identity in the post cold war world were of preeminent concern. In essence, the debate revolved around the question of whether the mainly American pressure to make a 'human contribution' should take precedence over adherence to the principles of 'pacifist Japan', as expressed by Doi.

As the opposition parties dominated the House of Councillors as a result of the LDP's loss of its Upper House majority in the 1989 election, and the socialists joined the communists in opposing the Bill, the only way for the ruling party to breach the restraint on overseas despatch of the SDF was by reaching a compromise with the middle-of-the-road Kōmei Party and DSP. With opposition to the Bill strong among the grassroots supporters of these parties, however, the LDP was at the time unable to forge an alliance in order to pass the legislation. This left the government no alternative but to withdraw the Bill. Even so, Ozawa was able to reach a compromise with the secretaries general of the Kōmei Party and the DSP on the creation of a separate organization from the SDF, to cooperate in UN peace-keeping activities in the future.[42] As we will see below, however, this was not an option pursued when the revised PKO legislation was brought before the Diet in 1991.

Beyond the Diet's control

The strength of the opposition to the Bill demonstrates that the opposition can, if not always defeat, at least delay and modify the policy of the government. Given this situation, the government adopted a tactic of building up *faits accomplis* (*kisei jijitsu*) in order to circumvent the democratic control exercised by the Diet. In other words, failure to gain the Diet's approval to despatch the SDF overseas did not mean that the government had abandoned the realization of this goal. What it did, instead, was to circumvent the Diet by expanding the constitutional interpretation of the permissible range of SDF activities, and implementing special Cabinet orders as a way to lay a legal foundation for the SDF's overseas despatch.

In the first place, after the start of the Gulf War in January 1991 Secretary General Ozawa continued to exert pressure on Prime Minister Kaifu to make a 'human contribution' to the resolution of the Gulf crisis. The specific approach taken by Ozawa was to push for the use of SDF planes to transport refugees, whereas the prime minister preferred to use civilian airliners. Under pressure from Ozawa, other party officials and a phalanx of supporters the prime minister agreed to go ahead with the despatch of SDF planes by using Article 100, Section 5, of the Defence Law.[43] This Article had been adopted in 1986 in order to permit the SDF to transport state guests, the prime minister, state officials and other VIPs, with the emperor and the imperial family being included in 1987 as a result of an amendment. In the same year the government purchased two Boeing 747s for such official government use.[44]

Shortly after the start of the Gulf crisis the International Organization for Refugees had requested Japanese assistance. The government responded by providing chartered airliners. With the outbreak of the war, however, Ozawa and others exerted pressure on the government to use Air SDF planes.[45] Despite the rejection of the Bill to despatch the SDF overseas in the previous Diet session, as we have seen, the Cabinet on 29 January adopted and implemented a Special Cabinet Order to allow the SDF to despatch up to five C-130 transporters. The ASDF then went on stand-by to await a request from an authorized international body for Japan to assist in the transportation of refugees. In the end, however, as the Japanese government received no request, the Special Cabinet Order was annulled by the Cabinet in April 1991. Nevertheless, by the use of such an order the government in effect implemented a new interpretation of the Constitution without gaining Diet approval for a change of this magnitude. Such actions, as with the despatch of minesweepers, were seen as a threat to Japanese parliamentary democracy.[46]

Second, the government introduced a Special Cabinet Order so as to provide a legal basis for a new interpretation of Article 99 of the Defence Law. In this case, the aim was to create a legal foundation for the despatch of Japanese minesweepers to the Gulf after the war had ended. We touched on Prime Minister Nakasone's attempt to despatch minesweepers in Chapter 3. More specifically, in August 1987 Nakasone declared before the House of Representatives Budget Committee:

> Action to clear mines is not the exercise of force. For instance, in cases where such obstructions occur on the high seas, in the Japan Sea or off the coast of Maizuru, it is of course lawful for the Marine SDF to clear them. Then, when we ask whether we can clear mines in places like the Persian Gulf or on the high seas, where passing Japanese tankers are in danger, I don't think there is much difference legally. This is still to clear obstructions for the safety of Japanese shipping. It is not legally equivalent to the exercise of force, and simply because it takes place a long way away, it is not the overseas despatch of military forces (*kaigai hahei*). This is my interpretation.[47]

At the US–Japan Summit in September 1987 Prime Minister Nakasone, with the strong backing of the Foreign Ministry, declared his intention to contribute to minesweeping in the Persian Gulf by despatching Japan's own minesweepers. Notwithstanding, this met with the fierce opposition not only of the socialists but also of Chief Cabinet Secretary Gotōda, who went so far as to threaten to refuse to sign any Cabinet decision authorizing the despatch.[48] At the time of the Gulf crisis, too, Japanese minesweeping operations were emphasized as being different from the use of force. As Prime Minister Kaifu stated before the House of Representatives, the clearing of mines 'does not correspond to the overseas despatch of military forces as prohibited by the Constitution'.[49] Further, in addition to the pressure from within the LDP to despatch Japanese minesweepers, especially the Watanabe faction (the heir to the Nakasone faction), such action came to be seen, more generally inside the party as well as in the business world, as a means to halt the deterioration of relations with the United States, which had been brought on by the Japanese government's dilatory response to the crisis. Thus after the war's end in April, for instance, the president of the Japan Federation of Economic Organizations (*Keidanren*), Hiraiwa Gaishi, under pressure from the Petroleum Federation and the Japan Shipowners Association, declared support for sending minesweepers to the Gulf.[50] This positive statement from the business community gave a major boost to the government's attempt to despatch the SDF to the Gulf on minesweeping operations.[51] With the ending of the war, public opinion was also more supportive of despatching the minesweepers, as we will see in Chapter 5. Minesweeping operations began in June 1991 and finished in early September, with the SDF having cleared 34 mines out of a total of approximately 1,200,[52] suggesting that the despatch of the vessels was of greater symbolic importance than the task performed. The strong links between the US and Japanese forces were evident in the minesweeping operations, with the MSDF reportedly operating under US Naval Command.[53]

UNITED NATIONS PEACE-KEEPING OPERATIONS BILL

Although the government was in this way able to circumvent the Diet in attempting to despatch two of the tri-service SDF – the Air SDF to ferry refugees and the Marine SDF to clear mines – the despatch of the Ground SDF had to await the passage of Diet legislation. Following on from the failure to pass the previous Bill, the Kaifu government in the autumn of 1991 again proposed legislation to the House of Representatives to enable the SDF to be despatched overseas, formally 'A bill regarding cooperation with United Nations peace-keeping activities and other activities' (hereafter, PKO Bill).[54] At the same time, a bill proposing the partial revision of the law on the despatch of personnel for international disaster relief operations was put before the Diet.[55] In line with Diet procedures, a special Diet committee to deliberate the PKO Bill was set up. The sessions continued for several months. In the end, however, the government cut off deliberations and rammed the legislation through the Diet with the support of the centrist opposition parties.[56]

Over the intervening months the previous agreement between the LDP, DSP and Kōmei Party on the setting up of a separate organization to the SDF gradually had been replaced by the acceptance of the SDF's despatch by the two centrist parties. The influence of these parties can be seen in the legislation's five principles for the participation of the SDF in UN peace-keeping: (1) a ceasefire agreement has been reached between the parties to the conflict; (2) the agreement of the parties to the conflict on Japan's participation in PKO activities and the peace-keeping forces; (3) strict observance of neutrality; (4) the withdrawal of Japanese forces from participation in cases where a situation arises in which any of these conditions are not met; (5) limits on the use of weapons to the necessary minimum for self-defence.[57] As was to emerge later in the Diet debates over the Bill, this agreement was an attempt to set restraints on the SDF within the bounds of the government's changing interpretation of the Constitution in order to satisfy the demands of the centrist parties and popular opinion.

Although the government was forced to compromise with the Kōmei Party and DSP in order to gain their support in passing the PKO Bill, the two parties differed over their own interpretations of the restraints to be imposed. In line with the idea of the civilian control of the military, for instance, the DSP favoured the overseas despatch of the SDF only after the Diet had approved the mission. The Kōmei Party, in contrast, was satisfied with a report to the Diet after its completion. Still, despite the DSP framing its position in terms of 'civilian control', a central element in the liberal approach to militarism discussed in Chapter 1, the party was actually more concerned with leaving open the possibility of being able to exercise influence in any future Diet deliberations on the overseas despatch of the SDF. For the Kōmei Party, the central issue was the implication of prior approval by the Diet in a changed political situation: if the ruling party regained control of a majority of seats in the House of Councillors, the argument ran, the SDF could be despatched abroad even if this action infringed the five principles.[58]

Nevertheless, the government's tactic of limiting the size and scope of SDF activities as a way to gain the centrist parties' support could not hide the further erosion of the Constitution's framework of restraint. The socialists, in particular, brought to the forefront of Diet debate the contradiction between the new legislation and previous government positions, and the difficulty of maintaining the five principles. For instance, questions were raised in the Diet on point 4 regarding the ability of the government to withdraw Japanese troops as, in participating in UN Peace-Keeping Operations, all would be placed under UN command.[59] Likewise, questions were raised on point 5 regarding limiting weapon use to self-defence, questioning whether in the field a distinction could always be drawn between the 'use of weapons' and the 'exercise of force'.

The strength of the opposition to the unfettered despatch of the SDF is clear from the delay in passing the legislation, which did not occur until June 1992. Thus, the Bill continued to be deliberated under Prime Minister Kaifu in the autumn of 1991, and for several months after Miyazawa Ki'ichi took over the reigns of power in November 1991. As a result of the need to take into account public opinion and the parliamentary opposition, the government was forced to accept a numerical limit of 2,000 personnel. Similarly, Ichikawa Kazuo, leader of the Kōmei Party, successfully proposed a freeze on Japan's participation in UN Peace-Keeping Forces. In the end, the SDF's participation in UN Peace-Keeping Forces was frozen for three years, with new legislation required in order to eliminate the freeze (appended Article 2). What this meant is that, instead of the SDF participating in activities such as ceasefire monitoring, collection and disposal of weapons, patrolling buffer zones, clearing land mines and assisting in the exchange of prisoners, they were restricted to behind-the-line operations involving transportation; communications; construction; health, sanitation and medicine; and assisting refugees, as in the case of their later despatch to Cambodia, Mozambique and Zaire. Quintessentially, this was the compromise necessary in order to maintain the SDF's image as other than a 'normal' military force. As we will see below in the case of the despatch of troops to Cambodia, however, on-the-ground SDF activities included some 'grey areas'.

Opposition to the PKO Bill

In contrast to the position taken by the two centrist parties, which cooperated with the government, the socialists, communists and the small Shaminren sought to prevent the Bill's passage. The position taken by these parties enjoyed popular support, at least in the beginning, as we will see in Chapter 5. At the same time, however, with the ending of the cold war and the call on Japan to make an 'international contribution', the weakness of criticism centring on whether or not certain SDF activities were in line with the principles of the Constitution became self-evident. More specifically, the opposition did not devote enough energy to defining in what ways Japan should make an 'international contribution', preferring instead to focus on the problems in the government's proposals. Further, the ending of the cold war had eroded any neat division between the socialist party and the labour union movement, which took as their premise the unconstitutionality of the SDF, on the one hand; and the ruling LDP, which took as its premise the constitutionality of the SDF, on the other. This can be seen, for instance, in the unwillingness of the labour unions to support the socialists' call for an all-out struggle against the PKO legislation. Indeed, with a *Rengō* (Japanese Trade Union Federation) group having fielded its own candidates and won several seats in the House of Councillors, the attitude of the labour unions to the SDF had already changed. *Rengō,* for instance, now accepted the existence of the SDF so long as they were under civilian control and were limited to strict territorial defence, and the three non-nuclear principles were retained.[60] What is more, in the spring of 1992 the then Deputy Prime Minister Kanemaru Shin had sought to gain the socialist party's support for a compromise bill limiting the SDF's despatch to Cambodia, and excluding participation in the PKF. Faced with the adamant opposition of the left-wing factions within the party, however, this proposal got nowhere, despite some interest on the part of the then head of the socialist party, Tanabe Makoto.[61]

Over the many years of trying to prevent the overseas despatch of Japanese troops in line with a rejection of 'a revival of militarism' as well as a rejection of a Japanese identity rooted in 'normal' military forces, opposition to the despatch of troops *per se* had become the goal in itself. In this sense, the despatch of the SDF went to the very heart of the question of Japan's identity, challenging that of 'pacifist Japan', as Doi phrased it. It is for this very reason that the tactics adopted by the socialists as a way to try to prevent the passage of the legislation went beyond the established practice of Diet democracy. Indeed, the socialists and the other parties voted at a snail's pace – the so-called 'ox-walk' – continuing for an unprecedented four nights and five days, with the 137 members of the socialist party and the 4 members of the Shaminren offering their resignation *en masse* in protest. These actions symbolized tactics of 'last resort': pragmatically, as a way to resist the inevitable result of the majority voting power of the ruling and centrist parties in the

Diet, as well as symbolically, as a way to appeal directly to the people as the final arbiters in the preservation of 'pacifist Japan', i.e. a peaceful regime. In a most fundamental sense, the tactics adopted demonstrated a rejection of parliamentary democracy defined simply in terms of a majority of votes in the Diet. Similar tactics had been used at the time of the 1960 revision of the security treaty, the 1965 normalization of relations with South Korea and the 1988 introduction of the consumption tax. In these cases, too, opposition was mounted, despite the ruling party's majority in the Diet. In the case of the PKO legislation, however, mass action was not forthcoming, popular opinion having by now swung round to greater support for the government's policy of making an 'international contribution'. For this reason, the tactics of 'last resort' became the object of widespread popular criticism.

Notwithstanding the absence of over one-third of the Diet members from the chamber, the government went ahead and passed the Bill with support from the DSP and Kōmei Party. The communist and other 'nay' votes amounted to seventeen. Despite their statements of opposition, LDP Dietmen Gotōda, Kujiraoka and other intra-party critics voted in favour of the Bill. In the end, therefore, legislation permitting the large-scale despatch of the SDF on PKO duties became law for the first time in June 1992. Despite their adoption of a tactic of 'last resort', once the legislation had been passed, the socialists paid little heed to the overseas activities of the SDF. As one socialist Diet member lamented:

> Should we really just leave things as they are once the legislation has been passed? It is exactly the same as the socialist party's attitude towards defence expenditures. By not fully discussing their details, giving as the reason the SDF's unconstitutionality, spending continued to increase as a result.[62]

The discourse of opposition

As we have seen, the ending of the cold war presented the LDP with the opportunity to give life to a new security discourse centring on the nation's responsibility to make an 'international contribution'. At the time of the Gulf crisis, however, this use of 'international contribution' as a way to legitimize the new role of the SDF could be challenged by government critics. In a similar way to the cold war 1980s, for instance, they could seek to undermine this appeal by emphasizing that, despite the rhetoric of an 'international contribution', the government's action did not go beyond making an 'American contribution'.[63] In other words, despite the transformation of the international system as a result of the ending of the cold war, the defence and security policies of the Japanese government were still being determined on the basis of the need to respond to the United States rather than the wider international community. Nevertheless, the rhetoric of 'international contribution' embodies a powerful appeal at the mass level, as ambiguity remains as to whether the contribution is 'military' or 'non-military'. Moreover, as we will see below, with the Cambodian prime minister requesting Japan to make a 'contribution' to Cambodian PKO activities, the political efficacy of this sort of opposition rhetoric declined in the wake of the ending of the Gulf War.

At the same time, opponents attempted to undermine the government's position by appealing to the old discourse of anti-militarism, without really developing an alternative discourse rooted in a non-military 'international contribution'. In this sense, the rhetoric of a 'revival of militarism' remained central to the criticism launched by government opponents, who saw the PKO legislation as a further step along this road. Such a perspective is evident among the socialists in opposing the overseas despatch of the SDF, as with Ishibashi Masashi, a former head of the JSP.[64] Yet the efficacy of the 'revival of militarism' critique depended very much upon the support of either the domestic audience, which had declined, or especially the former Asian victims of Japanese militarism. With the Cambodian prime minister requesting Japan's cooperation, however, such a rhetorical attack lost efficacy, even if Cambodia had suffered little at the hands of the militarists. Thus, as had often been the case in the past, although the concern of Japan's Asian neighbours over the SDF's despatch was employed as a reason to oppose the government, Asian willingness to accept the sort of constrained military role planned for the SDF challenged the efforts of government critics to characterize the policy as one aspect of 'a revival of militarism'.

Within this discourse of anti-militarism, the SDF were seen to be taking on the characteristics of a 'normal' military, with government opponents seeking to trigger a connection between the despatch of the SDF and pre-1945 practices. The then head of the socialist party, Tanabe Makoto, for instance, inferred that the despatch of the SDF could lead to the introduction of conscription.[65] Similarly, others emphasized this as a further step along the road to the SDF's full participation in collective security arrangements based on the US–Japan security treaty.[66] In such types of attack, explicit or implicit parallels were drawn between the present legitimization for the SDF's overseas despatch, and the despatch of the military in the militarist era. This was explicit, for instance, in the later discussions on the despatch of troops for the 'protection of overseas Japanese'. The logic was seen to be the same as in the militarist era when 'the war spread and troops were sent abroad in the name of rescuing "overseas Japanese" and protecting their life and person'.[67]

Finally, the link between the overseas despatch of the SDF and the threat to Japanese democracy was central, as we have seen in the case of the socialists' use of tactics of 'last resort' in the Diet. It was implied, for instance, that the lack of consensus in society on the exact type of contribution to make in the case of the resolution of the Gulf crisis, Cambodian peace-keeping operations, and so on, meant that government leaders should exercise restraint.[68] With a lack of consensus on sending the military overseas, but overwhelming support for making a non-military contribution to international society, the government's critics appealed to the legitimacy of policies premised on 'consensus'. In this we can see the critics' interpretation of Japanese democracy as being rooted in popular consensus, where rather than politicians taking strong leadership, implementing policies based on a majority of votes in the Diet, they act as the vehicle for implementing policies enjoying widespread support in society. At least this appears to be the case in regard to issues going to the heart of Japanese identity, as with the overseas despatch of the SDF.

THE SDF IN CAMBODIA

In the lead-up to the passage of the PKO legislation, government leaders held a number of meetings with the Cambodian Prime Minister Hun Sen, following Japan's role in helping to bring about the Paris Peace Accord of October 1991.[69] In March 1992, for instance, the prime minister visited Japan and held discussions with Prime Minister Miyazawa and Foreign Minister Watanabe Michio as well as leaders of the opposition. At the time, he made a request for the despatch of SDF personnel as well as financial support to reconstruct Cambodia.[70] In seeking to demonstrate that Japan was making an 'international contribution', Prime Minister Miyazawa was able to use the Cambodian prime minister's request as a way to build up support for the passage of the PKO legislation, thereby legitimizing Japan's new role in the region. As he stated in a press interview:

It is inappropriate for Japan, which is geographically close, not to be able to do anything at a time when the Cambodian peace is being finalised through UNTAC's [United Nations Transitional Authority in Cambodia] PKO. We have been requested by Cambodia to cooperate. I very much want to pass the PKO legislation in this Diet.[71]

Despite the periodic warnings from Asia of a 'revival of Japanese militarism', therefore, the despatch of the SDF to Cambodia did not lead to persistent criticism from the region. Indeed, according to Akashi Yasushi, the head of UNTAC, Japan's absence would have been 'odd', given that ASEAN (except Brunei), China, India, Pakistan and Bangladesh made up the main contributors to the operations.[72] In any event, the request from Prime Minister Hun Sen and then the formal request from the United Nations in September 1992 to send Japanese troops to Cambodia eroded the position of the government's opponents.

After sending an investigation team to Cambodia in July 1992, and members of the Defence Agency to Sweden for two weeks of training in September and October 1992, the government despatched the first engineer corps of 600 SDF to Cambodia.[73] The main purpose of this contingent was to repair the road and bridges of highway 2 and highway 3, which had been damaged as a result of the war. In December 1992, as a result of a decision by the Miyazawa Cabinet, these activities were expanded to include the provision of water and fuel, and the transportation of materials for UNTAC. Following a Cabinet decision in February 1993, the SDF's duties were further expanded to include medical assistance to UNTAC. A second corps of engineers was despatched to replace the first corps at the end of March to early April 1993, and commenced repairs of the road and bridges on highway 3. At the end of April 1993 another Cabinet decision was made to expand the scope of SDF operations to include such activities as the provision of accommodation and other facilities for UNTAC. Likewise, in the face of the worsening security situation, which led to the death of a Japanese UN volunteer and later to the death of a Japanese assistant police inspector, the Japanese SDF started to carry arms and wear bullet-proof vests and helmets. The troops then assisted in preparing for the election by transporting and erecting tents, providing food and accommodation for UNTAC officials involved in election work, transporting voting boxes and 'exchanging information on security'. After the successful holding of the election, with a turnout of nearly 90 per cent, the second corps of SDF engineers returned to Japan in September 1993.

As we can see from this brief description, although the primary purpose of the despatch of the SDF was to repair highways and bridges, the SDF's activities moved beyond this, and were gradually transformed from behind-the-line operations to 'grey area' operations related to the actual execution of military activities. For instance, the second engineering corps was involved in carrying out what some observers considered military patrols – the so-called 'exchange of information on security' – despite these types of activity being 'frozen' as part of peace-keeping forces (PKF) actiyities.[74] Critics again pointed to the erosion of constraints on the SDF, as whatever the perceived military need to carry out such activities in the field might have been, these were not approved in the Diet legislation. In this we can see how the controversy over the role of the Japanese military in the post cold-war era is set to continue, even after the SDF's withdrawal from Cambodia.

CONCLUSION

The above discussion demonstrates how the restraint on the overseas despatch of the SDF was eroded within a discourse centring on the responsibility of Japan to make an 'international contribution'. External pressure from the United States played a catalytic role in determining the initial response of the Kaifu government to the resolution of the Gulf crisis. At the same time, however, as in the case of Prime Minister Nakasone's push to expand military spending in the 1980s, the Japanese response to the Gulf crisis and the later decision to despatch troops to Cambodia cannot be understood without taking into account the domestic forces pushing for the overseas despatch of the SDF, with Ozawa Ichirō, in particular, pressing for them to play an international role as part of a new identity for Japan as a 'normal' military state. As we will see in the next chapter, the greater popular support for Japan to make an 'international contribution', even if this included the despatch of Japanese minesweepers, as supported by the business community, facilitated this task. Later, the call of Prime Minister Hun Sen for a Japanese presence in Cambodia helped to smooth the despatch of the SDF on peace-keeping operations. In all, the passage of legislation to permit the overseas despatch of the SDF went forward without a consensus existing in the Diet or at the mass level.

The institutionalization of this new role for the SDF is not to suggest the 'revival of militarism'. As we have seen, the crucial element in militarization in the early 1990s is the process of restoring legitimacy to the military as an instrument of state policy. Certainly, Japan's military role would not be considered 'excessive' by normal international standards. It should be noted, however, that the overseas despatch of the SDF has revived one of the classic concerns of analysts of 'militarism' – civilian control.[75] At heart, the real issue is the divergent concepts of democracy, as the ruling party's use of special Cabinet orders to circumvent the democratic control exercised by the Diet to bring about a major change in defence policy was seen as a failure of due democratic process by government critics. A similar concern was expressed at the time of the Danwakai's activities, suggesting a continuing connection in critics' minds between democracy and a peaceful regime. We also have seen how, after the SDF was despatched to Cambodia, the scope of activity was expanded, leading to criticism that the SDF were acting as PKF, despite the 'freeze' on such activity in Diet legislation. In both cases opponents mounted their criticism within the framework of civilian (Diet) control of the military.

Nevertheless, the opponents' criticisms and the opposition's control of a majority of seats in the House of Councillors did lead to a number of restrictions being placed on the SDF's activities. These acted as a restraint, at least to some extent. At the same time, however, the restructuring of the political party system in the interim suggests that the review of the PKO legislation due to take place in 1995 may lead to the abolition of these restraints. The Japan Frontier Party (Shinshintō), which was formed in December 1994, has called for a review of the freeze on the SDF's participation in UN PKF. This reflects the party's view that one of the SDF's main duties is to carry out international activities.[76] It is unclear at this time what effect the change in the make-up of the political parties will exert on the future role of the SDF. What is clear, however, is the importance of understanding popular attitudes as an indication of the way that the political parties may respond. In Chapter 5 we turn to the persistence and change in attitudes at the mass level.

5 Persistence and change in mass attitudes

We have seen in the previous chapters how Japanese defence and security policies have been a source of controversy in the post-1945 period. The experience of the war, both as a militarized aggressor and as a victim, especially of the nuclear attacks on Hiroshima and Nagasaki; the promulgation of a new Constitution, with an anti-militaristic Preamble and Article 9; the abolition of and then gradual build-up of military forces, culminating in the present-day SDF; and Japan's alliance with the United States, premised on the extension of the 'nuclear umbrella', have all helped to shape mass attitudes towards a whole range of defence and security policies. Thus attitudes at the mass level are a result of the longer-term influences of history and political culture as well as the shorter-term influences of specific domestic and international events and pressures. As such, they are manifest in public opinion polls and participation in political movements and demonstrations, as well as in voting patterns. Although election results most directly measure popular acceptance of, acquiescence in or rejection of government policies, nation-wide public opinion polls also provide valuable insight into popular attitudes towards these policies.

True, establishing a causal relationship between public opinion and the formulation of government policy is problematic. Some even go so far as to claim an 'absence of public opinion' in Japanese politics.[1] Nevertheless, the work of Weinstein, Umemoto and Berger points to an important role for public opinion in security-related policy areas.[2] Japanese writings on defence and security issues suggest that public opinion plays a similar role.[3] In this sense, 'mass opinion' is an important variable which influences the government's formulation of defence and security policies.[4] Broadly speaking, this is the backdrop against which government policies are formulated; more narrowly, public opinion polls can be used to actively promote, support or oppose specific government policies. Directly or indirectly, public opinion on defence and security issues constrains the government's flexibility in policy areas such as defence and diplomacy. Therefore, in order to come to an understanding of the level of support for both the establishment and erosion of constraints on militarization in Japan, the nature of mass attitudes needs to be examined. This should help to shed light on the broader issue of popular attitudes towards 'identity' and 'normality' in the post-1945 period.

Most of the data for this chapter are taken from the array of polls regularly carried out by the major national newspapers, the national broadcasting corporation, NHK, and the Prime Minister's Office.[5] Despite limitations arising from differences in sampling techniques, time between surveys and the wording of questions, which can result from political motivations, these polls offer the best source for analysing mass attitudes on defence and security issues. The results of these surveys are publicized through the media, which helps to shape attitudes. Although divisions exist in Japanese society due to differences in age, sex, occupation, political affiliation and so on, these are not our concern; nor are minor statistical variations between the different polls. Rather, we will focus on the broader trends in the polls in order to try to reach a clearer understanding of persistence and change in mass attitudes towards defence and security issues and policies. In line with the focus of Chapters 3 and 4, we are particularly interested in identifying these trends in the 1980s and early 1990s. Thus, we will examine polls on the revision of the Constitution and Article 9; the SDF's necessity, size and budget; the role of the SDF and the general question of Japan's 'international contribution'; and the US–Japan security treaty and nuclear weapons.

CONSTITUTIONAL REVISION AND ARTICLE 9

Public opinion polls on Japanese attitudes towards the Constitution are of interest to us in so far as the questions pertain to revision of the Constitution, generally, and revision of Article 9, specifically. Since the end of the Occupation a range of polls have been carried out on popular attitudes towards revision of the Constitution, with some focusing directly on Article 9. Although general questions on constitutional revision can obviously evoke responses not directly related to this Article, they do provide indirect evidence of support or opposition to the revision of Article 9, as this has been central to the debate on constitutional revision. Figure 5.1 presents the findings

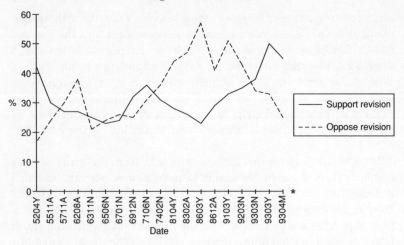

Figure 5.1 Revision of Constitution
*See end of note 5, pp. 220–1 for date and poll style

of representative nation-wide surveys from 1952 to 1993. What is striking about these results is the lack of an overall consensus on whether or not to revise the Constitution. This is especially true during the 1950s and 1960s, with approximately two-fifths to one-half of those polled either unable or unwilling to respond (the 'uncommitted'), but even in the 1970s, 1980s and early 1990s approximately one-quarter to one-third of the respondents did not come down on either side of the divide. What we do find, however, is that after the end of the Vietnam War in 1975 a growing number of people switch to opposition, with 40 per cent and occasionally a majority opposed to revision in the 1980s. We then find a sharp increase in support for constitutional revision in 1993, with the uncommitted moving to support this option. This seems to have ended the long-term opposition to revision evident during the cold war era.

Thus, the increased mass opposition to revision through the 'Nakasone 1980s' is in sharp contrast to the response in polls carried out after the despatch of the SDF to Cambodia. Three polls in the spring of 1993 highlight this dramatic change: 38 per cent in an NHK survey in March, 50.4 per cent in a *Yomiuri* survey in March, and 44 per cent in a *Mainichi* survey in April, support constitutional revision. With the *Yomiuri* poll showing a majority in favour of revision for the first time, if only by a whisker, the possibility that a popular

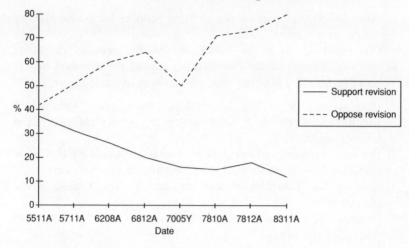

Figure 5.2 Revision of Article 9

referendum on the Constitution would vote for revision appeared on the horizon. Certainly, the *Yomiuri* regarded its own poll results as 'epochal', according to an editorial of 3 April 1993.

A similar increase in mass opposition to revision up into the 1980s can be found in the case of the polls available specifically on revision of Article 9 in order to establish a normal military. As is evident from Figure 5.2, when people were asked if they supported or opposed the revision of Article 9 in order to establish a 'regular military', three-quarters of those polled in the 1970s and early 1980s balked at the idea. This is in contrast to the situation in 1955, when 42 per cent opposed and 37 per cent supported revision. These responses indicate that, immediately after the creation of the SDF and the firming up of the '1955 system' pitting the 'revise the Constitution' LDP against the 'protect the Constitution' JSP, popular evaluation of the SDF and the Constitution was still fluid. Up into the 1980s, however, opposition steadily grew stronger at the same time as support for revision grew weaker. In other words, the uncommitted came down firmly on the side of opposing revision. A popular consensus thus emerged against establishing a regular military, at least into the 1980s. What is more, even if the 1993 polls on revision of the Constitution *per se* point to possible support for revision of Article 9, this does not mean that popular support to establish a 'regular military' has emerged in the post cold war era, despite the efforts of Nakasone and Ozawa to build support for a new identity for Japan as a 'normal state'.

This point seems to be borne out by the reasons given for supporting revision of the Constitution among those polled by the *Yomiuri* in March 1993. The multiple answers are as follows:

1. Because new issues like international contribution have arisen which cannot be dealt with under the present Constitution (56 per cent).
2. Because confusion will arise if responses are made by the interpretation and application of the Constitution (31 per cent).
3. Because the Constitution was imposed by the United States (23 per cent).
4. Because there is too much emphasis on rights and a neglect of duties (21 per cent).
5. In order to stipulate clearly the state's right of self-defence and establish a regular military (6 per cent).

As these answers suggest, support for revision is strongest in order to make an 'international contribution', not to establish a 'regular military'. In this sense, the consensus on mass opposition to setting up a regular military still appears to be firmly in place.

As we saw in Chapter 4, the key to the question of constitutional revision is the interpretation of Article 9, with respective LDP governments having taken the position that the SDF are not a 'regular military' and are therefore constitutional. The socialist-led coalition government of Murayama Tomi'ichi also accepted the constitutionality of the SDF in 1994. Figure 5.3 shows that a small increase has occurred over the years in support of the SDF's co-existence with Article 9, with nearly one-half of those polled accepting their constitutionality from the late 1970s onwards. A minority of about one-fifth balk at this interpretation. Despite this lack of consensus, the increase in support for the SDF *and* the Constitution indicates that, over the years, the government has marked up some success in garnering mass support for its own interpretation of Article 9; namely, that it does not prohibit the possession of 'minimum defensive strength'.

Therefore, so long as the 'SDF' and 'minimum defensive strength' appear to be compatible, no dramatic, short-term changes in mass opinion on the constitutionality of the SDF should be expected. But this seems to be what happened in June 1984 and September 1992, when in both cases the uncommitted opted for 'unconstitutional', increasing the 'no' response to nearly one-third. This perhaps means

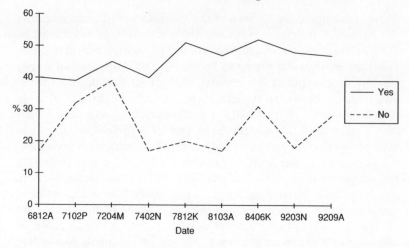

Figure 5.3 Constitutionality of Self-Defence Forces

that, at least initially, the uncommitted saw Nakasone's military build-up, on the one hand, and the decision to send the SDF overseas, on the other, as incompatible with 'minimum defensive strength', and thus expressed a clear choice. Certainly, even though polls in 1990–2 point to a growing willingness on the part of mass opinion to support the SDF's despatch in some capacity, as discussed below, over one-half still saw a constitutional problem. In *Asahi* surveys in November 1991 and April 1992, for instance, a majority of 59 and 54 per cent respectively agreed that there was a constitutional problem in the SDF participating in UN PKF (27 and 30 per cent saw no problem). Similarly, in an *Asahi* survey of July 1992 a majority of 58 per cent saw a constitutional problem in the overseas despatch of the SDF on PKO activities (26 per cent saw no problem). These responses indicate that, even among the supporters of the SDF's constitutionality, many saw their overseas despatch as problematic, despite the passage of government legislation. This may help to explain the support that we found for constitutional revision in the above-mentioned 1993 surveys.

Similarly, a number of surveys in the 1980s showed that up to two-fifths of those polled supported the revision of the constitution in order to clarify the right of self-defence and the constitutionality of the SDF. In a series of *Yomiuri* polls in April 1981, November 1984, March 1986 and June 1988, for instance, between one-fifth and one-quarter opted for revision of the Constitution in order to clarify the right of self-defence, with one-third to two-fifths regarding the SDF as constitutional, implying no need to carry out a revision. Likewise, in an *Asahi* survey of December 1980, when asked if they supported or opposed the revision of the Constitution in order to give clear constitutional recognition to the SDF, 44 per cent of those polled expressed support, 41 per cent opposition, and only 15 per cent were non-committal. An NHK poll of September 1982, moreover, shows that only 17 per cent thought the Constitution prohibited the possession of any arms, 42 per cent thought they were permitted for purposes of self-defence, so long as nuclear weapons were excluded, and 8 per cent were also prepared to accept nuclear weapons. Such responses seem to indicate that the popular constraint on the government's security policies is not so much in terms of adhering to a Japanese identity rooted in an unarmed, non-violent policy with no SDF, but is rather in terms of the SDF's type of equipment and role.

As discussed in detail below, this now includes making an 'international contribution'. In this sense, the Gulf crisis, the American pressure on Japan and the despatch of the SDF to Cambodia and elsewhere on PKO activities can be said to have provided a new opportunity for those political forces attempting to reshape popular attitudes towards acceptance of constitutional revision. As we mentioned in Chapter 4, revision of the Constitution has been a central plank of the LDP's party platform from the mid-1950s onwards. In the first election after the formation of the party and the reunification of the socialists in 1955, the opposition captured more than the one-third of seats needed to prevent a revision of the Constitution, and continued to do so until the breakdown of the 1955 system in 1993. Consequently, this policy was never put into practice. Although the question of constitutional revision has periodically arisen in the interim, it was really the Gulf crisis that sparked renewed interest. The *Yomiuri Shinbun* has been at the forefront of those domestic forces calling for a revision of the Constitution. With the above change in public opinion as the backdrop, in November 1994 the company published a concrete proposal to revise the Constitution, including Article 9.[6] At the same time, the blossoming debate on the Constitution and Japanese security in the post cold-war era highlights how the question of the revision of the Constitution now has broken out of the cold war straitjacket imposed by the 1955 system. It has certainly become far more complex. If our interpretation of the above polls is any indication, the increase in support for a revision of the Constitution is connected with increased popular recognition of the SDF's need to play an expanded role, not support for a regular military.

SDF'S NECESSITY, SIZE AND BUDGET

The above opposition to establishing a 'regular military' is in stark contrast to the opinions expressed in a range of surveys on the question of the necessity of the SDF. This question is relevant in the Japanese context, as we saw in Chapter 3, as one interpretation of Article 9 is that it prohibits the SDF's existence. Although this is the interpretation accepted by a majority of legal scholars,[7] at the mass level persistent and overwhelming support can be found for the existence of the SDF from the mid-1960s onwards. Figure 5.4 provides the results of the polls carried out by the Prime Minister's Office (PMO) between 1965 and 1984, when people were asked directly whether or not they thought the SDF were necessary. In all of these surveys three-quarters to four-fifths agreed, highlighting a powerful consensus on the necessity of the SDF, particularly after the ending of the Vietnam War. A similar high degree of support can be seen in a Jiji Tsūshinsha poll of October 1987, with three-quarters supporting and one-tenth opposing the SDF's existence. In this sense, the persistent mass opposition to establishing a regular

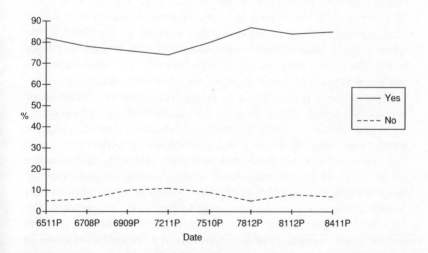

Figure 5.4 Necessity of Self-Defence Forces

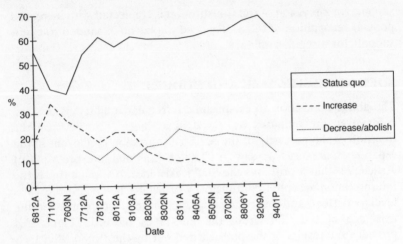

Figure 5.5 Strength of Self-Defence Forces

military goes hand in hand with persistent support for the existence of the SDF.

The interplay between these two positions appears in response to questions on the size and budget of the SDF, with mass support being expressed generally for constraints on the SDF as defensive forces, either passively, in support of the status quo, or actively, in support of defence cuts. As is evident from Figure 5.5, the polls point to majority support for maintaining the strength of the SDF at the 'present level' over the last twenty-five years, with around two-thirds in this category during the 1980s and early 1990s. In contrast to this persistent support for the status quo, approximately one-tenth to one-quarter of those polled fluctuate in supporting either a build-up or a reduction in the SDF's strength, with a dramatic change occurring during the Nakasone 1980s, when the uncommitted moved to support a reduction rather than a build-up in defensive strength. This support has continued into the post cold war 1990s. Thus, the maintenance of the SDF at the 'present level' enjoys strong popular backing, despite the actual build up of the SDF over the years, with support for increases and decreases seeming to fluctuate as a result of the uncommitted responding to the domestic and international political and security environments of the day. In this sense, the increase in support for the status quo can be said to arise from a popular tendency to give *post-factum* backing to the government's policies, with a small percentage of people from the 1980s onwards having come to favour defence cuts.

In the 1980s a variety of polls were conducted on whether Japan should bow to pressure from the United States to increase the SDF's defensive strength and take on new roles such as defending the SLOCs. In general the surveys show that about one-half of those polled were prepared to swallow the American demands in some form or other, especially when they were not linked to a specific military role like defending the sea lanes, with about one-third opposed. NHK polls in August 1981, March 1982 and February 1983 show about one-half (respectively 49, 50 and 53 per cent) prepared to accept and one-third (30, 33 and 34 per cent) set to reject the American demand to beef up the SDF. When a *Yomiuri* poll of August 1982 asked whether this should be done in order to assist the United States in the Middle East and the Indian Ocean, however, only 21 per cent agreed, with 40 per cent opposed. These results highlight how 'American pressure' can influence the uncommitted, especially towards support for increasing 'defensive strength', but not specific 'military roles'. This latter is more likely to evoke an image of the SDF as a 'regular military', challenging the identity of Japan as a demilitarized state.

Figure 5.6 shows similar persistent support of approximately 40–60 per cent for status quo spending on defence. Again, approximately one-tenth to one-quarter of those polled fluctuate in favour of more or less spending, with less spending favoured with the winding down of the Vietnam War, more spending at the time of a heightened sense of the 'Soviet threat', and then steady support for less spending after 1984. As in the case of popular attitudes on defensive strength, the low support for increased spending and a higher support for a decrease in spending has continued into the post cold war 1990s. The one-quarter support for a reduction in 1991 was short-lived, however: in 1994 this dropped back to one-fifth, about the same as in January 1988. In this sense, the ending of the cold war does not appear to have brought about a swell of popular opinion demanding that military spending should be slashed, with the uncommitted seeming to swing back to support of the status quo.

As we have seen in Chapter 3, defence spending was a major point of controversy during the 1980s, what with American pressure to boost spending and the Nakasone government's push to abandon the 1 per cent ceiling and to treat defence spending as 'sacrosanct'. It is thus not surprising to find a large number of polls devoted to defence spending during this period. What popular support existed

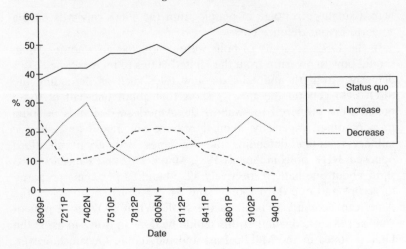

Figure 5.6 Defence expenditures

for keeping spending to 1 per cent of GNP before the ceiling was scrapped in January 1987? A series of *Yomiuri* polls between 1981 and 1984 suggest that 40–50 per cent of those polled regarded 1 per cent spending on the SDF as appropriate, with an increase from 41 per cent in August 1981 to 52 per cent in December 1984. Around one-fifth of pollees regarded 1 per cent as too much. The combined total of the supporters of the 1 per cent status quo and the supporters of reduced spending increased from 57 to 73 per cent between 1981 and 1984. As seen in Figure 5.6, a similar though less pronounced increase in the combined support for the status quo and cuts in defence spending occurs between 1981 and 1984 (62–71 per cent). Likewise, a high degree of support for the status quo or for a reduction in spending is evident in other polls: *Mainichi* polls show 71 per cent in November 1983 and 78 per cent in April 1985, and NHK polls show 55 per cent in March 1982 and 63 per cent in February 1985 expressing such opinions. Despite the differences between these surveys, opposition to an increase in military spending was clearly on the upswing.

Thereafter, polls in September 1985 show an increase in support for beefing up defence spending, with a *Mainichi* poll showing 22 per cent (compared to 12 per cent in April 1985) and an NHK poll showing 30 per cent (compared to 21 per cent in February 1985) prepared to accept the scrapping of the ceiling. This perhaps suggests the potency of the 'free-rider' argument or the efficacy of Nakasone's campaign to boost spending. Still, the largest percentage continued to support the status quo or a reduction. When we come to examine the results of a Jiji Tsūshinsha poll in October 1987, after the scrapping of the ceiling, again we find nearly two-thirds (60 per cent) support the status quo, with about one-quarter (23 per cent) calling for a reduction and 9 per cent calling for an increase in spending. As defence spending only went beyond the ceiling by 0.04 per cent, we could say that support was in essence still for spending at about the 1 per cent level. Indeed, an *Asahi* poll of October 1988 shows a majority of 54 per cent expressing support for low spending on the military, with 38 per cent opposed to spending over 1 per cent and 16 per cent calling for a reduction. At the same time, however, these results again seem to indicate the willingness of mass opinion to give *post-factum* support to government policies.

As we saw in Chapter 3, the 1980s were the years of the 'Soviet threat', 'sea-lane defence' and Prime Minister Nakasone's call to review the Constitution as part of his policy of 'settling the post-war account'. In this sense, the Nakasone years seem to have given rise to an increase in opposition to boosting military strength or defence expenditures, symbolizing popular concern over 'military big powerism' (e.g. abandoning the 1 per cent ceiling) combined with pre-war values (e.g. visit to Yasukuni Shrine). This concern over Nakasone's policies is clear from NHK surveys between 1983 to 1987, which show that over one-half of those polled (except for 49 per cent in September 1985) think the government is swinging to the right on constitutional and defence issues, with a high of 62 per cent in a June 1983 survey. This compares with 36 per cent in the case of the Suzuki Cabinet (March 1981 NHK survey). What is more, *Yomiuri* surveys show that between one-third and one-half of those polled list dissatisfaction over defence policy as one of two possible reasons for not supporting the Nakasone Cabinet, with a high of 58 per cent in an October 1985 survey. This is in marked contrast to the less than one-fifth who gave dissatisfaction over defence policy as one of their reasons for not supporting the Takeshita Cabinet, with only 16 per cent giving this as their reason in a February 1988 survey. Finally, as evident from PMO polls conducted every December, throughout the Nakasone era more than one-third of those polled considered that the nation was heading in a 'bad direction' on defence, with those thinking it was heading in a 'good direction' registering less than one-tenth. Clearly, the swing in mass opinion to oppose the increase in the SDF's strength and greater spending was directly related to the policies pursued by the Nakasone government.

THE ROLE OF SDF AND JAPAN'S 'INTERNATIONAL CONTRIBUTION'

Athough the 1980s were dominated by the question of boosting defensive strength, increasing military expenditure and expanding the range of SDF duties, in the 1990s the question of Japan's 'international contribution' has dominated the defence agenda. When people were asked to choose one specific area in which the SDF have made a contribution over the years, however, few chose 'national security' or 'international contribution' (included as an item in the PMO poll for the first time in 1991); instead, as in the 1970s, the overwhelming response has been 'disaster relief'. PMO polls in the 1970s, 1980s and 1990s all show that around three-quarters of those polled consistently choose this area, with 74 per cent in November 1972, 73 per cent in December 1981 and 73 per cent in January 1994. This low perception of the SDF's single most important contribution being the maintenance of national security is matched by a similar low level of popular demand for the government to devote future efforts in this area, as we will see below.

At the same time, however, these responses should not be taken to mean that the SDF are perceived as making no contribution to the peace and security of Japan. As an NHK survey of March 1981, an *Asahi* survey of May 1984 and an *Asahi* survey of October 1988 indicate, one-half to nearly two-thirds said that the SDF have made some contribution. Moreover, when people are not limited to responding in just one area of contribution, a high percentage endorse the SDF's role in national security, along with disaster relief and cooperation in public welfare. In a *Yomiuri* poll of July 1984, for instance, respectively 73, 93 and 87 per cent of the pollees thought that the SDF had made a 'major' or 'small' contribution in these areas. Clearly, the high percentage of responses in the 'disaster relief' category does not mean a lack of popular awareness of the SDF's defence role. Nevertheless, as the *Yomiuri* poll highlights, the SDF are *not* seen as making a significant contribution in this area: only 17 per cent thought that the SDF had made a 'major' contribution to national security, compared to 60 per cent support for disaster relief and 43 per cent for cooperation in public welfare.

Similarly, Figure 5.7 consistently shows more support for future efforts in the area of 'disaster relief' than in the area of 'national

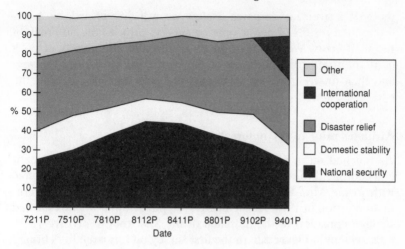

Figure 5.7 Area for future efforts by Self-Defence Forces

security', except for the early 1980s. A *Yomiuri* poll of June 1988 also shows stronger support for disaster relief, with 42 per cent supporting further efforts in this area and 35 per cent in the area of national security. Moreover, in the latest PMO survey of 1994, those polled give nearly as much support to the SDF's future effort in the new category of 'international contribution' as 'national security'. Indeed, the two seem to be correlated, with a large decline in support for national security between 1991 and 1994 (from 33 to 24 per cent), but with less impact on the 'disaster relief' category. As we shall see below, the SDF's 'international contribution' seems less controversial after the despatch of the SDF to Cambodia on PKO activities, despite initial opposition.

At stake is the question of whether Japan should make a military or non-military 'international contribution'. In this context, a number of surveys have been carried out from the mid-1960s onwards on mass attitudes towards the SDF's overseas despatch to cooperate with the United Nations (the only context in which the public have been questioned about overseas despatch). The need for the government to respond to the Gulf crisis generated renewed interest in this question among pollsters, with a number of surveys being carried out in the early 1990s. These polls highlight the nature of the persistence and change in mass attitudes towards the general question of Japan's international contribution as well as towards the specific question of the SDF's overseas despatch. Below we will first provide as background the results of public opinion surveys prior to the outbreak of the Gulf crisis. We will then go on to examine the results of polls carried out after the outbreak of the Gulf crisis but before the war, and then finally move on to discuss the polls carried out after the end of the war.

Attitudes prior to the outbreak of the Gulf War

As touched on in Chapter 4, until the early 1990s the government had continued to regard the despatch of the SDF as unconstitutional, with Prime Minister Satō having stated this as the official government position in 1970. At the mass level, public opinion polls showed strong opposition to the despatch of the SDF for twenty-five years, as is evident in Figure 5.8. In the first survey on this issue in February 1965, for instance, the PMO asked whether or not people supported the SDF's despatch in order to cooperate in some way with the United Nations, with a majority of 55 per cent opposed and less than one-tenth in favour. A high two-thirds to three-quarters of those surveyed persistently opposed and only up to one-quarter supported the SDF's despatch until the outbreak of the Gulf War. At the same time, however, the results of these polls are in marked contrast to two separate surveys carried out by the PMO in June 1983 and

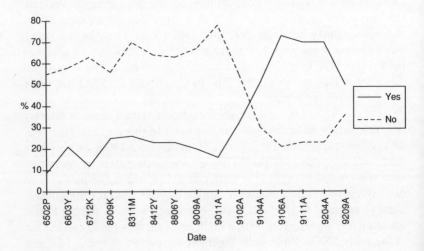

Figure 5.8 Overseas despatch of Self-Defence Forces

October 1986, which show that respectively, 42 and 39 per cent support and 23 and 25 per cent oppose cooperation with the United Nations. Crucially, the PMO surveys did not include the wording 'SDF' and 'overseas despatch', but instead talked about the 'despatch of personnel, provision of materials, financial cooperation and other forms of cooperation' and 'within the limits permitted by domestic law'. The implications of these surveys will become clearer below.

In the autumn of 1990, prior to the outbreak of the Gulf War in January 1991, mass opinion overwhelmingly supported a completely non-military contribution to the resolution of the crisis. In an *Asahi* poll of November 1990, for instance, over three-quarters (78 per cent) favoured a non-military contribution, with only 15 per cent in favour of sending the SDF. This is in marked contrast to American opinion at this time, when 65 per cent agreed to 'use force' and 46 per cent supported 'engage in combat'.[8] The strength of popular support for a non-military contribution is confirmed in a December 1990 *Asahi* poll: when asked what stance the government should adopt in international conflicts like the Middle East crisis, only 9 per cent favoured the SDF's despatch, with 33 per cent in favour of drawing the line at financial assistance, 29 per cent in favour of diplomatic efforts and 19 per cent in favour of despatching non-military support groups. Before the outbreak of the war, therefore, mass attitudes against the despatch of the SDF were even stronger than at the time of the Vietnam War.

Attitudes after the outbreak of the Gulf War

After the outbreak of the Gulf War, however, a change can be detected in public opinion, with a greater willingness to accept Japan playing a limited role involving the SDF. Thus, in an *Asahi* poll of February 1991, although a majority still opposed the despatch of SDF planes to transport refugees, one-third endorsed it. The lack of consensus on support for the SDF's participation in peacekeeping activities is clear from a PMO poll of February 1991, which shows that 46 per cent approved and 38 per cent disapproved of this role. Support for the overseas despatch of the SDF in order to contribute to disaster relief efforts is much stronger: in the same PMO survey a majority (54 per cent) was in favour and 30 per cent against.

Attitudes after the end of the Gulf War

After the end of the war, mass opinion for the first time expressed support for the SDF's limited involvement in some form of 'international contribution' involving military activity. In an *Asahi* survey of April 1991, for instance, a majority supported the despatch of the SDF on minesweeping duties, with 56 per cent in favour and 30 per cent opposed. This support was given despite the fact that over 40 per cent perceived a constitutional problem in despatching minesweepers overseas (46 per cent saw a problem; 33 per cent did not). The change in mass attitudes was even clearer by June 1991. This time, after the minesweepers had been despatched, an *Asahi* survey shows that over two-thirds (65 per cent) of those polled agreed that this was 'good', with only a quarter (24 per cent) not thinking so. Even after the government's major financial contribution to the resolution of the Gulf crisis and the despatch of the SDF on minesweeping duties, the same survey shows that 39 per cent of those polled still considered that Japan had not contributed enough, with 36 per cent regarding the level of contribution as appropriate and only 14 per cent responding that Japan had done too much. This seems to indicate that the domestic and international criticism of Japan as doing 'too little, too late' influenced mass attitudes.

The growing popular acceptance of Japan making an international contribution is clear from the fact that, when asked in the June 1991 *Asahi* poll whether Japan should play a more active role in the resolution of international conflicts, nearly two-thirds (61 per cent) agreed that this was necessary, with less than one-third (31 per cent) supporting approximately the same level of contribution. What bears note in this poll is the increase in support for the SDF to make this contribution: whereas only 9 per cent favoured the despatch of the SDF in December 1990, in the June 1991 survey 19 per cent supported their despatch in these kinds of crises. Indeed, only 21 per cent opposed the SDF's despatch *per se* with nearly three-quarters now willing to endorse their despatch in one form or other, with 46 per cent in favour of limiting the SDF's role to non-military support, 23 per cent accepting a military role under UN command and 5 per cent approving participation in military activities. A similar response can be found in the *Asahi* survey of November 1991: around three-quarters support the despatch, with 50 per cent in favour of limiting the SDF to non-military support, 19 per cent accepting a military role under UN command and 2 per cent approving participation in military activities. Finally, in an *Asahi* survey of April

1992 around three-quarters supported the SDF's despatch, with 47 per cent in favour of limiting their role to non-military support, 20 per cent accepting a military role under UN command and 4 per cent approving participation in military activities (24 per cent opposed the SDF's despatch overseas). Thus, in line with the longstanding popular support for limiting the role of the SDF, these polls demonstrate a persistent and marked preference at the mass level for Japan to make a non-military international contribution, even if the SDF are despatched overseas.

PKO legislation and the SDF's despatch to Cambodia

Mass attitudes after the passage of the PKO legislation and the despatch of troops to Cambodia highlight a continuing lack of consensus on the exact nature of Japan's 'international contribution'. In an *Asahi* survey of July 1992, for instance, people were divided almost equally among 33 per cent who supported the passage of the PKO legislation, 36 per cent who did not and 28 per cent who remained uncommitted. No doubt the split in the political world over support or opposition for the bill, as manifest most clearly at the time of the socialists' 'ox walk', had an impact on this large increase in the number of the uncommitted. By the time of an *Asahi* poll in September 1992 the uncommitted had moved to back the SDF's despatch to Cambodia, with a majority of 52 per cent now supporting and 36 per continuing to oppose this policy. When the supporters were asked why, the largest percentage (32 per cent) of the 52 per cent gave as their answer 'to fulfil responsibility in international society', which was triple the second response (9 per cent) 'to help Cambodian people'. Still, as heretofore, nearly three-quarters of those polled favoured Japan limiting its 'international contribution' to non-military areas.

In an *Asahi* poll conducted in May 1993, after the actual despatch of the SDF and others to Cambodia, we find that this decision was positively evaluated by 46 per cent, with 33 per cent opposed. As we discussed in Chapter 4, after the deaths of two Japanese nationals the SDF began to participate in activities that were criticized as going beyond the duties approved by Diet legislation, a position that a majority of those in the May poll seem to support: two-thirds (66 per cent) felt a sense of apprehension that the government was gradually expanding the role of the SDF despatched to Cambodia (20 per cent felt no apprehension). Faced with the reality of the SDF's activities in Cambodia (and after that the SDF's despatch to take part in peace-keeping operations in Mozambique), the same poll shows nearly two-thirds (60 per cent) opposed to the further despatch of the SDF on peace-keeping operations, with less than a quarter (21 per cent) in favour. Over two-fifths (42 per cent) felt that Japan's 'international contribution' in non-military areas alone was sufficient (31 per cent insufficient).

As can be seen from the above, by 1991 mass support for the overseas despatch of the SDF in some capacity or other had emerged, with the PMO survey of January 1994 pointing to a growing consensus on the despatch of the SDF for peace-keeping activities: 48 per cent endorsed this role (up from 46 per cent in 1991), with nearly two-thirds (62 per cent) supportive of their despatch for such tasks as disaster relief (up from 54 per cent in 1991). Opponents had respectively declined from 38 per cent in 1991 to 31 per cent in 1994, and 30 per cent in 1991 to 22 per cent in 1994. The burgeoning support for the SDF playing such a role can be seen from the fact that 22 per cent of those polled supported the SDF putting greater effort into 'international contribution' in the future.

Looked at from another perspective, however, the polls also highlight the persistent strength of popular opinion in support of Japan making a non-military 'international contribution'. If we take the approximately one-fifth to one-quarter of people who opposed the SDF's despatch in the above-mentioned *Asahi* surveys as still favouring some form of non-military contribution, together with the 40–50 per cent who support the non-military contribution of the SDF, then 67 per cent in the June 1991 survey, 74 per cent in the November 1991 survey and 71 per cent in the April 1992 survey can be said to favour Japan making a non-military contribution. Indeed, an *Asahi* poll of September 1992 shows that nearly three-quarters support Japan limiting its global contribution to non-military areas. The two-thirds in support of the SDF making a contribution to disaster relief in the 1994 PMO survey clearly points to a greater willingness to support the SDF in playing this role. This suggests that the fault-line in Japanese mass attitudes in the wake of the Gulf War has moved from the question of whether or not to support the despatch of the SDF to the more fundamental question of the nature of Japan's 'international contribution', even if the SDF are involved. The preference still seems to be for non-military contributions.

US–JAPAN SECURITY TREATY AND NUCLEAR WEAPONS

The above discussion of mass attitudes in regard to the SDF gives only the conventional part of the Japanese defence equation; the US–Japan security treaty provides the nuclear input. As is evident from Figure 5.9, support for the combination of the SDF and the security treaty as the most appropriate defence equation for Japan has increased gradually over the past twenty years, with a majority after the mid-1970s. A range of surveys prior to the mid-1970s show strong grassroots opposition to the security treaty, especially at the time of the treaty's revision in 1960. Even in the late 1960s only around a quarter of those polled expressed support for the treaty (*Mainichi* poll of June 1968). The possibility of Japan becoming embroiled in war as a result of the treaty was a constant fear played on by the socialist and communist opposition. In an *Asahi* survey of August 1965, for instance, nearly two-thirds (60 per cent) feared that Japan may be embroiled in an expanded war. The termination of the Vietnam War, along with Chinese support for the treaty after the normalization of relations with the US, eroded the efficacy of this argument. In the years since the war's end, mass support for the status quo defence formula has increased to two-thirds or more, with 69 per cent expressing support in 1994. The lack of backing for the other options suggests a consensus on the status-quo combination of

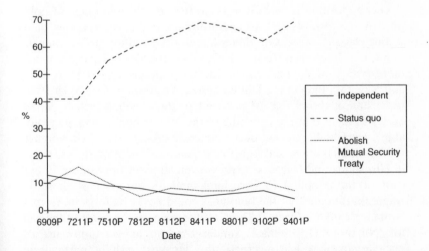

Figure 5.9 Japan's national security strategy

the SDF and the security treaty. The influence of the ending of the cold war was in this sense short-lived: after the 1991 PMO survey had shown a small decrease in support for this formula, support bounced back in 1994, with those in favour of abandoning the treaty and reducing the SDF showing the same trend. The SDF plus security treaty formula seems set to continue to enjoy mass support in the post cold war era, too. Certainly, a large majority of mass opinion continues to evaluate the role of the security treaty positively, with over two-thirds regarding the treaty as 'useful to Japan' from the 1960s onwards, with over two-thirds (68 per cent) endorsing the usefulness of the treaty in the PMO survey of January 1994.

Despite such strong support for the value of the treaty *per se*, a consensus does not exist on the treaty's nuclear aspect, with approximately one-third to close to a majority seeing the 'nuclear umbrella' as unnecessary, about the same amount as see it as necessary. This perhaps indicates a large degree of support for a denuclearized, if not demilitarized, treaty, especially in the post cold war era. This is a security option that we will touch on in the Conclusion. For instance, in an *Asahi* poll of June 1981, a *Yomiuri* poll of November 1984 and an *Asahi* poll of June 1985, respectively 45, 36 and 34 per cent of those polled thought it was necessary, whereas 41, 46 and 46 per cent thought it unnecessary. This lack of consensus reflects the dual structure of mass attitudes on nuclear issues: on the one hand, support for the (nuclear) security treaty; on the other, strong opposition to nuclear weapons.

This opposition is evident in the results of a whole range of polls on attitudes towards the past and future use of nuclear weapons, their testing, Japan's possession thereof, and a recognition of the dangers of nuclear deterrence. To start with, mass attitudes in Japan are much more critical of the past use of nuclear weapons against Hiroshima and Nagasaki than in the United States. An *Asahi* poll of April 1982, for instance, shows that 63 per cent of those polled in the United States thought that the dropping of the atomic bombs was 'unavoidable', whereas 49 per cent of the Japanese thought that the bombings were 'inhumane and unforgivable'.[9] As a 1975 survey shows, those in Hiroshima and Nagasaki express even stronger opposition: 70 per cent of those polled in Hiroshima and 78 per cent of those in Nagasaki thought that the bombings could never be forgiven from a humanistic point of view.[10] These attitudes are at the heart of the call for 'No more Hiroshimas!' Similarly, so far as the future use of nuclear weapons is concerned, the Japanese exhibit particularly strong anti-nuclear attitudes when compared with other countries.

In an *Asahi* poll of November 1983, for instance, Japan followed Switzerland in expressing the second highest opposition (58 per cent) to the use of nuclear weapons, even if nuclear weapons had already been used in an attack. The American public expressed the lowest rate of opposition at 14 per cent. Likewise, an *Asahi* poll of July 1957 shows 87 per cent opposed to the atmospheric testing of nuclear weapons.

Opposition to the possession, not only use, of nuclear weapons is also deeply rooted at the mass level. This is clear from periodic polls carried out from the late 1960s onwards showing strong opposition to Japan going nuclear and support for the three non-nuclear principles of not to produce, possess or introduce nuclear weapons into Japan. In general, two-thirds or more have tended to oppose the possession of nuclear weapons, with a minority of around 10–15 per cent in favour. In a Kyōdō Tsūshin poll of December 1967, for instance, 60 per cent opposed and 14 per cent supported the possession of nuclear weapons. Similarly, at the beginning of the 1980s an *Asahi* poll of March 1981 shows that nearly three-quarters (71 per cent) oppose and 16 per cent approve Japan's possession of nuclear weapons. The same high level of consensus can be found in regard to the three non-nuclear principles, with around three-quarters in support, as seen in an *Asahi* poll of June 1981 (76 per cent), a *Mainichi* poll of November 1983 (64 per cent) and an *Asahi* poll of June 1985 (78 per cent). In the same 1985 *Asahi* poll, moreover, nearly three-quarters (72 per cent) of those polled thought that the Japanese government should follow the example of New Zealand and deny entry to any vessels or planes suspected of carrying nuclear weapons.

Nevertheless, even though there is a popular consensus on the three non-nuclear principles, at the same time between two-thirds and three-quarters of those polled do not believe that the third principle of 'not to introduce' nuclear weapons is being honoured. An *Asahi* poll of June 1981, a *Mainichi* poll of November 1983, a *Yomiuri* poll of November 1984, an *Asahi* poll of June 1985 and a *Yomiuri* poll of July 1988 showed that 79, 65, 65, 73 and 72 per cent respectively of those polled did not believe the government's declared position that no nuclear weapons have been introduced into Japan. When pollsters asked questions that reduced the third non-nuclear principle to 2.5 principles, i.e. permitting introduction in the form of 'transit', then one-third to two-fifths of those polled were prepared to accept 'introduction', with a *Yomiuri* poll of August 1981, a *Yomiuri* poll of November 1984 and a *Yomiuri* poll of July 1988 showing 37, 34 and 35 per cent respectively supportive of 'transit', with 43, 47 and 49 per cent in favour of the strict observance of the three principles. Thus, strong opposition to the reduction of these principles still exists, despite the demands of the US–Japan security treaty.

Finally, mass opposition to nuclear weapons can be seen from the fact that nuclear deterrence in the cold war 1980s was not so much viewed as a deterrent in preventing a US–Soviet nuclear war as a threat to peace. Approximately two-fifths to one-half of those polled viewed nuclear deterrence as a threat to peace in a *Mainichi* poll of November 1983 (41 per cent), a *Yomiuri* poll of November 1984 (49 per cent) and an *Asahi* poll of October 1988 (54 per cent), with approximately one-third supporting the role of nuclear deterrence. This seems to indicate that, among those who express support for the (nuclear) security treaty, this is more passive acquiescence than active support. In any event, the opposition to the use and possession of nuclear weapons and a rejection of nuclear deterrence are persistent features of mass attitudes in Japan.

SIGNIFICANCE OF MASS ATTITUDES

The above discussion of opinion poll results over the past decades has shed light on persistence and change in mass attitudes towards defence and security policies and issues during the cold war and early post cold war years. What, then, can we say about the significance of mass attitudes in Japan? In the first place, these surveys have brought into stark relief the underlying structure of mass attitudes, with a persistent anti-militaristic core at their base. At the most fundamental level this is rooted in an inveterate opposition to participation in any form of aggressive wars. This was manifest most saliently during the cold war in opposition to the revision of Article 9 in order to set up a 'regular military', and opposition to the despatch of the SDF overseas, with the consensus on support for the SDF being in terms of the status quo, i.e. 'minimum self-defence' and an emphasis on their non-military as opposed to military role, as seen in the high evaluation of the SDF's 'disaster relief'. In other words, over the past 40 years of the SDF's existence, a national consensus has gradually emerged on the legitimacy of certain defence and security policies, leading to a greater acquiescence in, if not outright acceptance of, a number of roles for the SDF within a structure of constraint.

This support for 'self-defence' but not 'aggression' symbolizes how the experience of the 'regular military' in Japanese history has been interpreted to mean a need to place restrictions on the role of the SDF. Such attitudes are an outcome of integrating the wartime actions of the military into an anti-militaristic identity for Japan. These attitudes indicate a deep resistance to the military taking on such a role again and are more than a mere opposition to becoming embroiled in war. The historical link between the overseas despatch of Japanese military forces and their participation in aggressive wars has meant that individuals and political forces opposed to militarization have struggled to pass on the lessons of the war, from which arose a deep-rooted antipathy towards despatching the SDF overseas as independent military forces. These attitudes are the basis for the LDP government's adoption of the ban on the overseas despatch of the SDF, the 1 per cent ceiling, the general low military profile of the SDF and so on.

Second, these mass attitudes reflect a deeper recognition that, in the nuclear cold war, the despatch of the SDF could possibly have exacerbated the danger of nuclear war. The strong opposition to the use, testing, production, possession and introduction of nuclear weapons symbolizes how the experience of being atom-bombed has been interpreted as calling for popular resistance to nuclear weapons. These attitudes are the basis for the LDP government's adoption of the three non-nuclear principles. Moreover, as we have seen, despite popular support for the security treaty, no consensus exists on its nuclear aspect, with many rejecting the role of nuclear deterrence. In essence, this reflects the fact that mass opinion does not accept a major role for the security treaty in maintaining peace. *Asahi* polls of October 1978 and December 1994 respectively show much greater recognition of the experience of the war (29 per cent and 24 per cent) and the 'peace Constitution' (17 per cent and 25 per cent) than the security treaty (18 per cent and 17 per cent) in maintaining the peace. Indeed, the Constitution was considered to be the most important reason in the 1994 survey.

True, the popular opposition to the SDF's overseas despatch on military duties and the support for the 'nuclear security treaty' can be interpreted as an unwillingness to 'share the defence burden', as a 'nuclear allergy' or as a general failure to make an 'international contribution'. In this sense, it took the Gulf crisis to bring about a change in popular attitudes on the need for Japan to make a direct contribution to international society, as well as the indirect contribution already being made by the provision of bases and payments to the United States. At the same time, however, the popular acceptance of the overseas despatch of the SDF in the post cold war era indicates that, at heart, popular opposition was in regard to the despatch of the SDF as an instrument of state policy in seeking military solutions to policy problems. Under the slogan of making an 'international contribution', therefore, the government was able to delink the despatch of the SDF to take part in aggressive war, the almost sole purpose for which the imperial military was despatched and the popular fear during the cold war, and their despatch to make an 'international contribution'. Indeed, the government has shown that, by using the SDF for non-military purposes, Japan is able to win the support or even praise of the international community, rather than its opposition or opprobrium.

Still, popular support remains strong for Japan to make a non-military international contribution, as is evident in PMO surveys on the role that Japan should play in international society. In a survey of September 1993, for instance, when people were asked to select two options, the top three choices were to contribute to the resolution of global problems such as global environmental problems (48 per cent), the healthy development of the world economy (29 per cent) and the maintenance of international peace by mediating regional conflicts and in other ways making a contribution including human support (29 per cent). The mass support for Japan making a non-military contribution is clear from an *Asahi* poll of November 1991, when only 14 per cent opted for Japan taking on a military as well as economic and political role in the world, with 29 per cent favouring Japan continuing to play a leadership role in economics and a majority (52 per cent) opting for a political as well as an economic role. This was in contrast to those polled in the United States, where over two-thirds (69 per cent) favoured Japan taking on military responsibilities. Likewise, the deep-seated Japanese opposition to the use of the military can be seen in the case of the North Korean nuclear issue, with a May 1994 *Mainichi* survey showing nearly three-quarters (71 per cent) in support of resolving the problem through dialogue. Finally, an *Asahi* poll of September 1994 shows support for Japan's permanent membership of the UN Security Council at 70 per cent, but only so long as the government is not asked to play a military role. Support drops to 57 per cent if a military contribution is requested.

Thus, although the strong preference at the popular level is for a non-military contribution, it is opposition to the unfettered use of a 'normal' military as an instrument of state policy that is at the heart of popular attitudes. In other words, it is the deep-seated nature of anti-militaristic attitudes that explains why support is most saliently for a non-military rather than a military contribution, with continuing support for constraints to be placed in the way of militarization to prevent Japan becoming a 'normal state' in terms of the normalization of the SDF. Indeed, the end of the cold war seems to have accelerated the decline in popular support for the SDF devoting future efforts to safeguarding Japanese security, as the PMO surveys demonstrate, with support declining from 44 per cent in November 1984 to 38 per cent in January 1988, to 33 per cent in February 1991, to only 24 per cent in January 1994.

So why do we find a change of opinion after the end of the cold war? There are four reasons. In the first place, the end of the cold war and the outbreak of the Gulf crisis cast doubt on the simple equation 'overseas despatch implies participation in an aggressive war'. The international support for Japan to play some kind of military role, even in East Asia, demonstrated that the overseas despatch of the SDF in the post cold war era need not be for aggression. Indeed, it could even gain the approval of the international community. Second, with the end of the cold war the fear that the overseas despatch of the SDF would exacerbate the nuclear stand-off between the East and West was no longer valid. The international cooperation between the United States and the Soviet Union at the time of the Gulf War symbolized the changed international situation. Third, the international criticism of Japan, together with the domestic support for Japan to play a larger political and even military role in international society, as touched on in Chapter 4, played a significant role in bringing about a change in attitudes. As the 1993 *Yomiuri* survey on the revision of the Constitution indicates, the strongest reason for popular support for revision was in order to deal with calls for Japan to make an 'international contribution'. Fourth, the post cold war era has exposed the quintessence of Japanese mass attitudes towards war and peace: at heart they are anti-militaristic, opposing militarism at home, aggressive wars abroad and the use of nuclear weapons. In other words, mass attitudes are not 'pacifist' in a western sense – that is, rooted in a belief in unarmed, non-violence – and are prepared to accept a role for the SDF under constraint.

Finally, despite the continuing strength of these anti-militaristic attitudes, we must also note how many people are prepared to give *post-factum* support to government policies. This can be seen to be the case in support for the SDF and the Constitution, support for defence spending after breaking through the 1 per cent ceiling, turning a blind eye to the infringement of the third non-nuclear principle, supporting the despatch of the SDF in a 'non-military' capacity and so on. This tendency to give *post-factum* legitimacy to the government's security policies marks a level of success on the part of the government in trying to shape popular opinion on security issues.

CONCLUSION

We have seen from our discussion of persistence and change in mass attitudes how the interplay between the anti-militaristic Constitution, the build-up of the SDF and the maintenance of a nuclear security treaty with the United States has created a complex amalgam of attitudes, with increased support for certain, but not all, policies supportive of militarization and restoring legitimacy to the military occurring over the years. During the post cold war era, this was partly achieved by employing a discourse of 'international contribution' to legitimize the change in the role of the SDF. This facilitated the erosion of the restraint on the overseas despatch of the SDF. But the use of 'international contribution' as a way to legitimize a major change in security policy is only one of the techniques employed by political leaders over the years. At times of controversial decisions, in particular, politicians have used a rich variety of discourses and rhetorical devices in order to support the build-up of the SDF, changes in the other major element of Japan's defence formula, the US–Japanese security treaty, and generally to shape an information environment supportive of government policies.

This suggests the need to investigate in more detail how political leaders have worked over the years to eliminate attitudinal impediments through the use of political rhetoric and discourse. This does not mean that these efforts are always successful: as we have seen, strong resistance to the possession of nuclear weapons and the setting up of a regular military has persisted over many years. Whether in success or failure, however, it is important to shed light on the specific mode of rhetoric and discourse employed in Japan in trying to legitimize militarization and demilitarization. In Chapter 6, therefore, let us first examine what rhetorical devices have been used in order to try to undermine the powerful anti-nuclear attitudes we have identified above, and then go on in Chapter 7 to discuss the evolution of the anti-nuclear discourse.

Part III

6 Militarization and language

The strength of anti-militaristic and anti-nuclear attitudes at the mass level means that, perhaps more than in other industrial democracies, government leaders in Japan have tended to employ evasive political rhetoric in discussing military affairs. In this way, any sense of a radical departure from the status quo can be eschewed, and popular acquiescence in defence and security policies maintained. Gaining public acquiescence in these matters is facilitated by one plain fact: the public cannot check at first hand how their taxes have been spent to build up the nation's military might, nor do they – nor, for that matter, do their political and military leaders – possess a reliable yardstick with which to measure any purported enhancement in national security resulting from a boost in military spending or a build-up in military power. To the overwhelming majority of those in whose name the military is strengthened, therefore, 'reality' in so far as security is concerned is what political leaders say about it. For 'reality' in this sense is embedded in the information environment of which their articulations are an integral part.[1] It is from this perspective that we need to take account of the role that language plays in legitimizing defence and security policies at the mass level in Japan.

There are two particular reasons for focusing on militarization and language. First, most research on the Japanese military treats language merely as a tool, thereby ignoring the political role that language *per se* plays in legitimizing militarization processes. For political leaders can act to direct mass opinion towards acquiescence, acceptance or denial of militarization processes, depending on the mode of discourse and rhetoric selected. This means that, far from being a mere tool to describe an objective reality, language constitutes reality.[2] The point should become clearer as we go on to examine how perspective in language use highlights certain aspects of reality at the expense of others.

The second reason is the salience of rhetorical forms of linguistic expressions in the discourse of political leaders in general. Despite the frequency with which rhetorical devices such as euphemisms and metaphors are employed, however, further work still needs to be carried out on their political function, particularly in legitimizing defence and security policies.[3] Such studies are even rarer in the case of Japan.[4] In order to deepen our understanding of the political use of rhetorical devices in facilitating militarization, therefore, we will analyse how euphemisms and metaphors have been employed by a number of Japanese prime ministers and other political leaders.

Specifically, after discussing 'perspective' in language use, we will examine the way that euphemisms have been utilized in order to obfuscate certain aspects of reality – as in the use of 'advance' for 'invasion' in referring to Japan's wartime actions in China – and how the euphemism 'partnership' was replaced in the 1980s by 'alliance' in connection with US–Japan relations. We will then go on to metaphor, introducing the function of metaphor in general before proceeding to examine a number of representative metaphors that former prime ministers Suzuki Zenkō and Nakasone Yasuhiro employed in order to try to promote popular acceptance of Japan's military build-up and closer military ties with the United States in the 1980s. Finally, we will analyse in depth the 'nuclear allergy' metaphor used by Prime Minister Satō Eisaku in the late 1960s, as this is crucial to our understanding of the rhetorical techniques used in order to undermine anti-nuclear attitudes at the mass level in Japan.

PERSPECTIVE IN LANGUAGE USE

A broad division can often, though not necessarily always, be made between a 'top-down' perspective and a 'bottom-up' perspective on political reality.[5] By 'top-down' perspective we have in mind the perspective of the aggressor, the ruler, the strong; by 'bottom-up' perspective we refer to the perspective of the victim, the ruled, the weak. The titles of two of Honda Katsuichi's books, *The Logic of the Killer* and *The Logic of the Killed*, capture the essential difference between the perspectives of the aggressors and of the victims in war.[6] For war is extreme enough to lay bare the role that perspectives can play in structuring reality for political purpose, particularly when supported by euphemistic or metaphorical expressions.

Take the 'top-down' perspective adopted by the Nazis against the Jews. In *Mein Kampf*, for instance, Adolf Hitler's perspective is of a member of a highly civilized race looking down despisingly on the Jews as 'parasites', 'bacilli' or 'poison spreaders'.[7] The perspective of the doctors who worked for the Nazi 'biocracy' is embedded in a similar discourse. As one doctor phrased it: 'out of respect for human life, I would remove a gangrenous appendix from a diseased body. The Jew is the gangrenous appendix in the body of mankind.'[8] This dehumanization of the enemy was practised in the Pacific War, too, as historian John Dower makes abundantly clear in *War Without Mercy*: on the one hand, the Allies looked down on the Japanese as subhuman, as apes or vermin; on the other hand, the Japanese viewed the Allies as monsters, devils or demons.[9]

Of course, the role that perspectives play in structuring reality for political purposes is not limited to making the killing of the enemy easier in the extremities of war. For in the cold war discussions of future nuclear war, the 'top-down' perspective of the users of nuclear weapons bears different implications to the 'bottom-up' perspective of their victims. The contrast between the dominant nuclear discourse in the United States and in Japan is here instructive.[10]

In the United States, the central role of nuclear strategists in producing the nuclear discourse has promoted a user's perspective as the most pervasive, albeit not the only, perspective on nuclear war. To these strategists the existence and threatened use of nuclear weapons ensured that the Soviet Union was deterred from attacking the United States. Should a nuclear war occur, the resulting civilian deaths often appeared as an inevitable cost of employing nuclear weapons.[11] Adopting a user's perspective thus led some strategists to view the results of nuclear war in terms of the survival of weapons or nuclear damage to the state more than in terms of the survival of the civilian population.[12] Despite this, at the mass level Americans seem to have adopted the user's perspective, as seen in the support expressed for the past and future use of nuclear weapons, as touched on in Chapter 5. The Japanese case is contrastive, as the victims' perspectives on nuclear war still hold considerable sway at the mass level. Such perspectives were formed as a result of the atomic-bomb experiences of Hiroshima and Nagasaki being integrated into a dominant anti-nuclear rather than pro-nuclear discourse. This means that, in contrast to the United States, the public in Japan primarily has been exposed to an anti-nuclear discourse, as we will discuss in Chapter 7.

These dominant discourses exert an influence on the perspective coexisting with nuclear weapons. A political leader may not intentionally adopt a perspective with the express purpose of directing the public towards the acceptance or rejection of nuclear weapons; however, as a result of adopting one of these perspectives, individuals are likely to be influenced in their own views. The role of the mass media is here crucial: in the United States, their role has tended to be to promote a pro-nuclear user's perspective, whereas in Japan an anti-nuclear victim's perspective has tended to dominate in the media.[13] In this way, the media are not neutral but contribute to making one or the other of these perspectives seem 'normal' at the mass level.

In discussing the problem of security, therefore, the perspective adopted at the mass level as well as in the media can serve to promote a perspective on nuclear war useful for supporting or undermining miltarization processes. Two types of rhetorical devices can serve political leaders particularly well in seeking the public's acquiescence in militarization – euphemism and metaphor.

EUPHEMISM

Euphemisms are used as substitutes for direct, harsh or blunt expressions of an unpleasant nature. Instead of choosing the direct expression 'die', for instance, we often choose to employ the euphemistic expression 'pass away'. As this euphemism helps to distance both the speaker and hearer from the unpleasantness of death, 'pass away' facilitates communication. At the same time, however, euphemisms are frequently employed in order to deceive for political purpose.[14] Euphemisms for killing and murder carried out on behalf of the state such as 'final solution', 'liquidate' and 'terminate with extreme prejudice' should be viewed in this light.

The use of euphemisms for political purposes surfaces in George Orwell's novel, *Nineteen Eighty-Four*, where the first two of the ruling party's three slogans state the opposite of what we normally take to be the meaning of the words: 'War is Peace', 'Freedom is Slavery', 'Ignorance is Strength'.[15] The names of government ministries – the Ministry of Peace, Ministry of Truth, Ministry of Love, Ministry of Plenty – are euphemisms, for each is respectively in charge of war, lies, hate and scarcity. These are examples from science fiction where the government employs euphemistic expressions in order to obfuscate the unpleasant function of government ministries.

But we need not go far to find governments in the real world putting euphemisms to work. In the United States, for instance, the Department of War was made much more easy to live with by renaming it the Department of Defense shortly after the end of the

Second World War. The constitutional ban on the possession of 'war potential' and military forces ensured that the Japanese government organ in charge of the military was named euphemistically when it was set up in 1954: Japan Self-Defence Agency. The change in 1984 to 'Defence Agency' symbolized the greater acceptance of the agency's function by this time. Even so, euphemistic expressions are still used for weaponry, as in the case of 'equipment' (weapons), 'special vehicles' (tanks), 'technical brigade' (artillery brigade), 'guard ship' (frigate) and so on. We saw in Chapter 5 how, in despatching the SDF overseas in the early 1990s, the government stressed that this was done in the name of *haken* (despatch of 'personnel'), not *hahei* (despatch of military forces). Finally, at the beginning of the 1980s Britain's Ministry of Defence resorted to the homely 'life insurance' euphemism in an attempt to gain public acquiescence in the NATO governments' decision to accept the deployment of American cruise missiles. The front page of the Ministry of Defence brochure declared cruise missiles to be 'A vital part of the West's life insurance'.[16] This expression was meant to keep thoughts of the actual use of these weapons from the people's minds, and to promote the nuclear deterrent as performing a similar function to a life insurance policy.

Euphemisms in wartime can be used to try to make the war more acceptable at the mass level. In the Vietnam War, for instance, a 'surgical strike' against a 'strategic hamlet' was a euphemistic way of referring to bombing raids against villages. Similarly, in the 1991 Gulf War the euphemisms 'surgical strikes' against 'military targets' were meant to prescind thought of civilian casualties, although graphic evidence emerged to challenge the euphemisms. 'Pacification' is another example of a euphemism from the Vietnam War. George Orwell's description of 'pacification' from an earlier period gives a sense of what a 'bottom-up' perspective would show: '[d]efenseless villages are bombarded from the air, the inhabitants driven out into the countryside, the cattle machine-gunned, the huts set on fire with incendiary bullets'.[17] In fact, according to the euphemism, the Vietnam War was not a war but a conflict – the Vietnam Conflict. A similar euphemism still exists for the Korean War – the Korean Police Action. These euphemisms are meant to structure reality so as to facilitate the acceptance of state policies and interpretations at the mass level.

The political role that euphemisms can play in structuring nuclear reality is evident from a comparison of the expressions 'collateral damage' and 'massacre'. Both can be used to describe the same reality: dead civilians in a nuclear war. The two expressions bring to mind quite different associations, however: the former, associations of unintended damage in the pursuit of planned objectives; the latter, associations of wilful murder on a mass scale. The euphemism 'collateral damage' rather than 'massacre' is used in the pro-nuclear discourse. For those involved in planning nuclear war or legitimizing its possibility to the public, 'massacre' is not in fact a practical, although it may well be a potential, choice of expressions. For critics, however, such an expression is both a practical and a potential choice. Yet they may opt to use the self-same euphemism: some, for instance, may adopt such an expression in order to gain credibility with the defence establishment as a means of trying to influence policy choices; others, in contrast, may use the euphemism as a means to gain respectability and prestige as an expert, depending on the audience, for 'massacre' can bring to mind the emotionalism of the uninformed. For others, however, the euphemism 'collateral damage' would be expected to have a different referent point in reality. It is in this latter sense that we can speak of the political role of euphemisms in structuring political reality.

Euphemisms in Japanese school textbooks

The use of euphemisms in order to structure reality for political purpose surfaces in the Japanese Ministry of Education's attempt to pressurize authors and publishers into changing certain politically sensitive expressions, particularly in regard to war–peace issues. The 'textbook problem' will be taken up in the Conclusion, but here we wish to shed light on the political use of euphemism by examining the use of euphemisms in connection with the war. The case in question is that of June 1982. At the time, Japanese newspapers announced that, in new history and high-school textbooks to be used in high schools from the next school year, Japan's 'invasion' (*shinryaku*) of China during the 1930s had been changed to 'advance' (*shinshutsu*).[18] It came to light later that, in fact, the newspapers' charge of the change from 'invasion' to 'advance' had not occurred in the case of China, although 'invasion' had been changed to the less emotive 'incursion' (*shinnyu*); in other cases, the use of any of these expressions had been avoided by authors who felt compelled to rewrite the material, and in the case of reference to Southeast Asia, 'advance' had indeed been substituted for 'invasion'.[19] In spite of this misreporting, however, as such changes had previously occurred as a very consequence of the Ministry of Education's role in certifying textbooks, the mass media in Japan, China, the two Koreas and other East Asian countries continued to criticize the government, and the governments of China and South Korea lodged formal protests with the Japanese government. Some regarded the textbook issue as indicative of the revival of Japanese militarism.

The Ministry of Education reluctantly succumbed to the domestic and especially foreign pressure aroused by the media and allowed textbook authors, upon application, to replace 'advance' with 'invasion' one year earlier than was customarily allowed for textbook revisions. Although the pressure from overseas forced the government to 'give consideration to neighbouring countries' in the future, this did not immediately alter the fundamental character of the textbook certification system, as seen in 1986, when an ultra-conservative textbook was authorized prior to domestic and foreign protest.[20] The political nature of the problem is symbolized by the case of Minister of Education Fujio Masayuki, who was relieved of his post by Prime Minister Nakasone for publishing an article in which he said, among other things, that the Korean side was at least partly responsible for Japan's annexation of the peninsula.[21]

Why is the use of the direct expression 'invasion' or the euphemistic expression 'advance' in Japanese school textbooks such a point of controversy? There are at least two reasons: first, textbooks are regarded as efficacious tools to shape the attitudes of the future generation. Anti-militaristic attitudes among the young are considered more likely to develop as a result of providing details on Japan's aggressive action on the Asian mainland than as a result of obfuscating them with euphemisms. It would be naive to suggest that the only course the Japanese government needs to follow in order to raise youngsters prepared to acquiesce in militarization processes is to resort to euphemistic expressions meant to hide the ugly side of Japanese history. The problem is obviously more complex. But the attention that the Ministry of Education pays to even the expressions employed by textbook authors does suggest a connection between language and education and the acceptance or rejection of a role for the military as a legitimate instrument of state power.

The second reason concerns the role that the textbook plays in legitimizing a particular interpretation of history to Japanese schoolchildren. Depending on the expression selected, different aspects of reality will be revealed or concealed, highlighted or obfuscated, and this will in some way influence attitudes and understanding. The euphemistic expression 'advance' is meant to conceal or obfuscate the facts and implications of Japanese wartime aggression. Two important implications arise from such an aggressor's perspective: (1) Japan bears responsibility for the war; (2) the war was morally wrong and should be reflected upon. Leading Japanese newspapers like the *Asahi Shinbun* generally tend to regard Japan as the aggressor in China. At the popular level, however, quite a large percentage of the population seem prepared to accept the Ministry's role in certifying textbooks, and thus pressurizing authors into substituting 'advance' for 'invasion', suggesting that the public feels more comfortable when Ministry bureaucrats take a hand in shaping the textbook contents.[22] Such attitudes lend support to the Ministry of Education's aim of undermining the view that Japan's wartime acts of aggression were wrong and need to be squarely faced.

Legitimizing 'advance'

The government attempted to legitimize the change from 'invasion' to 'advance' by appealing to 'objectivity' and 'neutrality'. The Minister of Education, for instance, stated in the Diet that textbook authors were asked to 'amend' (*kaizen*) the expression 'invasion', as 'advance' or 'incursion' is more 'objective'.[23] One member of the Cabinet went on to suggest that to refer to an 'advance' as an 'invasion' is 'to distort reality, and Japanese children will lose respect for their forefathers'.[24] In seeking to legitimize the textbook certification system as a whole, both now and in the future, Prime Minister Suzuki asserted: 'The textbook certification system is necessary in order to ensure neutral education and prevent the appearance of textbooks being influenced by ideological prejudice.'[25]

Second, the government sought to legitimize the use of 'advance' by referring to comparable deeds carried out by other countries. Here the Western imperial powers were cited to show that Japan, far from being the only nation with a history of imperial conquest, is no different from other 'advanced countries'. In descriptions of the Western imperialists' Opium War with China, the Minister of Education pointed out, textbooks used 'advance', whereas in the case of Japan's war, 'invasion' was the preferred option.[26] If the West's aggression could be referred to as an 'advance', then why not Japan's too?

Third, members of the Cabinet lambasted the governments of China and South Korea for 'interference in domestic affairs'.[27] This line of attack served to switch the issue: what was now at stake was not whether 'advance' or 'invasion' felicitously described Japan's war in China, but whether it was legitimate for China and South Korea to attempt to influence the educational policy of a sovereign state. For the Cabinet the interpretation of Japanese history was a domestic matter to be determined on the basis of Japanese values. By charging the governments of China and South Korea with 'interference in domestic affairs', therefore, the notion of a purely Japanese inter- pretation of history, irrespective of international public opinion, could be given precedence.

Legitimizing 'aggression'

The attempt to legitimize the use of 'advance' on the grounds of 'objectivity' and 'neutrality', the similar actions of Japan and the Western imperial powers and the accusation of 'interference in domestic affairs' were challenged, both directly and indirectly, by government critics. Their central point was disarmingly simple: Japan was indeed an aggressor. First, Prime Minister Suzuki's appeal to 'objectivity' and 'neutrality' was challenged on the grounds that, without a specifically ideological premise to his own criticism, refer- ence to ideologically prejudiced textbooks could not be mounted.[28] The prime minister's statement was taken as evidence of an ideo- logical premise at the base of the textbook certification system itself: far from being used to ensure 'objectivity' and 'neutrality', as Suzuki claimed, it was in fact used to impose the ideological bias of the ruling party.

Second, critics challenged the attempt to relativize Japan's 'advance' into China by employing the Western imperial powers as a counterbalance. This was done by referring to (1) international norms, (2) repentant aggressors and (3) Japan's 'reference coun- tries'. The Japanese government was thus taken to task for 'lacking international common sense' and being otherwise at odds with inter- national norms.[29] The repentant aggressors, West Germany and Italy, were used in order to legitimize 'aggression'. It was pointed out, for instance, that whereas the heads of governments in these two nations had forthrightly acknowledged the Axis Powers' aggression, Japanese prime ministers, from Prime Minister Satō onwards, had not.[30] The reference countries, the United States and Europe, were a further way for critics to legitimize 'aggression'. The following exchange between a Ministry of Education textbook inspector and a textbook author calls attention to how the 'United States' and 'Europe' were put to political use in this regard:

INSPECTOR: The use of the expression 'Japanese invasion of China' is unsuitable. Change it to 'advance' or 'incursion'.

AUTHOR: If you ask me to do that, it will become a problem in the United States and Europe![31]

What the author here implies is that, irrespective of the inspector's own attempt to say otherwise, Americans and Europeans recognize Japan's invasion of China for what it was: aggression.

Third, the Cabinet member's attempt to cover up the basic issue, achieved by treating the Chinese and Korean protests as 'interference in domestic affairs', i.e. as an issue between *states*, was challenged from a perspective regarding the issue as one between *peoples*. It was pointed out, for instance, that even though the question of Japan's wartime responsibilities may have been settled between governments, this does not mean that the governmental agreements were based on the understanding of the Chinese and Korean people.[32] In short, for many Asians who suffered as a result of Japan's invasion of the mainland, wartime memories remain alive.

The government and its critics put forward the above arguments in order to legitimize their respective interpretations of Japanese history. By making the expressions used in Japanese school textbooks a political issue, critics challenged the government's use of political power to structure reality. The active role that the Chinese and Korean governments played in criticizing the use of a euphemism to obfuscate Japan's invasion of Asian countries points to the importance of international as well as domestic criticism in influencing government policy.

Death of a euphemism

The fierce controversy over the use of 'advance' or 'invasion' to refer to Japan's past relations with China is in marked contrast to the relatively smooth transition in the expression used to refer to Japan's relations with the United States at this time. In consideration of anti-militaristic attitudes at the mass level, expressions highlighting the military relationship between Japan and the United States were not usually employed by political leaders until the 1980s. Along with the gradual build-up of Japan's military might, as discussed in Chapter 3, expressions symbolizing the military ties between the two countries started to come into wide usage at this time. This new situation is typified in the transition from 'partnership' to 'alliance' in referring to the US–Japan relationship.

The preference of LDP leaders heretofore had been to eschew expressions with military connotations; hence, 'partnership', popularized during the 1960s at the time that Reischauer was US ambassador to Japan, had been commonly employed by political leaders to refer to Japan's relations with the United States. Why was this expression used to refer to the US–Japan relationship? It is precisely because of the controversy surrounding the security treaty with the United States.

As we have seen in Chapter 3, the security treaty ties Japan into US nuclear strategy, a point of controversy between the government, which holds that the US nuclear deterrent offers protection to Japan, and the opposition forces during the cold war, particular the socialist and communist parties and various peace movements, which continually raised doubts about the value of the treaty to Japan's security. During the Korean War and the Vietnam War, the bases in Japan were used for the rapid deployment of conventional US forces to other parts of Asia, as during the Gulf War they were used to deploy forces to the Middle East. Likewise, the nuclear value of the treaty to the United States has been perennial, as Japan provides the United States with facilities for nuclear-capable ships and planes, as well as for communication centres to coordinate the information needed to plan and wage nuclear war. As we have seen, in the 1980s Japan was called upon to play a larger role in both the United States' conventional and nuclear strategy, and this new role was legitimized by the use of a plainly military term – alliance.

Following the May 1981 meeting between President Reagan and Prime Minister Suzuki, the word 'alliance' appeared in the US–Japan joint communiqué for the first time.[33] Despite the patent military associations of the word, the prime minister, endeavouring to bridge the perceptual gap developing between Japan as the 'partner' of the United States and Japan as the 'ally' of the United States, chose to focus on the economic, political and cultural ties between the two nations, playing down any military implications behind the term 'alliance'.[34] The ensuing controversy over the use of the word 'alliance' nevertheless forced the resignation of the foreign minister. Why did 'alliance' appear in a US–Japan joint communiqué for the first time in 1981?

First, by implying a commonality of interests, the word 'alliance' functions to de-emphasize the significance of conflict, yet emphasize the significance of cooperation, between Japan and the United States. It is not surprising, therefore, to find a stress on Japan as an 'ally' and as a 'member of the West' when major conflicts between the two nations could no longer be settled unilaterally by the United States: defence – American demands to boost military spending and purchase US military equipment; trade – restrictions on Japanese exports and demands to accept more US imports. For Japan to increase its military expenditure, 'voluntarily' restrict Japanese exports and boost American imports, can all be more easily legitimized at the mass level as natural forms of cooperation between allies.

Second, the word 'alliance' suggests the existence of a common enemy. Traditionally, the Soviet Union was an enemy of Japan. Likewise, in the nuclear confrontation of the 1980s the Soviet Union was the enemy. It was therefore relatively easy to fuse together the 'traditional enemy' of Japan and the 'nuclear enemy' of the United States as the 'common enemy' of them both. Here the word 'alliance' functions to emphasize the significance of conflict, yet de-emphasize the significance of cooperation, between Japan and the Soviet Union. The popularly accepted point of conflict between the two at the time was and still remains the unresolved question of sovereignty over the Northern Territories. This is a common point of agreement, on both the governmental and mass levels, and such negative feelings, strengthened by the Ministry of Foreign Affairs' Northern Territories Day, the Ministry of Education's close scrutiny of textbooks on this issue and the actual behaviour of the Soviet Union (e.g. invasion of Afghanistan), as well as the widespread antipathy towards the Soviet Union, formed the basis for a perspective on the Soviet Union as the 'common enemy'.[35] The possibility of cooperation, such as arises from the complementary needs of the two economies, is not highlighted. In this way, the word 'alliance' works in a similar way to metaphor in structuring reality in a way to make the military relations with the United States appear 'normal'.[36]

METAPHOR

Metaphors are most familiar as rhetorical devices in literature, as with 'men are wolves'. But the influence of metaphors extends far beyond the boundaries of literature. We will examine how they are employed politically below. Before that, let us briefly discuss metaphor more generally.

Despite its time-honoured usage, no consensus on a single definition of metaphor has emerged. Two views predominate: the 'comparison view' and the 'interaction view'. According to the comparison view, a metaphor is a condensed or elliptical simile, where words such as 'like' or 'as' have been omitted. The comparison view implies that what is transferred through metaphor '*must already be "known" or present* in some way before metaphorical meaning can be grasped'.[37] This gives rise to the view that a metaphorical statement can be replaced with a literal statement. The metaphor 'Richard the Lion-hearted', for instance, can be rephrased as 'Richard is brave'. The 'comparison view' thus holds that metaphors do not purvey new information; rather, because an identical logical and affective meaning can be restated literally, they are simply held to draw out *already existing* similarities.

In contrast, the 'interaction view' of metaphor, as proposed by Max Black, suggests that a literal substitute simply does not convey the same meaning as the metaphor.[38] In Black's analysis of the metaphor 'the poor are the negroes of Europe', for instance, the word 'negroes' is the 'focus' of the metaphor; the remainder of the sentence, the 'frame'. He writes: 'in the given context the focal word "negroes" obtains a *new meaning*'.[39] He goes on to state: 'It would be more illuminating in some of these cases (i.e. of metaphors imputing similarities difficult to discern otherwise) to say that the metaphor *creates* the similarity than to say that it formulates some similarity antecedently existing.'[40] Thus, unlike the 'comparison view', the 'interaction view' of metaphor holds that new meaning is *created* by metaphor.

Despite the different implications of these two views in terms of a metaphor's power to create new meaning, common to both is its function in connecting, in our minds, the hitherto unconnected. We go through a process of seeing X, or a certain aspect of X, as belonging to Y; or, again, we are influenced in our view of X by Y. At first, of course, we may reject the metaphor in favour of the literal truth of the statement; thus, 'men are wolves' may be rejected because men are bipeds whereas wolves are quadrupeds. At the second stage, what is essential for the success of the metaphor – connecting the hitherto unconnected – occurs, and a dual sense comes into play. At this stage the latent wild nature of men is focused upon to make the metaphor a success. At the third and final stage the metaphor may become part of everyday language, 'a dead metaphor', as in the case of the 'leg' of a table; again, it may fall into desuetude or undergo metamorphosis.

Disease metaphor

A metaphor's political role in highlighting or obfuscating certain aspects of reality at the expense of others is evident in the case of disease metaphors. Disease metaphors are especially powerful as political metaphors as they evoke the normative implication of the need for a *cure*.[41] This suggests why disease metaphors permeate the discourse of the radical right. In *The Blue Book of the John Birch Society*, for instance, Robert Welch writes of 'disease', 'virus', 'festering, and 'cancer'.[42] The cancer metaphor, in particular, is central to the Right's discourse. This should come as no surprise, for as Susan Sontag points out: 'cancer is being magnified and projected into a metaphor for the *biggest enemy*'.[43] We thus find Welch crying out to stop the communists 'from agitating our cancerous tissues, reimplanting the virus, and working to spread it'; 'the cancer of collectivism', of which Europe is dying, is already of 'considerable growth' in the United States. The cure is to 'cut out' the cancer for, like individuals, civilizations 'will eventually succumb to the degenerative disease of cancer'.[44] By speaking metaphorically in this way about the 'communist menace' Welch does not evoke the brutal image of a rightist knife slashing a communist throat; rather, he evokes the civilized image of a surgeon's scalpel cutting out abnormality from an unhealthy body.

Of course, communism has not been the only target for disease metaphors. The following is a quote from US Justice Douglas's opinion on urban renewal in the 1950s: 'The experts concluded that if the community were to be healthy, if it were not to revert again to a blighted or slum area, *as though possessed of a congenital disease*, the area must be planned as a whole.'[45] Nor does the radical right monopolize the cancer metaphor: in his description of the Nixon presidency, for instance, John Dean conveys to Nixon 'his fear of a cancer on the presidency'.[46] Again, during the Vietnam War, Clark Clifford, President Lyndon Johnson's last Secretary of Defense, declared: 'We're going to step in there and excise this cancer before it gets to the metastatic phase and spreads throughout . . . that part of the world.'[47] That the cancer metaphor has been exploited at the highest levels of political leadership is evident from President Reagan's usage of the metaphor: 'The cancer that has to be excised is Nicaragua.'[48] We again face the disease–cure link.

METAPHORS OF JAPANESE PRIME MINISTERS

In Japan, too, political leaders have employed a variety of metaphors in order to promote their policies. As a prelude to a more detailed analysis of the 'nuclear allergy' metaphor employed by Prime

Minister Satō, let us briefly examine a number of metaphors used by prime ministers Suzuki and Nakasone to legitimize the military build-up in the 1980s.

Hedgehog

In his 1981 visit to the United States, Prime Minister Suzuki announced that Japan should become a 'hedgehog'.[49] This metaphor functions to bring together, in our minds, the similarity between a country (Japan) and a mammal (hedgehog). In contrast to the aggressive image evoked by the American eagle, the Russian bear or the British lion, the Japanese hedgehog evokes the image of a small, defensive creature, not preying on others but going about its business in a slow, orderly manner. What does the hedgehog do if, on one of its nocturnal outings, it meets an enemy? As is well known, it rolls up into a ball so as to present its defensive spines outward, not taking any aggressive action.

The metaphor thus creates the image of Japan as a non-aggressive, difficult-to-attack country prepared to defend itself, by purely defensive means, should it be attacked. The political efficacy of the metaphor is threefold. First, the prime minister's metaphor fits perfectly with popular support for the constitutionality of 'defensive' forces. Second, the possibility of Japan's military build-up again leading to Japanese aggressive militarism, the fear harboured by many in 1980s East Asia, is counterbalanced by the strong image of defence evoked by 'hedgehog'. Third, American criticism that Japan is a 'free-rider' not willing to defend itself is less easily maintained, for the metaphor implies that Japan will bear more of its own defence burden. In this way, Suzuki was able to foster an image of Japan with an identity as a 'Switzerland of Asia', thereby obfuscating the integration of Japan into US global strategy then under way.

Shield and spear

Prime Minister Suzuki also made use of the 'shield and spear' metaphor to evoke the similarity between a warrior's and a country's means of defence and attack.[50] The militaristic implications of the metaphor are softened, however; unlike the warrior, who single-handedly defends himself with his shield and attacks with his spear, the modern Japanese political leader prefers a division of labour – the Japanese Self-Defence Forces as the shield, the American military as the spear. The purely defensive image of the hedgehog is thus replaced with an image of both defence (Japan) and offence (United States).

As Japan is the 'shield', the 'shield and spear' metaphor still serves to make a military build-up appear defensive; more importantly, however, it serves to justify the maintenance and strengthening of Japan's military ties with the United States as normal. Two points are salient: first, the burgeoning combined military exercises between the Self-Defence Forces and the American military we discussed in Chapter 3 can be legitimized – the two should be as well coordinated as a shield and spear in the hands of a warrior; second, the possibility of the United States ever attacking Japan is made more difficult to think about – the spear is always pointed outwards at the 'enemy'. Thus, the metaphor reinforces awareness of the fact that Japan and the United States are, indeed, allies.

Unsinkable aircraft carrier

Not until after the formation of the Nakasone Cabinet did an explicitly militaristic metaphor meant to support the military build-up enter the Japanese security discourse.[51] This is the controversial metaphor 'unsinkable aircraft carrier', which Prime Minister Nakasone used during his 1983 visit to the United States in an interview with the *Washington Post*.[52] The similarity evoked here implies that, as with an aircraft carrier, Japan should become a forward-attack platform against the Soviet Union.[53] Japan's role thus becomes one of patrolling the straits near the home islands in order to defend the United States and Japan from a Soviet attack. In line with the metaphor's implications, however, Japan would in times of crisis be expected to blockade the straits and play a role in interdicting Soviet Backfire bombers. As we discussed in Chapter 3, this suggests that Japan would break out of the constitutional constraint on the SDF and take part in 'collective defence'; that is, 'offence'.

No doubt the implication of deploying Japanese military forces in such new roles was the reason that 'unsinkable aircraft carrier' did not prove a particularly efficacious metaphor in support of the military build-up. For on his return to Japan Prime Minister Nakasone had to face a barrage of questions in the Diet regarding his use of the metaphor.[54] When he gave as his reason for this 'slip of the tongue' his career as a naval officer during the Second World War, the opposition pointed out that, as Japanese aircraft carriers in the war had been sunk, his choice of metaphor was hardly felicitous.[55] The prime minister also suggested that his use of 'unsinkable aircraft carrier' was meant in the same sense as saying 'unsinkable archipelago',[56] although as Ōe Kenzaburō pointed out, this makes no sense as, unlike an aircraft carrier, an archipelago does not sink.[57]

In this way, Prime Minister Nakasone was exposed to criticism from a variety of quarters. Nevertheless, this does not mean that the metaphor was totally devoid of political significance. Two points deserve mention: first, he employed the metaphor in the United States, and this served to strengthen US expectations that Japan would act even more like an aircraft carrier, that is, as a US forward base in the cold war 1980s. Nakasone's choice of the United States as venue for his comment can be seen as an attempt to blunt American criticism of Japan as a 'free-rider'. Second, the metaphor serves to obfuscate the fragility of Japan as an island nation in the nuclear era. Japan remains highly dependent on food, oil and other essential resources from overseas, and is unable, as is any other nation, to defend itself against nuclear war. As reported by the *Washington Post*, this latter point was emphasized by the Soviet News Agency, TASS, shortly after the metaphor appeared in print, when it rhetorically asked: 'Is it not clear that, in the present nuclear age, there can be no unsinkable aircraft carrier?'[58]

House insurance

It was no doubt as a result of the sharp domestic response to his militaristic metaphor, reminding many Japanese that, metaphor aside, Japan had been 'sunk' once already, that the prime minister softened his militaristic rhetoric.[59] In the wake of the negative reactions to his 'unsinkable aircraft carrier' metaphor, the prime minister made use of the 'insurance' metaphor.[60] This homely metaphor suggests a similarity between house insurance against emergencies like fire, and military expenditure against emergencies such as an attack. It implies that, as Japan has become more prosperous, it needs to take greater precautions against emergencies. So there should be a greater willingness on the part of Japan to shoulder an increase in insurance premiums commensurate with this new status, for the economy is like a home needing adequate protection. With this metaphor the principle of keeping military expenditure below 1 per cent of GNP, which as we have seen earlier was supported by a majority at the mass level, could be challenged on the basis of a homely argument: supporters of the symbolic 1 per cent ceiling failed to recognize that, by moving up in the world, Japan had incurred an obligation to pay adequately for security in the new neighbourhood. In a country where owning one's own home is a national dream, the metaphor was naturally more appealing than the militaristic 'unsinkable aircraft carrier' metaphor.

The defence ('hedgehog'), defence–offence ('shield and spear'), offence ('aircraft carrier') and defence ('insurance') metaphors employed by prime ministers Suzuki and Nakasone served to support Japan's military build-up in different ways. One of the purposes of utilizing such expressions was to make militarization more accept-able at the mass level. Nakasone's oral juggling on the use of 'unsinkable aircraft carrier', his resort to the 'insurance' metaphor and his reduced preference for militaristic expressions during the latter part of his administration point to the power of public opinion to constrain the militarization of language. It must be stressed, however, that precisely because Japanese political leaders may hesitate to use expressions with militaristic connotations, as with Prime Minister Suzuki, an awareness of how other metaphors may be used to obfuscate militarization processes is essential.

Nuclear allergy metaphor

This brings us to a more detailed study of the 'nuclear allergy' metaphor employed by Prime Minister Satō in the 1960s. This metaphor originally appeared as 'nuclear-*weapons* allergy' in an article written by the Washington correspondent for the *Asahi Shinbun* in 1964. Initially, the metaphor was simply employed to char-acterize the Japanese public's sensitivity to the expression 'nuclear weapons' at a time when the Japanese government first agreed to the port call of one of the United States' Nautilus-class nuclear-powered submarines. The correspondent comments:

> As the American government is fully aware of the extreme sensi-tivity of the Japanese people to the expression 'nuclear weapons', it adopted a prudent attitude towards this problem throughout, taking great pains not to give the impression of having, in a word, 'put pressure' on the Japanese government.[61]

In a sense, this was the precursor to the Tomahawk problem of the 1980s. It essentially concerned the planned deployment of Subroc anti-submarine nuclear torpedoes on all Nautilus-class submarines because, according to the position adopted by the Japanese govern-ment, the 'introduction' of US nuclear weapons is prohibited without 'prior consultation' between the two governments, as we have seen in Chapter 3. The metaphor appears in this connection:

the State Department would only comment 'we have heard nothing about Subroc'. In the background seems to be the American government's desire for the Japanese to put greater trust in the United States, expecting that, if enough time goes by, Japan's 'nuclear-weapons allergy' will be eliminated.[62]

The appearance of the metaphor in the above context suggests that it was simply used in order to characterize the attitude of the American government towards Japan; or, more precisely, towards the Japanese people. It is not at this stage a *political* metaphor for the promotion of a pro- or anti-nuclear policy. This is doubly clear: first, the metaphor is used neutrally, that is, neither to promote nor oppose the goal of integrating Japan into the American nuclear-strategic framework; second, the metaphor as such lacks political efficacy for realizing either of these goals. The reason for this can be found in the metaphor itself: it contains the negative word 'weapons'. If the metaphor had originally been intended to facilitate the nuclearization of Japan then, as discussed later, 'nuclear allergy' rather than 'nuclear-weapons allergy' would have been more efficacious politically. On the other hand, if the original purpose had been to oppose Japan's integration into the American nuclear-strategic framework, then in order to locate popular anti-nuclear sentiments in a political context suggesting everyone's right to oppose the government's security policy, the word 'allergy' would not have been used. The reason is self-evident: the negative connotation of the word 'allergy' constrains the metaphor functioning to resist militarization. In short, the nuclear-weapons allergy can be said to have been employed as a rhetorical, not political, device.

In any event, for whatever reason the metaphor 'nuclear-weapons allergy' did not survive. Instead, the element (weapons) constraining the effective functioning of the metaphor as a *political* metaphor disappeared, and the metaphor 'nuclear allergy' entered the security discourse. The *Asahi* reporter Kishida Junnosuke comments on the implications of the metaphor as follows: 'Words like this, which are ambiguous and can mean any number of things . . . are very convenient for attacking the other party. It is the same as in the days when calling someone "red" was effective.'[63] The nuclear-allergy metaphor, like other disease metaphors, was effective in bringing to mind the need to cure the 'abnormal citizens' who opposed port calls by the US navy. Precisely because the 'nuclear' in 'nuclear allergy' is ambiguous, those political forces in favour of promoting the popular acceptance of port calls as 'normal' were able to put the nuclear allergy metaphor to work in order to switch the issue from the original one of whether Japan's further integration into US nuclear strategy would contribute to Japanese security, to the superficial one of whether port calls by nuclear-powered submarines were safe:

> The first thing to become a problem in port calls by nuclear-powered submarines was safety. Those in favour of the port calls pointed to the fact that nuclear-powered submarines had made more than a hundred port calls in Japan and overseas without any accidents. They took those who doubted their safety to task for suffering from 'nuclear allergy'. The opponents repeated that there is no guarantee that, just because an accident had not occurred so far, one would not occur in the future, and would not be satisfied until the safety of nuclear-powered submarines had been established scientifically. The main point of the discussion was placed on safety, but the real point of controversy was whether following US nuclear strategy was a plus or a minus for Japan's security.[64]

In this context, the ambiguous 'nuclear allergy' metaphor could be used with greater political flexibility than the explicit nuclear-*weapons* allergy metaphor.

At the same time, opponents of the government's policies could, and did, use the self-same metaphor. As the negative connotation of the word 'allergy' normatively implies the need for a cure, however, the metaphor was of limited political value to those opposing the port calls. What opponents did, therefore, was to challenge such a metaphoric description of popular anti-nuclear sentiments. This is how the nuclear-allergy metaphor appears in an editorial in the *Asahi Shinbun* in October 1967. At the time, the government had agreed to the first port call of the aircraft carrier *Enterprise*, despite popular discontent. The editorial comments: 'The United States, as the user of bases in Japan, should not merely call this sentiment among the people a nuclear allergy ... and make light of it.'[65]

Three points should be made. First, as an interview with the *Asahi Shinbun*'s Washington correspondent indicates, both 'nuclear-weapons allergy' and 'nuclear allergy' were probably first used as metaphors – at least in print in Japan – by the Japanese staff of the *Asahi Shinbun*.[66] Second, although the editorial implicitly supports the anti-nuclear sentiments, by taking on the job of criticizing the metaphor as 'made in America', it still uses the self-same expression that was being used as a political metaphor to denigrate such feelings. This means, third, that a powerful 'countermetaphor' supportive of popular anti-nuclear sentiments which challenged the 'normality' of nuclear weapons did not become part of the dominant security discourse.[67] Let us analyse each of these points in detail in order to clarify the power of nuclear allergy as political metaphor.

Power of metaphor

In regard to the first point, to imply American responsibility for the use of the nuclear-allergy metaphor at this time served the purposes of both the opponents and supporters of Japan's militarization. For those political actors opposed to the government's security policy, opposing the United States, whether as a nuclear superpower or as an 'imperialist' power, was an important political task during the cold war. Opposition to the United States as the creator of the nuclear-allergy metaphor meant opposition to the United States in the symbolic world of politics.

For those political actors in favour of further integrating Japan into the American nuclear-strategic framework in Asia–Pacific, in contrast, to imply American responsibility for the use of the metaphor facilitated the labelling of opponents as sufferers from an allergy and politically locating them as *abnormal, unhealthy* elements in a healthy body-politic. For many Japanese at the time, the United States acted as a 'reference country', suggesting standards for normal attitudes and behaviour in international society. Accordingly, for Americans to characterize anti-nuclear sentiments, attitudes and behaviour as 'allergic' meant that those wanting Japan to appear on the international stage as a normal, healthy political actor must work to eliminate the anti-nuclear sentiments at the mass level. For it is 'international common sense' to allow the US government a free hand in regard to nuclear policy. Direct appeals to the legacy of Hiroshima and Nagasaki could be branded as 'unrealistic' or 'abnormal' in the context of the cold war nuclear confrontation. At the peak of the use of nuclear allergy as political metaphor (1966–8), opposition to the government's policy of eliminating the 'nuclear allergy' implied opposition to the established norms of 'international common sense'.[68] By the early 1990s, as we saw in Chapter 4, the desire to become a 'normal' state in line with 'international common sense' had come to mean Japan itself making a direct military contribution to international society.

Function

In order to shed light on how the metaphor actually worked, as a metaphor, let us turn to a more detailed examination of the second point – the use of the nuclear-allergy metaphor even by supporters of popular anti-nuclear attitudes. This naturally is related to the appeal of the metaphor. For the metaphor successfully makes a connection between the reaction of an allergy sufferer to an allergy-inducing allergen, and the reaction of the Japanese people to the 'nuclear allergen'. So we can easily go through the process of seeing X (allergy) or certain aspects of X as belonging to Y (Japanese people). In this way, the hitherto unconnected can be connected in our mind and the metaphor can enter the second stage of its life.

What makes the metaphor so appealing is the similarity between an allergy sufferer and the Japanese people. Medically speaking, the process of becoming allergic is that a host, say you or me, is exposed to an allergen, and becomes sensitized as a result. On re-exposure to the allergen, the host has an abnormal reaction, such as a bout of sneezing, known as an 'allergic reaction'. We can see how the metaphor works when we apply this process to the case of Japan. The Japanese were exposed to the 'nuclear allergen' with the dropping of the atomic bombs on Hiroshima and Nagasaki, becoming sensitized as a result (Figure 6.1). On re-exposure to the 'nuclear allergen', an abnormal reaction occurs among the people

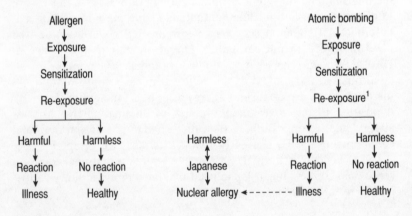

Figure 6.1 Making of the nuclear metaphor

Note: [1] Re-exposure to nuclear-powered (undoubtedly nuclear-weapon loaded) ships and submarines, nuclear weapon tests, etc.

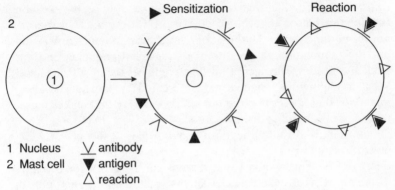

1 Nucleus $\vee$ antibody
2 Mast cell $\blacktriangledown$ antigen
           $\triangle$ reaction

Figure 6.2 Allergic reaction (antigen + antibody = reaction)

(Figure 6.2). This abnormal reaction is the Japanese people's 'nuclear allergy'.[69]

This points to the success of nuclear allergy as metaphor. Nevertheless, the metaphor obfuscates a number of elements making nuclear allergy as a *political* metaphor especially powerful only when used by those political actors seeking to label opponents of Japan's nuclearization as sufferers from an allergy and politically abnormal. Two things, in particular, deserve consideration. First, the allergen causing the allergic reaction is completely *harmless* to all but the allergy sufferer, medically speaking the host of the specific allergic agent. For an allergy is 'an abnormal reaction with characteristically unusual symptoms occurring in man or lower animals from contact with an agent that ordinarily is *innocuous* to most individuals of that species'.[70] Since nuclear allergy as metaphor functions to connect the hitherto unconnected – the ordinarily harmless aspect of the allergen and things nuclear – we are led to see nuclear weapons as being *harmless*. This is the first reason that the metaphor is of limited political use to oppose nuclearization.

The other reason is that, with the transfer of the image of harmlessness to nuclear weapons and other things nuclear, the image of abnormality can be transferred to those Japanese who oppose re-exposure to the 'nuclear allergen'. The transfer of this latter image facilitates structuring reality in the following way: what is abnormal in international society is not the threat of nuclear war and the existence of nuclear weapons, but the threat of nuclear opponents and the existence of anti-nuclear attitudes. In short, the problem of the nuclear disease – to stick to the disease metaphor – has been transferred from the weapons to those who oppose the weapons. It is for this reason that the proposed cure for the nuclear disease is not the elimination of the threat of nuclear war and nuclear weapons, but the elimination of the threat of nuclear opponents and anti-nuclear attitudes. The agent ('nuclear') replaces the host ('Japanese'). What is highlighted, shaded and obfuscated by the nuclear-allergy metaphor thus serves to structure reality in a way that makes nuclear weapons easier to live with.

Let us now turn to the third major point – the absence of a powerful countermetaphor positively appraising the public's opposition to nuclear weapons. Three reasons can be given for this. First, the ambiguity of the nuclear-allergy metaphor.[71] This put the metaphor at the centre of the political stage, kept it alive and no doubt made the creation of a countermetaphor for promoting de-militarization difficult. Second, as Charlotte Linde has suggested: '[W]hether in national politics or in everyday interaction, people in power get to impose their metaphors.'[72] Certainly the call that Prime Minister Satō made in 1967 for the 'elimination' of nuclear allergy ensured the metaphor a central place in politics at the time of the debate on the reversion of Okinawa – a critical turning point in the nuclear relations between Japan and the United States. Third, there was simply a lack of awareness on the part of those trying to promote demilitarization of the political implication of using metaphors. In any event, the absence of a powerful countermetaphor meant that the nuclear-allergy metaphor could be easily used to label government opponents as 'allergic'.

Medical context

Two consequences followed from the above. First, on the level of images, the salience of the nuclear-allergy metaphor in the security discourse facilitated the location of the nuclear issue in what is metaphorically a medical context. Of specific importance here are the images of 'doctor', 'patient' and 'cure' in Japan. The relationship between a doctor and a patient is generally authoritative and hier-archical. The doctor, who is an expert possessing specialized knowledge, is seen to be in a position to be able to judge the appropriate cure for a patient's illness. One of the cures for a patient suffering from an allergy is 'desensitization'. This cure is based on the principle of gradually exposing a patient to larger and larger amounts of the allergen in order to reduce or entirely eliminate the abnormal allergic reaction (Figure 6.3).

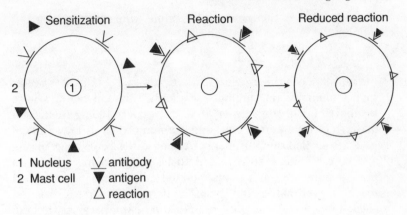

Sensitization   Reaction   Reduced reaction

1 Nucleus   ∨ antibody
2 Mast cell ▼ antigen
          △ reaction

Figure 6.3 Desensitization

To locate this in the metaphoric context: the doctor should be regarded as Prime Minister Satō, the patient as an opponent of Japan's nuclearization, the cure as the gradual exposure of the opponent to the 'nuclear allergen'. The speech by Prime Minister Satō calling for the elimination of the people's nuclear allergy is a point of focus for explicating the political efficacy of the metaphor. This speech was made in 1967 at a special session of the Diet devoted to the problem of the return of Okinawa to Japan. Of critical concern at the time was the question of whether Okinawa would revert to Japan without nuclear weapons (*hondonami*, the same as the mainland), or whether the Satō government would have to accept the return of Okinawa with nuclear weapons (*kakutsuki*). A question was put to the Prime Minister by Kuroyanagi Akira, a Kōmei Party opposition Diet member, in the House of Representatives Special Committee Meeting Concerning the Okinawan and Other Problems, 22 December 1967:

> it is said that the nation, the whole of Japan, is suffering from a nuclear allergy. I have heard that within the Liberal Democratic Party, also, discussions are being held on how to eliminate the people's nuclear allergy. In short, the nuclear threat and nuclear matters are fearful. I think this is certainly so. At the same time, there are some scholars who say that we have arrived at a time when we should go one step further and should correctly understand nuclear matters and should provide a correct understanding

thereof. What is the view of the Prime Minister regarding this opinion?[73]

Prime Minister Satō replied:

> the question of nuclear allergy has been raised. I think it is necessary to eliminate this, the nuclear allergy. I think it can be said to be the result of not having a correct understanding of nuclear matters. If there were correct understanding, then there would not be the so-called nuclear allergy. Again, in regard to peaceful use and so on, I think there ought to be a higher appreciation of nuclear power. So, as was just pointed out, I think it is necessary to strive even harder for correct understanding. Yet, this is not solely in respect of weapons, so in this sense it is necessary to have correct understanding.[74]

For Satō, then, a cure for 'nuclear allergy' was necessary in order to promote the administration's policies in regard to both nuclear weapons and nuclear energy. It came to light in November 1994 that, for the two-year period from 1967 to 1969, secret research was carried out at the request of the Cabinet Research Office on the pros and cons of Japan going nuclear. A secret research report concluded that:

1. Japan had the capability to produce a small quantity of plutonium bombs;
2. if Japan went nuclear, this would invite suspicion among its neighbours, and diplomatic isolation would be inevitable;
3. it would be difficult to maintain deterrent power with a small number of weapons;
4. it would be an enormous financial burden;
5. it would be difficult to gain public support.

The conclusion was therefore not to go nuclear.[75] The prime minister's secretary, Kusuda Minoru, tells how Satō's call for the elimination of the nuclear allergy, which stirred up a political storm, was part of the administration's political strategy, at least for the development of nuclear energy if not for nuclear weapons:

> In a situation where a national sentiment of what could be called a nuclear allergy existed, there had up until this time been something like a political current in favour of avoiding as far as possible any reference to nuclear matters, but Prime Minister Satō, with the three non-nuclear principles as support, dared to challenge this taboo.[76]

By employing nuclear allergy as political metaphor, the prime minister was able to eschew concrete images of his administration's attempt to reshape popular opinion on nuclear matters, with some success.[77] Essentially, the goal was to develop a security discourse where nuclear matters were no longer 'taboo', as in the early 1990s political leaders are seeking to reshape popular opinion to make constitutional revision no longer 'taboo'.[78] What the nuclear-allergy metaphor does is to create the image either of eliminating the *allergy* in a medical context; or, failing this, of a doctor curing a patient's disease. It creates no empathy for those who are suffering from the allergy; that is, no support for those opposing nuclearization.

Three methods of 'desensitization' were adopted. First, the people were gradually exposed to the 'nuclear allergen'; that is, the number of port calls by US nuclear submarines and surface vessels was gradually increased. By the 1980s, except for the voices raised in protest against the Tomahawk deployments, protest against US port calls had all but disappeared. Second, as previously touched on, criticism against the anti-nuclear sentiment (emotion) was made from the standpoint of international common sense (reason). Third, as suggested by Prime Minister Satō, the people were provided with a 'correct' understanding of nuclear issues, with political leaders emphasizing the safety of US visits and the necessity of the security treaty with the United States in order to maintain Japanese security.

Political efficacy

In this way, Prime Minister Satō was able to use the nuclear-allergy metaphor effectively against those who opposed Japan's closer military ties with the United States. Although his opponents challenged the idea of their need for a 'cure', they did so in a metaphorical medical context. Precisely for this reason, the argument that raged during the height of the nuclear-allergy controversy revolved around the question of whether the allergy was 'healthy' or not, a 'legitimate illness' or not, an illness to be 'spread' or not, and so on.[79] In other words, the controversy revolved not around the specific issue of whether US submarines were carrying nuclear weapons when making port calls to Japan, but around the general issue of whether the Japanese 'nuclear allergy' was healthy or not. The nuclear-allergy metaphor thus served to direct the nation's eyes to the 'nuclear problem' in a broad sense, i.e. the non-military as well as military use of nuclear energy.

At the same time, however, a major problem was obfuscated by the use of the allergy metaphor. As Kishida states, this was the need to hold full discussions on internationally competitive technology for the 'peaceful use' of nuclear energy, which is closely linked to nuclear-weapons technology:

> If avoiding this kind of discussion is also called 'nuclear allergy', then it is necessary to rid ourselves of it. However, strangely enough, in problems likely to lead to competition with the United States, great care is taken to avoid the use of the expression 'nuclear allergy'.
>
> The reason is related to the process through which the expression 'nuclear allergy' came into being. Originally, 'nuclear allergy' was an expression that became used popularly as a result of port calls by US nuclear-powered submarines. Frankly speaking, those who took a critical or uncooperative attitude towards US nuclear strategy were taken to task for having a nuclear allergy. The expression was used in order to attack that attitude as if it were the result of ignorance or an unhealthy constitution.[80]

In this way, the nuclear-allergy metaphor was used selectively, and politically, in order to brand those who opposed US nuclear strategy, but not to characterize those who avoided discussion of nuclear technology with military application. The political efficacy of the metaphor is plain here: it served to structure the nuclear discourse in such a way that the 'nuclear problem' was not defined as the danger of applying nuclear technology developed for non-military use to the development of nuclear weapons, but the danger that those Japanese who failed to understand the difference between 'peaceful use' and 'military use' of nuclear energy would threaten Japan's relations with the United States. The following comments by the well-known nationalist politician, Ishihara Shintarō, follow Prime Minister Satō in characterizing the problem as ignorance, when in fact it was disagreement over government policy:

> I think the Japanese people are confusing nuclear-weapons allergy and nuclear allergy. When I speak of nuclear development I strictly mean development for peaceful use. For this purpose, too, it is necessary to educate those Japanese with nuclear allergy – more correctly, nuclear ignorance – who are apt to fear even nuclear [energy] for peaceful use.[81]

As we have seen above, Prime Minister Satō and other political leaders used the nuclear-allergy metaphor as a tool to avoid a democratic discussion on the security policy being pursued by the government. By the prime minister locating the anti-nuclear sentiments of the people in a metaphorical medical context, calling forth the entailment of a cure, he stirred a strong reaction among the atomic-bomb victims and anti-nuclear activists. At the same time, however, by branding his opponents as 'allergic' he was able to isolate them. Of course, just because those opposed to militarization were branded 'allergic' does not mean that, as a result, they immediately stopped protesting against the port calls of US naval vessels. But the use of the metaphor at least can be said to have been politically efficacious in bringing to people's minds the linkage anti-nuclear–allergic–illness–cure. For those political forces aiming to promote the acceptance of militarization, therefore, the nuclear-allergy metaphor served its purpose, for nuclear opponents could be branded as being ill and ignorant.

CONCLUSION

It should be clear from the above discussion how euphemisms and metaphors can be employed by political leaders in order to facilitate the acceptance of their policies. In the case of Japanese school textbooks, the purpose of the certification system seems to have been to pressurize authors to eschew the direct expression 'invasion' and use the euphemism 'advance' as part of the process of obfuscating the ugly side of Japanese history, not as a way to maintain 'objectivity' and 'neutrality' in Japanese education. As we will discuss further in the concluding chapter, the certification system has been used in order to promote a certain image of Japan's identity. In so far as anti-militaristic attitudes at the mass level are rooted in the experience of the war, how the war experience is interpreted for future generations is an important element in determining their attitudes towards war and peace. The use of the certification system to sanitize Japanese history thus can be understood as one aspect of the attempt to regain legitimacy for the military among the younger generation. In this we can see the importance that Prime Minister Nakasone placed on rehabilitating Japan's war against Asia as part of the 'settling of the post-war accounts'. By rekindling pride in Japanese history he no doubt hoped that the future generations would be the carriers of a new Japanese identity, with the state enjoying a pride of place as an economic, political and 'normal' military big power in international society.

In the case of metaphors, we have seen how Japanese prime ministers have employed these rhetorical devices in order to hide certain aspects of reality, as with the 'hedgehog' metaphor, which obfuscates the offensive capabilities of Japanese military forces, as well as to expose certain other aspects of reality, as with the 'allergy' metaphor, which highlights the similarity between the reaction of an anti-nuclear activist and an allergy sufferer. These metaphors have played at least some role in facilitating the implementation of government policies. In the first place, the 'hedgehog' metaphor made Japan's military build-up in the 1980s appear more acceptable, both domestically and internationally; in the second, the 'allergy' metaphor undermined faith in anti-nuclear attitudes as 'normal' by attacking the normative premise of anti-nuclearism.

At the same time, however, we need to pay attention to the overall structure of the macro security discourse in which these euphemisms and metaphors have been deployed. We have already seen in Chapter 2 how peace thought developed in the early years after the war. This was one factor helping to create an environment where a powerful anti-militaristic – more specifically, anti-nuclear – discourse could be widely disseminated. Prime Minister Satō's call to eliminate the nuclear allergy takes on significance precisely because there was a healthy scepticism about nuclear weapons in Japan at the time. The experience of the atomic bombings of Hiroshima and Nagasaki has meant that, for many Japanese, the nuclear pact that the government sealed with the United States has been a major source of concern, not a guarantee of Japanese security. The call to eliminate the nuclear allergy was a call to eliminate this concern.

One of the reasons for popular sensitivity to nuclear issues stems from the character of the dominant nuclear discourse in Japan. As Prime Minister Satō's call to eliminate the nuclear allergy suggests, the experience of being atom-bombed was integrated into an anti- rather than pro-nuclear discourse. It is to the nature of this anti-nuclear discourse that we turn now.

7 Demilitarization and language

The attempts by Japanese political leaders to employ metaphors in order to facilitate the acceptance of their policies and to define normal or abnormal nuclear attitudes have posed a challenge to the anti-nuclear discourse in Japan. By 'anti-nuclear discourse' we mean the corpus of texts, mostly on the atomic bombings of Hiroshima and Nagasaki, produced from the perspectives of the victims of the 'first limited nuclear war'. These perspectives, constituted by language and embedded in the information environment, have been of critical importance in configuring the 'macro discourse' which evolved out of the oft-times competing interpretations of the meaning of being atom-bombed.[1] For there is nothing intrinsic to the atom-bomb experience *per se* that gives it significance in creating an anti-nuclear identity, rather than for supporting coexistence with nuclear weapons. What has been crucial to the evolution of the anti-nuclear discourse in Japan has been the centrality of the atom-bomb experience as the starting point to oppose nuclear weapons as the core of this identity. The fact that the atomic bombings of Hiroshima and Nagasaki have not, in general, been taken as a lesson that Japan, too, should possess nuclear weapons, is evidence of how an anti-nuclear rather than a pro-nuclear discourse has taken root.[2] This chapter discusses the evolution of this anti-nuclear discourse.

But what is 'nuclear' discourse? As we will go on to explicate later, 'nuclear' discourse brings to mind a metaphorical 'nuclear chain' with radiation as the critical link between human beings as aggressors and victims. This relationship is most clearly manifest in the actual use of atomic bombs against the men, women and children of Hiroshima and Nagasaki, but the chain between human beings as users of nuclear weapons and as victims of their use links uranium mining, weapon research and development, production, testing (atmospheric, underground), deployment (land, sea, air), transportation, use (past, present, future) and victims of use, with all the infrastructures, from physical to ideological, necessary to those vested with the power to use nuclear weapons. Certain links in the 'chain' will be highlighted at the expense of others in pro-nuclear and anti-nuclear 'dominant' or 'hegemonic' discourses, with the former centring on the users' perspectives and the latter on the victims' perspectives on nuclear weapons. In discussing the nuclear discourse in Japan, therefore, we are interested first in the links of the 'chain' highlighted in the discourse; second, in the perspectives adopted on nuclear weapons; and third, in radiation as the critical link between human beings as aggressors and victims. The *hibakusha* (essentially, those exposed to the atom bombs) have played a central role in the evolution of the anti-nuclear discourse in all three respects, especially in terms of the perspectives adopted on nuclear weapons.[3] Their role in the anti-nuclear discourse will be elucidated by examining the competing interpretations of the meaning of being atom-bombed and its impact on the evolution of the nuclear discourse in Japan.

COMPETING INTERPRETATIONS OF THE ATOMIC BOMBINGS

Three interpretations of the atomic bombings have vied, with varying degrees of success, for space in the nuclear discourse: first, the bombings as a sacrifice in fighting the war; second, the bombings as a sacrifice in ending the war; third, the bombings as the link between aggressors and victims.

Sacrifice in fighting the war

The first and least influential interpretation is the one adopted by those Japanese who support the prosecution of the last war: the atomic bombings of Hiroshima and Nagasaki were a sacrifice made in fighting the war. This interpretation gains validity only in so far as Japan's war in Asia–Pacific can be legitimized; that is, there must be a value over and above the sacrifice of Hiroshima and Nagasaki. This has continued to remain difficult to establish at the mass level. The reason is straightforward: the defeat in the war, both moral and physical, spelled the destruction of the pre-war ideological and value system as well as the state. As a result, the attempts made to legitimize the war by right-wing, ultra-nationalistic groups and politicians in the years since the defeat have tended to focus on regaining the 'morality of the state'. Of crucial importance in this respect has been Yasukuni Shrine.

Located in Tokyo, Yasukuni Shrine is a Shintō shrine dedicated to the war dead – more specifically, those who died in the name of the state, including Class A war criminals found guilty of prosecuting the last war – which gives meaning to death in action by elevating Japanese souls to the rank of *eirei* (heroic souls of the war dead). Murakami Shigeyoshi explains *eirei* as follows:

> It became popular to refer to the enshrined deities of Yasukuni Shrine as *eirei* after the Russo-Japanese War. *Eirei* was originally a beautified name for *reikon* (soul) ... However, after the Russo-Japanese War, *eirei* became the beautified name for the souls of those who died through loyalty to the emperor. The enshrined deities of Yasukuni Shrine further lost their individuality and became a group of deities called '*eirei* for the defence of the country'. From childhood the people were taught that loyalty to the emperor and enshrinement as a deity at Yasukuni Shrine was the highest honour for a subject.[4]

This role of Yasukuni Shrine in deifying the war dead has given the shrine a central place in the political attempts made over the years to maintain the spirit of militarism and build up pride in the Japanese state.[5] Although the link between the state and the shrine was formally severed as a result of the principle of the separation of state and religion in the 1947 Constitution (Article 20), prime ministers started to visit Yasukuni again from the mid-1970s onwards, when Prime Minister Miki Takeo became the first post-war incumbent to pay his respects in 1975. In order to avoid the constitutional issue, this visit was made in his 'private capacity' as an individual, not in his 'official capacity' as prime minister, a tactic followed by prime ministers Fukuda Takeo and Suzuki Zenkō. As we mentioned in Chapter 3, however, Prime Minister Nakasone Yasuhiro broke out of this mould in 1985 when he paid his respects at the shrine in his official capacity as the prime minister of Japan. Strong criticism from Japan's neighbours, especially China, nevertheless forced him to forgo a visit to the shrine in his following two years in office.

It is logically necessary to justify the deaths of those sacrificed in the name of the state for fighting the war before trying to justify the deaths of the mainly non-combatants killed in Hiroshima and Nagasaki. The sacrifice of Hiroshima and Nagasaki can in this sense only be legitimized to a majority of Japanese if the morality of the state in fighting the war can first be established. This has been attempted by perverting the standards for judging war responsibility: supporters of the war praise the subjective quality of Japanese soldiers – i.e. their purity of heart – not their objective actions, and point to the objective results of the war – i.e. the release of Asians from the yoke of European imperialism – not the aim of Japanese leaders to dominate Asia.[6]

Sacrifice in ending the war

In the second interpretation the sacrifices of Hiroshima and Nagasaki are seen as part of ending, not fighting, the war. Two variants of this interpretation deserve particular mention. First, years after he had ordered the attacks on Hiroshima and Nagasaki, US President Harry S. Truman morally justified his decision by claiming that the atomic bombing of Japan had ended the war quickly and saved half a million American lives, as well as British and Japanese lives.[7] This 'user's perspective' on the atomic bombings implies that the sacrifice of those in Hiroshima and Nagasaki was on a smaller scale than the potential loss of life likely from an invasion by Allied troops. Second, for conservative Japanese governments, Hiroshima and Nagasaki have been the sacrifices suffered for peace and prosperity as a member of the 'West'. Each of these interpretations appeals to a value scale acceptable to many Japanese: the first gives precedence to the utilitarian principle of saving lives; the second gives precedence to present, rather than past, relations between the victor and victim.

The use of nuclear weapons for peace is a powerful argument at the centre of any pro-nuclear discourse. It is powerful in Japan, too, yet not hegemonic. Why? There are a number of reasons, as discussed below, but of cardinal importance is one simple fact: the pro-nuclear discourse centres on *death* in Hiroshima and Nagasaki as the sacrifice made to end the war. It is precisely the fact that many *hibakusha* – used here in the narrow sense of the survivors of the atomic bombings – lived, and have struggled to give meaning to their existence, that the pro-nuclear discourse has been challenged and the anti-nuclear discourse has gained a hegemonic position.[8] In short, to accept the dropping of the atomic bombs as a legitimate action in ending the war is to deny a meaningful existence to the survivors. For many *hibakusha* to have a meaningful existence, therefore, key elements of the pro-nuclear discourse must be delegitimized, and the link with the bomb through radiation must be given a new meaning.

It is in this process that the third perspective on the atomic bombing has taken shape.

LINKING AGGRESSORS AND VICTIMS

The delegitimization of the pro-nuclear discourse has been manifest concretely in attempts to carry out four interrelated tasks: first, to undermine the interpretation that the atomic bombs were dropped in order to end the war and save lives; second, to show that the Japanese government, too, bears responsibility for the bombings; third, to challenge the international acceptance of nuclear weapons; fourth, and most importantly, to establish a victim's perspective on the atomic-bomb experience.

Japanese 'guinea pigs' and cold war strategy

A strong tendency exists on the part of those opposed to the atomic bombings of Hiroshima and Nagasaki to deny the bomb's role in expediting the end of the war and saving lives.[9] Much can be said for balking at this interpretation: Rufus Miles and others have examined the record and come to the conclusion that, far from saving over half a million lives as later claimed by Truman, or 'over a million casualties' as asserted by Secretary of War Stimson, or the 'loss of a million American lives and half that number of British', as in the mind of Winston Churchill, 'the number of American deaths prevented by the two bombs would almost certainly not have exceeded 20,000 and would probably have been much lower, perhaps even zero'.[10] Our purpose here is not to argue the validity of this critique, but instead to stress the need, in establishing a powerful anti-nuclear discourse, to reject the utilitarian principle of 'saving lives' as a moral justification for the atomic bombings of Hiroshima and Nagasaki. It is precisely as a result of the need to morally justify American actions in carrying out the bombings that the myth of the enormous number of lives saved is firmly established in the nuclear discourse of the United States.[11] The close ties between the US and Japanese governments have meant that, as we saw in Chapter 6 with Prime Minister Satō's use of the nuclear allergy metaphor, a continual competition has occurred in Japan over the central ground of the nuclear discourse. Yet seldom has 'lives saved' been used at the mass level to justify the atomic bombings. Far more salient has been to argue either that the bombs were essentially for experimental purposes, or that they were used as part of American cold war strategy against the Soviet Union.

In the most comprehensive study of the atomic damage in Hiroshima and Nagasaki to have been carried out, the authors conclude:

> the A-bomb attacks were needed not so much against Japan – already on the brink of surrender and no longer capable of mounting an effective counteroffensive – as to establish clearly America's post-war international position and strategic supremacy in the anticipated cold war setting. One tragedy of Hiroshima and Nagasaki is that this historically unprecedented devastation of human society stemmed from essentially experimental and political aims.[12]

Maruyama Masuteru rhetorically asks: 'Couldn't the dropping of the atomic bombs on Hiroshima and Nagasaki . . . be said to be a terrible, enormous test on live subjects (*jintai jikken*)?'[13] This perspective undoubtedly gained new adherents after the US Department of Energy released information in December 1993 admitting that, in order to investigate the influence of radioactivity as part of the nuclear weapons development programme of the late 1940s and early 1950s, it had carried out experiments which included using several hundred US citizens as 'guinea pigs': some were injected with plutonium, and pregnant women were given medicine laced with radioactive elements.[14] At the same time, others have focused more on the political goals of the United States in the emerging cold war situation. In this respect, Itō Takeshi concludes: '[S]cholars both in Japan and overseas are almost unanimous in the opinion that, against the backdrop of the Soviet–American cold war already under way at the time, the strategic purpose of the atomic bombings was to deter the Soviet Union.'[15]

Whatever the validity of focusing on the Japanese as 'guinea pigs' or on the cold war strategic designs of the United States in terms of historical interpretation, in terms of forming an anti-nuclear discourse, such a perspective does not possess the same moral legitimacy as does the utilitarian principle 'to end the war and save lives', and thus serves to deny any moral basis to the atomic bombings of Japan. In short, the atomic bombings of hundreds of thousands of human beings for the purpose of testing the destructive power of a new weapon or gaining a future power position in international society lacks the moral claims of 'to end the war and save lives'. It is this point, more than the validity of interpretations, that is of most significance in our discussion of the evolution of the anti-nuclear discourse.

Discourse of ascribed responsibility

The *hibakusha* have taken various legal and political actions in order to try to establish the American and Japanese governments' responsibility for the atomic bombings. They are trying to ascribe responsibility in the following respects:

> First, responsibility for the damage created by the atomic bombings – the Japanese state's responsibility for starting and prosecuting the war, the illegality under international law of the dropping of the atomic bombs by the American state; second, responsibility for increasing the extent of the damage – the Japanese state's responsibility for not taking appropriate measures after the bombings (e.g. information provided by the government played down the damage), the US government's responsibility during the Occupation period for concealing the extent of the damage and ignoring the *hibakusha*, the post-war Japanese governments' responsibility for not taking up the *hibakusha* issue (e.g. the A-Bomb Victims Medical Care Law was not passed until twelve years after the end of the war), and responsibility, under the San Francisco peace treaty, for relinquishing the right to seek compensation for damages; third, the political responsibility of the Japanese government to promote abolition of nuclear weapons.[16]

In this way, the *hibakusha* link the atomic bombings of Hiroshima and Nagasaki to Japan's aggressive war and the legal norms of international society, charge the Japanese and American governments with increasing the damage by withholding information and, in so far as the Japanese government is concerned, delaying assistance to the *hibakusha*, and look to the Japanese government to shoulder a special responsibility in promoting nuclear disarmament.[17] Likewise, many *hibakusha* regard the provisions of the San Francisco peace treaty — specifically, Chapter 5, Article 19 of the Treaty of Peace signed by Japan in 1951 – where the government relinquished the right to seek compensation from the Allied Powers, as making the Japanese government responsible for providing aid to the victims of Hiroshima and Nagasaki.

Accordingly, one of the concrete political aims of the *hibakusha* has been to gain financial assistance from the government for medical treatment as well as for livelihood. Partial success was achieved by the promulgation of the A-Bomb Victims Medical Care Law (1957), the A-Bomb Victims Special Measures Law (1968) and the A-Bomb Victims Relief Law, passed by the Diet in 1994 after the socialists became part of the coalition government.[18] In pushing for the implementation of such laws, the *hibakusha*, their non-victim supporters and some of the political parties, especially the socialists, have played a significant role in integrating the atomic bombings of Hiroshima and Nagasaki into the nuclear discourse as a problem of the present and future and not simply of the past. In particular, the *hibakusha* have striven to delineate sharply the experiences of Hiroshima and Nagasaki from those of what some might regard as the equally terrible suffering caused by conventional weaponry, as with the great fire raid on Tokyo in May 1945, which caused more immediate deaths. So, for instance, the death count continues to this day, as the names of the *hibakusha* who die as a result of radiation-related and other illnesses are added to the 'Books of the Past', with 221,407 in Hiroshima (1992) and 102,275 (1994) in Nagasaki.[19] Such activity maintains a symbolic link between the past, present and future: for the *hibakusha*, the atomic bombs continue to explode on into the future. In this way, the atomic bombings are not simply viewed as a problem of the Second World War, but as a problem of the nuclear era.

Challenging the acceptance of nuclear weapons

The *hibakusha* have taken the lead in trying to undermine the international acceptance of nuclear weapons as normal, taking legal action in order to challenge the legitimacy of these weapons, as well as political action in order to globalize the significance of being atom-bombed. In 1955, for instance, Shinoda *et al.* sought to challenge the legality of using nuclear weapons in their case against the government of Japan. Although the plaintiffs held the United States primarily responsible for the atomic damage, they were forced to bring the case against their own government as no claims could be made against the United States due to Article 19 of the Treaty of Peace. In his 1963 ruling the judge allowed no compensation; significantly, however, he ruled that the atomic bombings were contrary to the international law of the day.[20] This ruling helped to put the moral weight of international law on the side of those opposed to nuclear weapons. The approach taken by the *hibakusha* can also be considered a challenge to the Japanese government's position of not compensating civilians killed or injured during the war.[21] In 1958, moreover, three 'Hiroshima Maidens' joined Marshall Islanders in filing suit in Washington to halt nuclear testing, although the US District Court turned down their case in 1962. In this way, as we shall see below, the *hibakusha* have taken action against the damage arising from nuclear weapons in the present as well as in the past.

Second, in seeking to globalize the significance of Hiroshima, *hibakusha*, especially as organized through the Japan Council of Hibakusha Organizations (Nihon Hidankyō, established 1954), have over the years played a lead role in spreading the message, 'No More Hiroshimas!'. In the 1960s, for instance, the Hiroshima–Nagasaki Peace Study Mission (1964) was organized in order to send twenty-six *hibakusha* on a goodwill mission to the United States and Europe. In the 1970s, photographic exhibitions of the atomic bombings were organized in Europe and the United States – for instance, at the United Nations Special Session on Disarmament in 1978 – and photographic albums, films and books on the bombings were sent overseas. In the 1980s, these activities were intensified, with a major exhibition of the atomic bombings organized at the UN Second Special Session on Disarmament in 1982, and a large contingent of *hibakusha* sent as part of the Japanese delegation of over 1,000 persons which delivered the results of an anti-nuclear signature campaign.[22] In the early 1990s the *hibakusha* supported the loan of exhibits on the bombings made to the Smithsonian Museum in Washington as part of the fiftieth anniversary of the war's end. In all these efforts, as was made vividly clear in the protests mounted by US war veterans against the Smithsonian Museum exhibits from Hiroshima and Nagasaki, the *hibakusha* and other activists have been attempting to promote a victim's perspective as the core of the nuclear discourse.[23]

VICTIM'S PERSPECTIVE

The most significant challenge to the pro-nuclear discourse comes from the centrality of the victims of Hiroshima and Nagasaki in the anti-nuclear discourse. It is this, more than anything else, that has led to the strength of the anti-nuclear identity in Japan. But who are victims of what? The evolution of a victim's perspective can be divided into five main periods: (1) 1945–51; (2) 1952–4; (3) mid-1950s–early 1960s; (4) early 1960s–late 1970s; (5)the cold war 1980s. Our examination of the victims' perspectives which surfaced during these years should provide insight into the evolution of the anti-nuclear discourse in Japan.

1945–51: censorship and taboo

The period from 19 September 1945 until the coming into force of the Treaty of Peace on 28 April 1952 was a period of severe, albeit not total, restriction on the publication and dissemination of information on the atomic damage and casualties in Hiroshima and Nagasaki. Censorship, self-censorship and suppression of such information resulted from the imposition of the Press Code by the Occupation Authorities as well as from the history of censorship in Japan. Occupation censorship extended formally from 19 September 1945 to 31 October 1949, but continued to exert influence past this date, not least in the self-censorship exercised by the Japanese during the remainder of the Occupation and early post-Occupation years.[24]

The primary objective of the Occupation censors in so far as the atomic bombings are concerned was to restrict information implying that the bombing of Hiroshima and Nagasaki was inhumane and a violation of international and humanitarian laws as well as to convey the impression, especially to the American public, that atomic-bomb damage was not extensive and ended quickly.[25] The Press Code was used in order to suppress personal accounts of the bombings written by the victims. A story by a fifteen-year-old girl, *Masako Does Not Collapse*, for instance, was suppressed for fear it 'would disturb public tranquillity in Japan and that it implies the bombing was a crime against humanity'.[26] The authorities' attempt to make the victim's perspective taboo can be seen from the censor's deletion of 'many innocent people were killed in Hiroshima and Nagasaki', with the implication that no Japanese is innocent.[27] In the case of Nagai Takashi's *The Bells of Nagasaki*, the perspective of the atomic-bomb victims was relativized by appending 'The Sack of Manila', which describes Japanese atrocities in the Philippines.[28] Finally, death by radiation, which provided the most powerful condemnation of the atomic bombings, was denied as 'Japanese propaganda'.[29]

Likewise, at the Far Eastern Military Tribunal held from May 1946 to November 1948, Japanese were tried in the name of 'justice' and 'civilization' for wartime acts of aggression and cruelty, a fate not awaiting the users of the atomic bomb. The restriction of information, the emphasis on Japanese war crimes through the Allies' 'war-guilt campaign', the need to rebuild and the overall impact of foreign Occupation all meant that a powerful anti-nuclear discourse centring on a victim's perspective did not develop at this time. The *Asahi Shinbun* sums up the situation in an editorial on the sixth anniversary of the Hiroshima bombing:

There is detailed information on the damage caused by the atomic bomb in the report of the US Strategic Bombing Survey and also in translations of American and British publications. In regard to the limitless human tragedy brought about by the heat and blast of the atomic bomb, however, it seems hardly anything has been disseminated. Although transmitting this very information is the task allotted to the Japanese, we have not to this day set our eyes on any scientific reports of the bombings compiled by Japanese. We have still to see a comprehensive account put together on the pitiful experience of the *hibakusha*. . . . Even if most Japanese have an abstract understanding of the damage caused by the bomb, they probably do not know its true terror.

As in this period concrete knowledge of the atomic bombings was not widely available to the Japanese,[30] the victims' perspectives on the atomic damage were largely limited to those *hibakusha* who viewed themselves as victims. This sense of the *hibakusha* being specifically victims of the bomb, more than victims of the war as other Japanese, was promoted by the work of Kurihara Sadako, Shōda Shinoe and others. These two writers were able to publish literature and poetry describing the *hibakusha*'s suffering by submitting to the changes imposed on their work by the Occupation censors: after a gathering of about sixty writers in December 1945, Kurihara and her group in March 1946 started to publish *Chūgoku Bunka*, the first issue of which was devoted to the atomic bombing. The last issue (no. 18) was published in 1948, after which the name was changed to *Liberté*, with five issues (October 1948–November 1949) being published. Kurihara also put out a collection of her own writings, *Kuroi Tamago* (Black Eggs) in 1946; and in 1947 Shōda published 150 copies of *Sange* (Penitence or Confessions), a collection of tanka poetry. At the time of these nascent attempts to grapple with the meaning of the atomic bombings, however, the majority of Japanese, as well as the *hibakusha*, viewed themselves as the survivors of the war more than its victims. For the information environment was filled largely with images of the Japanese as the aggressors in the war, as symbolized by the Allies' war-guilt campaign and the executions carried out as a result of the findings of the Far Eastern Military Tribunal.

1952–4: anti-Americanism

It was after the publication in July 1952 of the magazine *Asahi Graph* (6 August issue), which included graphic, heart-rending pictures of the cruel effects of the atomic bombs on human beings, that the *hibakusha* of Hiroshima and Nagasaki began to be viewed more widely as victims by the Japanese. At the same time, however, the shock of seeing the sheer cruelty of the bombs' effects on the men, women and children of Hiroshima and Nagasaki, as depicted in *Asahi Graph* and in films like *Hiroshima, Children of the A Bomb, Glad to be Alive* and so forth, just a few short months after the end of the American-dominated Occupation, meant that many Japanese viewed the *hibakusha* as victims of the *American* bombings. In other words, the cruelty of the atomic damage linked the plight of the *hibakusha* to the agent of the atomic bombings, the Americans, de-reifying the bomb as the agent of destruction. As Kasugai Kunio comments:

> By coming into visual contact with the cold-blooded brutality of the atomic bombings after the peace treaty came into effect, an emotion was rapidly kindled of opposing the A-bomb as the enemy to be hated for such terrible damage, and this tended to be transformed into an emotion of anti-Americanism. In a word, by reliving the tragedy of the brutal atomic bombings, racial enmity was recalled, and the fearful atomic bomb and 'hateful America' came to overlap.[31]

As seen in the censoring of atomic-bomb material, fear of such kinds of reaction was a key motive behind the Occupation Authorities' restriction on publication of information giving concrete details on the cruelty of the atomic bombings. But this did not later lead to a focus on the particular – the impugning of the American atomic bombings – but the universal – the banning of *all* nuclear weapons. Such an approach surfaced in the next period, when the Japanese came to see themselves as victims.

Mid-1950s–early 1960s: radiation as violence

This period corresponds to the growth of a truly national peace movement in Japan. Two incidents are particularly important to our discussion: the Bikini incident of 1954, and the death of twelve-year-old Sasaki Sadako in 1955.

Bikini incident

The twenty-three crewmen aboard the fishing vessel *Lucky Dragon No. 5* were exposed to 'radioactive fall-out' as a result of a US hydrogen bomb test at Bikini atoll in the Marshall Islands on 1 March 1954. All of the crew suffered from radiation symptoms, with the radio operator dying in September. The catch had to be buried by health officials due to contamination. Shortly thereafter, Yaizu, home port of the *Lucky Dragon No. 5*, passed a resolution calling for 'a ban on all military use of nuclear energy'.[32] Other local governments throughout the nation quickly followed suit. Even both Houses of the National Diet, despite American pressure and resistance by the ruling conservative party, passed resolutions calling for international control of nuclear energy. At the grassroots level, Sugi no Ko Kai, a reading circle of housewives in Suginami Ward (Tokyo), started a signature collection campaign, which together with other groups succeeded in gathering eighteen million signatures in a few short months. The national movement as a whole collected around thirty-two million signatures – over half of the registered voters in Japan.[33] The goal of the movement, which had originally focused on the immediate problem of Bikini, was gradually expanded to take up the issues of the production, testing and future use of nuclear weapons, as well as the need to enact a national relief law for the *hibakusha*.[34] From the following year the annual World Conference Against Atomic and Hydrogen Bombs was held in Hiroshima, 6–8 August. In this way, the Bikini incident led to the growth of a nation-wide anti-nuclear movement with a universal goal – the banning of all atomic and hydrogen bombs. Neither concrete information on the death, injuries and destruction in Hiroshima and Nagasaki nor the efforts of the *hibakusha* to champion their cause had been able to galvanize a national movement. The way that the Bikini incident was integrated into the anti-nuclear discourse helps to explain the growth of the movement at this time. In short, the incident concretely focused attention on radiation as the critical link in the metaphoric 'nuclear chain'.

As a result of the centrality of radiation to the Bikini incident, the nuclear issue was highlighted not as a problem of the past war – the atomic bombings – nor of a minority – the *hibakusha* – but as a concrete, individually realizable problem of the nuclear era and of all Japanese. The goals of the movement were certainly international – a ban on the testing, manufacturing and use of nuclear weapons – but the ability of all Japanese to visualize themselves as *hibakusha*, that is, to see themselves as contaminated by radiation – physically, through eating polluted fish; psychologically, through identification with the sick and dying crewmen – meant that radiation as a link in the 'nuclear chain' was universalized, nationalized and subjectivized as a *threat* by individual Japanese.

The threat was concretely manifest in the discourse to evolve at the time in the following three ways. First, the Bikini incident was symbolically linked to Hiroshima and Nagasaki by dubbing it the 'third nuclear attack' on Japan.[35] It is precisely the link with radiation that permits the mind to accept the incommensuration between the death and devastation in Hiroshima and Nagasaki during war and the contamination of twenty-three crewmen near Bikini atoll during peace. Second, slogans linked the international, national and individual levels: the call for an international ban on nuclear tests went hand in hand with the national demand for the Japanese government to aid the *hibakusha* and the individual demand to eat non-polluted fish. Third, the anti-nuclear expression 'ashes of death' became common parlance for the English 'radioactive fall-out'.[36] This was the expression used by the reporter who first covered the return to port of the *Lucky Dragon No. 5*. This expression functions metaphorically to connect the deaths and suffering from the use of the atomic bombs against Hiroshima and Nagasaki with the death and suffering from the hydrogen bomb test at Bikini. In this way, the Bikini incident helped to place radiation at the centre of the discourse in terms of the past as well as the present and future.

Individuation of radiation as violence

Sasaki Sadako is the name of a twelve-year-old Hiroshima girl who died from leukaemia as a result of the residual radiation she received in the bombing at the age of 2. While hospitalized, she had received a paper crane in an anonymous letter and, in line with the ancient Japanese belief that folding 1,000 paper cranes would aid her recovery, she set out to fold *senbazuru* in her hospital bed, reaching 964 before her death on 25 October 1955.[37] The 'Girl of the Paper Cranes', as she has been called in English,[38] is important to our discussion for three reasons. First, her death by radiation received as an infant helped to crystallize the sheer inhumanity of atomic weapons in that they continue striking innocent victims on into the future. The individuation of atomic death in this one child symbolized to the Japanese how radiation links atomic death in the past, present and future. Second, the paper crane came to take on a new symbolic form. With the death of Sasaki Sadako and her classmate Iwamoto Yoshie the previous year, Hiroshima children started to collect funds to erect a memorial to all atomic-bomb victims who were children, a statue of Sadako holding aloft a golden crane, upon whose wings the message of peace is carried to the world, being unveiled in 1958. The crane came to link children symbolically to Hiroshima: children in the Folded Crane Club, active since the same year, produced a bilingual mimeograph, *Crane*, and schoolchildren from throughout Japan and from around the world still continue to place annually approximately four million folded cranes on the statue when on excursions to Hiroshima.[39] Third, this means that new generations of children have to some extent been linked symbolically to the atomic bombings by the 'Girl of the Paper Cranes'. In this way, the threat from radiation came to be individualized in the death of a child.

Early 1960s–late 1970s: victims of the bomb or of the United States?

It is at the beginning of this period that an open split occurred in the Japanese peace movement. This is important to our discussion of discourse because, as a result of this split, the question of whether to oppose all nuclear weapons and tests, or whether to oppose them selectively, became salient. To state the conclusion first: popular opinion supported the inclusiveness of the demand for a ban on both; that is, both 'capitalist' and 'socialist' tests and bombs should be opposed.

The controversy surrounding the revision of the US–Japan security treaty in 1960 went to the heart of the question of Japanese identity, bringing to the surface latent political and ideological differences between the various groups making up the anti-nuclear movement. At the founding World Conference Against Atomic and Hydrogen Bombs in 1955, Japanese peace groups were united under an umbrella organization, Gensuikyō (Japan Council Against Atomic and Hydrogen Bombs), which was formed in September 1955 in the wake of the peace activities following the Bikini incident. But the ruling Liberal Democratic Party's stand in favour of extending the security treaty, and the Japan Communist Party's and Japan Socialist Party's determination to oppose the revision in favour of an independent security policy, brought the question of opposition to nuclear weapons at the international level down to the question of the concrete policy to be adopted at the national level.

The anti-treaty stance of the communists and socialists and their union and other supporters led to the withdrawal from Gensuikyō of conservative groups and the formation in November 1961 of Kakkin Kaigi (National Council for Peace and Against Nuclear Weapons). More importantly, in 1963 the socialists walked out of the World Conference owing to a difference with the communists over opposition to nuclear tests, formally establishing together with Sōhyō (General Council of Trade Unions of Japan) and other groups a new organization Gensuikin (Japan National Conference Against Atomic and Hydrogen Bombs) in February 1965. The communists were disinclined to oppose Soviet nuclear testing or support the partial nuclear-test ban treaty, which China opposed, viewing the possession and testing of nuclear weapons by socialist countries as necessary to maintain peace – to the communists, 'imperialist' American weapons and tests were the crux of the problem.

The split in the movement appeared for a short time to be on the mend, when joint action between Gensuikyō and Gensuikin started at the time of the United Nations First Special Session on Disarmament in 1978, lasting until the mid-1980s. In the late 1980s and early 1990s, however, the rift reopened, with the two groups holding separate annual conferences in Hiroshima. The most damaging result of this politicization of 'peace' was the alienation of ordinary citizens from the institutionalized anti-nuclear movement. What must be noted, however, is the ability of Gensuikin, not Gensuikyō, to maintain popular legitimacy in terms of the goals espoused. In other words, opposition to the testing and possession of *all* nuclear weapons, irrespective of whether they were 'capitalist' or 'communist', was a goal shared at the mass level. This made one thing perfectly clear: mass opposition to nuclear weapons and testing sprang from anti-nuclearism, *not* anti-Americanism. The *Asahi Shinbun* editorial (6 August 1970) on the twenty-fifth anniversary of the Hiroshima bombing explains the situation in the following way:

> The Japanese, who have thrice experienced atomic explosions, two at Hiroshima and Nagasaki, and another at the time of the *Lucky Dragon No. 5*, have not processed their experiences at the level of a racial problem or anti-Americanism, but on the level of disavowing war in general and eliminating nuclear weapons – that is, at the level of the whole of humankind. The vast majority of Japanese rejected the attempt to whip up hate towards a specific country in the name of ideology.

The rejection of the communist position in favour of universal opposition to nuclear weapons is clear here.

The cold war 1980s: who are the *hibakusha*? The discourse of law and the discourse of protest

The approach that the *hibakusha* themselves have taken towards their status as victims of the atomic bombings has helped to crystallize the victims' perspectives in the anti-nuclear discourse. For in the process of building an identity, the *hibakusha* and others involved in opposing nuclear weapons have brought into sharp relief the question 'Who are the *hibakusha*?' The boundaries of the meaning given to this term have thus been brought into focus.

According to the A-Bomb Victims Medical Care Law, the *hibakusha* are:

1. those who were in the cities of Hiroshima and Nagasaki and in certain nearby areas (the law names the relevant areas, which are where the 'black rain' fell) when the atomic bombs were dropped;
2. those who entered the cities of Hiroshima and Nagasaki to search for relatives, for rescue operations and so forth, within two weeks from the day that the bombs were dropped;
3. those who received radiation through disposal of the dead, rescue work and so forth, in areas other than those stipulated in point 1;
4. those in any of the above categories who were at the time *in utero*.[40]

There are a number of reasons why this legal definition of *hibakusha* proved inadequate for promoting an anti-nuclear discourse centring on the victims.

This inadequacy can be summed up by saying that the law is based strictly on the principle of exclusion. In other words, the law aims to define a discrete category of living beings who, as a result of the atomic bombings of Hiroshima and Nagasaki, have been exposed to a large enough quantity of radiation to create at least the suspicion of them being susceptible to ill-effects at some point during their lifetime. In contrast, the *hibakusha* – at least those actively opposed to nuclear weapons – have been the driving force to make the meaning *inclusive*.[41] In other words, they aim to establish a universalistic concept of *hibakusha* in order to build a shared *political* identity among all those who have suffered as a result of the atomic bombings, nuclear testing and so on.

Three points are salient: first, the boundaries of the legal definition of *hibakusha* have been challenged. Of most importance here has been the movement to secure the same rights for Korean *hibakusha* as for Japanese. For the law had actually functioned in a more exclusionary (discriminatory) way than the actual wording. The legal battle of Son Jin-doo, who in 1978 won his fight for Koreans to be treated as Japanese and receive medical care – that is, the inclusion of Koreans in the legal definition of *hibakusha* – was instrumental in highlighting the dual victimization of Koreans in Hiroshima and Nagasaki: as victims of Japanese imperialism, on the one hand, and as victims of the atomic bombings, on the other.[42] This served to link the colonization of Korea to the atomic bombings: 'the Korean *hibakusha* ... were long the victims of repressive policies before falling victim to the atomic bombs'.[43]

Second, intellectuals, particularly *hibakusha* intellectuals, have worked to expand the boundaries of the definition. For instance, Itō Takeshi, a *hibakusha* social scientist, defines *hibakusha* as follows:

> The definition of '*hibakusha*' according to the law can be summarized as the two principles: (1) someone who is presently alive; (2) someone who was exposed to large quantities of radiation as a result of the atomic bombings. When I use '*hibakusha*' the meaning is broader than this legal definition in that I include those who were killed as a result of the bombing ... Moreover, '*hibakusha*' from nuclear weapon tests and '*hibakusha*' from the peaceful use of nuclear power, and '*hibakusha*' as used here, while the same in the sense that they were all harmed by exposure to radiation, are greatly different in other respects.[44]

In this way Itō – a *hibakusha* according to the legal definition – expanded the definition of *hibakusha* in order to embrace others who have suffered harm as a result of exposure to radiation in the years since the atomic bombings of Hiroshima and Nagasaki.

Third, as is evident in the 'Itō definition', focusing on radiation more broadly as well as on the atomic bombings of the two cities and those affected functions politically to embrace others outside Japan in a shared political identity. The political motivations of activists are evident in 1977 at an NGO-sponsored International Symposium on the Damage and After-effects of the Atomic Bombing of Hiroshima and Nagasaki, when the chairman of the international organizing committee declared: 'We are all *hibakusha*. We are all the survivors of Hiroshima and Nagasaki.'[45] This expands the definition of *hibakusha* to its logical, universalistic conclusion, as symbolized by the title of the appeal proclaimed at the symposium: 'Life or Oblivion: A Call from the *Hibakusha* of Hiroshima and Nagasaki to the *Hibakusha* of the World'.

But if we are all *hibakusha*, then are we all victims? And, if so, then who are the aggressors? Itō steps back just slightly from this universalistic definition to provide his own political definition of *hibakusha*:

> The atomic bombing of Allied prisoners of war in Nagasaki, the problem of the Korean *hibakusha*, whose atomic damage overlaps with the problem of colonial control and their forced move [to mainland Japan], and other such problems, are different in social implication to Japanese *hibakusha*, even though all suffer from the same atomic damage. Further, the relationship between aggressors and victims established by the atomic bomb does not end with 'the dropping of the atomic bomb'. For example, the Occupation forces' policy of maintaining a taboo on the atomic bomb during the Occupation period is clearly a continuation of the relationship. If I go even further, the damage arising from the Bikini nuclear tests demonstrates nothing other than the result of the continuation and expansion of this relationship. And, in the sense that nowadays the possibility of becoming *hibakusha* extends to all of humankind, we can even say that the relationship continues between the leaders of the nuclear-weapon states who are vested with the authority to decide on the use of nuclear weapons, and the potential *hibakusha* (in a word, all of humankind except these leaders).[46]

In his attempt to isolate the users of nuclear weapons from the rest of humankind, Itō has failed to give enough consideration to two questions, one related to war responsibility as addressed in the Nuremburg Trials, which raises doubts about whether all of those involved in so many ways in the 'use of nuclear weapons' should be excluded, either logically or morally from his definition; the other, which is the flip side of the first question, is whether these leaders would themselves not be exposed to the nuclear aftermath, even if a nuclear shelter may protect them at first, meaning that they can also become '*hibakusha*'. In any event, the approach taken by Itō is important in order to illustrate how the *hibakusha* have quite clearly aimed at developing a *political* definition of victim and aggressor, with Itō himself coming down in favour of excluding from the definition of *hibakusha* only those vested with the authority to start a nuclear war.

CONCLUSION

For the pro-American conservative governments in control of Japan during the cold war era, anti-nuclearism at the mass level has created at least some impediment to policy-making in regard to nuclear relations with the United States. How those in favour of accepting the militarization of Japan have attempted – with some success – to destroy the basis for anti-nuclear attitudes by attacking the critical link – radiation – by using the metaphor 'nuclear allergy' to brand the people's anti-nuclearism as 'abnormal' was discussed in Chapter 6. But the continued strength of anti-nuclear and more generally anti-militaristic attitudes suggests that the anti-nuclear discourse has been an important factor in promoting such attitudes and actions as the core of a demilitarized Japanese identity. What conclusions can be drawn in regard to demilitarization and language in Japan?

It would appear that nuclearization processes may have been slowed – if not reversed – by actions promoting an anti-nuclear discourse centring on a victim's perspective. This perspective must be seen as a critical element for opponents of nuclear weapons in building a sense of shared identity with people in different parts of the world. It was certainly at the heart of the successful grassroots attempts made in the late 1980s and early 1990s to institutionalize a world conference of nuclear victims aimed at creating political awareness of nuclear victimization. At the second conference held in Berlin in 1992, for instance, approximately 450 participants from over 60 countries came together to appeal the plight of victims of uranium mining, nuclear accidents, nuclear tests, the atomic bombings and so forth. With an estimate of up to 30 million nuclear victims world-wide, the efficacy of a victim's perspective is plain to see.[47]

Second, our discussion of the evolution of the anti-nuclear discourse has brought into sharp relief the question of the specific link in the metaphorical 'nuclear chain' that Japanese activists have focused upon in order to promote an anti-nuclear discourse linked to praxis. The discourse in Japan evolved around the links 'radiation' and 'victims'. This is not, of course, to ignore the obvious role of the atomic bombings, but rather to emphasize how these experiences became a link in the chain between aggressors and victims. The developments mentioned in the last paragraph suggest the emergence first of a sense of the Japanese as *the* victims of the bomb, with a 'limited' number of mainly Japanese victims, to a nascent sense of a global threat arising from the preparation and production of nuclear weapons, as seen at the time of the Bikini incident, developing to a point where political activities in the 1990s can be premised on the idea that thirty million victims exist. This implies the possibility of extending the scope of potential victimization to almost all humanity, as proposed in the 1977 NGO symposium. It does not seem unreasonable to claim that it was partly as a result of the Bikini 'ashes of death' being integrated into an evolving anti-nuclear discourse that the halt of nuclear testing in the late 1950s, and the achievement of a ban on atmospheric testing in the Limited Nuclear Test Ban Treaty of 1963, were put into effect.

Third, the success of the anti-nuclear movement in Japan in emphasizing a universalistic approach to the nuclear problem – opposing all nuclear weapons – compared to the failure of the communists in trying to promote an exclusionary approach – opposing only US nuclear weapons – re-emphasizes the importance of the inclusionary approach to 'victims' in the nuclear chain. Nevertheless, the growth of the peace movement at the time of the Bikini incident, together with the general lack of an active peace movement in the post cold-war era, also seems to indicate the importance of a concrete threat to everyday life being perceived by individual Japanese before large-scale anti-nuclear action takes place.

Finally, as seen in the coining of the metaphor 'ashes of death', rhetorical language played a crucial role in the anti-nuclear discourse, too. To what extent expressions such as 'nuclear allergy' and 'ashes of death' became rooted in the security discourse is closely related to how popular attitudes, state structures, and internal and external pressures interacted during the cold war era. In the concluding chapter let us touch on this question as a prelude to discussing the debate in the early 1990s on Japan's future role in the world.

Conclusion

In the preceding chapters we have examined militarization and demilitarization in contemporary Japan paying attention to the intertwined issues of 'identity' and 'normality'. This approach was taken in order to shed light on the 'soft side' of these two processes. The experience of being demilitarized during the Occupation has meant that, for the cold war conservative regimes, Japanese (re)militarization was at heart a process of restoring legitimacy to the military as an instrument of state policy, especially during the period we have examined. Of course, this is not to deny the importance of the 'hard side' aspects of militarization, as without the essential ingredients the military could not be normalized. As seen with the increase in Japan's military expenditures, quantitative and qualitative improvement in weaponry and deeper integration into US nuclear strategy, these aspects were particularly salient during the 1980s. It is rather to emphasize the need to take due account of the erosion of the legal and normative constraints imposed on employing the SDF as a 'normal' military force, as seen more clearly in the early 1990s, when the ban on the SDF's overseas despatch was scrapped. This 'normalization' is a necessary step for those political forces struggling to transform Japan into a military big power, enjoying the fruits but shouldering the burden of big powerism, where the military is employed in upholding a regional and global order as defined under the hegemony of the United States, if not as a step towards making Japan an independent military power.[1] In this sense, the proposal of Ozawa Ichirō for Japan to cooperate with the United Nations should be understood more as a call to contribute to the United Nations under the hegemony of the United States than as a Japanese commitment to strive for the realization of multilateral interests seeking to embrace those outside the Security Council. Needless to say, in the first place the same path can be taken in seeking to make Japan an independent military power.[2]

Nevertheless, the experience of the war, especially the atomic bombings, and the popular support for the anti-militaristic Constitution, have continued to inform mass opinion and constrain the government in trying to become a normal military state. Whereas anti-nuclear attitudes grew out of a realistic assessment of the meaning of the nuclear era, anti-militaristic attitudes embody a dual rejection of militarism, both at home and abroad. The persistent strength of these attitudes suggests that the experience of the war and the meaning of constitutional principles have been integrated into a discourse on security and defence, giving priority to non-violent forms of contribution to the realization of security goals. The Heiwa Mondai Danwakai, the *hibakusha*, opposition political parties and a wide variety of peace, anti-nuclear and other social movements over the years have struggled to give a positive meaning to the lessons of the war, the atom-bomb experiences and the principles of the Constitution. In this sense, although the United States won the war, dropped the bomb and introduced the Constitution, it was the people who gave them positive meaning as part of a new Japanese identity centring on anti-nuclearism and anti-militarism.

What are the key elements in the attitudes nurtured by the activities surrounding these experiences? With varying degrees of emphasis these are *not* to (1) take part in aggressive wars; (2) use, possess or provoke the use of nuclear weapons; (3) establish a 'regular military' or use force in trying to solve international problems. On the other hand, such attitudes (1) support the SDF, especially for domestic 'disaster relief'; (2) agree to their overseas deployment, but not for 'normal' military activities; (3) accept the security treaty, but acquiesce in, if not oppose, its nuclear aspects. That Japan did not develop nuclear weapons, directly fight in the Vietnam War, suffer military dictatorships (unlike many other US allies in the region) or deploy aircraft carriers and other weapons for 'power projection' is related in no small part to the development of these attitudes at the mass level, and not simply to the existence of the US–Japan security treaty. In this sense, as Kuno Osamu pointed out, political victory is victory 'outside the arena of thought'.

It is true that, for many, the US–Japan security treaty system is the main restraint on Japanese defence and security policy.[3] Certainly, the treaty has functioned to integrate the SDF into a bilateral force structure dominated by the United States, thereby restricting independent actions by the SDF. It is also true that, especially in the post cold-war era, concern is mounting in US policy-making circles over the possibility of a militarily independent Japan, outside the control of the United States.[4] But this does not mean that the US–Japan security treaty system is 'the single anchor for Japan's new culture of anti-militarism'.[5] The anchor is much more firmly at rest in the anti-nuclearism and anti-militarism of the Japanese people. In other words, the US–Japan security treaty is secondary to the attitudes and actions of the people in maintaining a peaceful regime. As we will see below, one task in realizing a demilitarized identity is to strive to transform the treaty as part of a new regional security framework in tune with the realities of the post cold-war era.

Thus, even though in the early post cold-war 1990s popular attitudes did not reject out-of-hand an international role for the SDF, the preference remained for Japan to contribute by non-military means. The government was able to make the SDF's overseas despatch more acceptable at the mass level by articulating a discourse centring on 'international contribution'. In this context, the United Nations posed a challenge to the Constitution: in defining a new identity for Japan in the early 1990s, the United Nations as a positive international symbol of the new post cold-war order could be set against the Constitution as a positive domestic symbol of the old cold war order. Such a change in the mode of legitimation is not new. In the cold war era, a variety of euphemisms and metaphors were employed by political leaders in order to legitimize the SDF's growth and changing role. But the symbol of the United Nations and the rhetoric of 'international contribution' were a powerful combination, demonstrating that overseas despatch need not be for aggression. As popular attitudes are rooted in the rejection of a 'normal military' using force, one of the main issues over the past years and in the future is to what extent these attitudes are also manifest as actions to constrain the government's own actions and policies. In this sense, the roles of peace education and peace action are an essential part of the struggle over defence and security policies, and the broader question of Japanese identity in the nuclear yet post cold-war era.

EDUCATION AND ACTION

We have seen already in Chapter 6 how the Ministry of Education has sought to employ the textbook certification system as a means to inculcate certain attitudes in the future generations, with certification at the heart of attempts to obfuscate a critical perspective on

Japan's war in Asia. This symbolizes the way that education in the cold war era was an integral part of the struggle over Japanese identity, with social studies textbooks at the crux of the competition over transmitting information and values on war and peace to the young.[6] The role of education in this task led both the supporters and opponents of creating a 'normal state' to focus on the textbook as a means to promote their respective values. Thus, the Ministry of Education, backed by political forces calling for a stronger sense of patriotism in the younger generation, was set against the Teachers' Union, backed by the peace education movement and other political forces, which tried to pass on the lessons of the war as a way to promote values seeking to deny militarization.

The Japan Teachers' Union and peace educators strove to thwart the Ministry of Education's interference in the content of education, as exemplified by textbook certification. Their actions derive from a rejection of the sort of education carried out under militarism. The fear has been that, as in the days when militarists transformed school education into a vehicle for raising patriotic citizens loyal to the emperor and state, the education system again has been used to produce students prepared to acquiesce in the government's defence and security policies. The kind of textbook certification practised, as seen in the effect on the texts, suggests that information on the 'ugly side' of Japanese history has been restricted, and the government's policies on defence and security have been given prominence.

A case in point is the 'certification' of Ienaga Saburō's textbook.[7] In 1965 Ienaga Saburō, at the time a professor at the Tokyo University of Education, brought a suit against the government, charging that the 'certification' of his history textbook was in fact 'censorship', in contravention of Article 21 of the Constitution, which states in the second clause 'No censorship shall be maintained, nor shall the secrecy of any means of communication be violated'. The reason for the changes in his textbook, as seen by Ienaga, was the Ministry's 'political intention to keep the ideal of abolition of war in the present constitution from permeating into the people's minds, and thus to remove barriers to rearmament'.[8]

Likewise, in 1981 the Japan Teachers' Union produced a report comparing the pre-inspection and post-inspection textbooks to be used in high-school social studies courses from 1982, which pointed to the changes implemented by the authors and publishers after the texts had been subject to certification.[9] The following sections are relevant to our discussion: (1) defence, the Self-Defence Forces and the Northern Territories; (2) pacifism and international society;

(3) nuclear weapons and war; and (4) patriotism and the Constitution. The report draws the following conclusions, which are indicative of the workings of the certification system:[10]

1. stress on the legality of the Self-Defence Forces and elimination of any reference to Japan as the country with the strongest 'defensive power' in Asia;
2. elimination of the history of the peace movement since the Meiji era and references to the need to respect peace;
3. elimination of material dealing with the reality of war; obfuscation of any perspective to allow students to think about the existence of a military–industrial complex and the arms industry;
4. covering up of the individual's sense of alienation and powerlessness *vis-à-vis* the state; emphasis on strengthening patriotism.

Later, when high-school textbooks were subject to certification in 1986, the ministry approved the Nihon o Mamoru Kokumin Kaigi's (National Conference for the Defence of Japan) *Shinpen Nipponshi*,[11] a history textbook criticized for being a 'militaristic textbook centring on the emperor', which plays down the Nanjing massacre.[12] These sorts of change in the content and emphasis of text material, along with the publication of *Shinpen Nipponshi*, were behind renewed criticism of the textbook certification system and the version of history being taught in Japanese schools.[13]

Due to the earlier East Asian as well as domestic criticisms, the textbook certification system was made more open in 1983. But problems still occurred, as in 1986, leading to a full revision of the system in 1989. This followed the establishment of an *ad hoc* commission on education under Prime Minister Nakasone.[14] The revision simplified procedures and extended the period of certification for new texts to every four years instead of every three.[15] Despite these and other changes, as authors and publishers still fear the consequences of the textbook failing to be approved for school use, not least the loss of sales revenue, critics charge that a subtle form of control and 'self-censorship' continues unabated, as seen in the appearance of state-defined military heroes in all primary-school history textbooks approved for use in 1991.[16]

High-school texts were first approved under this new system in 1992, although social studies was no longer a compulsory subject after a revision of the course of study in 1989.[17] Representative examples of the type of comments made during the certification process include the need to exercise care in using expressions implying that Japan was responsible for the Marco Polo Bridge incident in 1937; that mentioning the 'violation of women' at the time of the Nanjing massacre is inappropriate from an educational point of view, and care should be taken in discussing the number killed, as no scholarly consensus exists; that the legal basis for the existence of the Self-Defence Forces needs to be stated; and that the US use of bases in Japan is under certain restrictions as a result of the US–Japan security treaty.[18] Likewise, in so far as the more recent controversy over the despatch of the SDF is concerned, comments included the inappropriateness of referring to Japan as a 'base for the Gulf War' as well as of using the expression 'overseas despatch of troops' (*kaigai hahei*) about the SDF.[19] Both might create misunderstanding, the inspectors argued.

The change in the attitudes and actions of the Ministry of Education can be seen by referring back to a publication from the early years of the Occupation, when in 1947 the ministry published a booklet for middle-school students, *The Story of the New Constitution*. In explaining the new Constitution, the booklet relates how two things have been decided to ensure that Japan will never again wage war:

> The first is that Japan will never possess anything with which to make war, no army, battleships, or planes. From now on Japan will not have any land, sea, or air forces. This means Japan's renunciation of war potential.
>
> The second thing that was decided is that, if a conflict occurs with another country, Japan will not through war try to defeat or get its own way with that country. We will rather carry out discussions calmly to reach a decision . . . Also, even if we do not go so far as war, it was decided in the Constitution that Japan will never threaten another country by using its own power. This is the renunciation of war potential.[20]

The change in the government's interpretation of the Constitution meant that, as we have seen above, certification of textbooks during the following decades centred on obfuscating the dark side of war, emphasizing the legal basis of the SDF and in general presenting the ruling party's perspectives. By the late 1960s teachers in Hiroshima were surprised to find that, even in one of the atom-bombed cities, many of the students did not know the details of the atomic bombings, with a majority not even knowing that Nagasaki also had been bombed.[21] From thenceforth, the Japanese peace education movement started in earnest. Over the years, the teachers involved have striven to pass on the memory of the war by concretely teaching their students about the atomic bombings, the everyday-life situation of the *hibakusha*, the dangers of nuclear war and other issues of importance in peace education. The Japanese emphasis can be seen from the issues considered of relevance to peace education, as taken up in articles in the journal *Heiwa Kyōiku* (Peace Education). In the 1980s, for instance, the topics included 'The Self-Defence Forces and National Defence Education', 'What to Teach in the Face of the Threat of a Future Nuclear War', 'How to Teach about Urban Bombing', 'Educational Topics and the Danger of Nuclear War', 'How to Teach about the Fifteen-Year War' and others in the peace–war framework. With the fiftieth anniversary of the war, similar topics are also a focus of attention in 1995.

In addition, as the number of pages in the certified textbooks dealing with issues of war and peace were reduced over the years, peace educators took countervailing steps to produce other teaching materials. Representative examples include *Hiroshima: This is Our Cry*, for teaching about the cruelty of war and the importance of peace by focusing on the atomic bombing of Hiroshima; *Hiroshima: Thinking about the Atomic Bombs*, for stimulating students to think about the atomic bombings and the growth of the peace movement; and *To the People of Tomorrow: Peace Essays by Hiroshima Children*, a collection of essays by children dealing with the war.

Beyond the production of text materials, a close relationship has been developed between peace education and peace action. This perspective can be seen in the proposal of the Hiroshima Peace Education Research Institute's 'The Aims of Peace Education'. The Institute was set up in 1972 with the aim of 'creating the contents of, and developing a movement for, peace education'.[22] In this respect, the Institute specifically aims to: (1) inform students of the inhumanity and cruelty of war and to make them understand respect for peace and the dignity of life; (2) seek the causes of war and make them scientifically aware of the forces giving rise to war and its true character; (3) elucidate the power to protect peace. Finally, it is hoped that the students will come to understand how to prevent war and build peace by investigating and gaining first-hand knowledge of the peace movement and peace action.

Such activities in the classroom and production of text materials are thus part of a broader, mass-based movement for peace for many of those involved in peace education. This link between peace education and peace action goes back to 1950–1, when many teachers followed the lead of the Japan Teachers' Union and participated in the movement supporting the Danwakai's proposal for an 'overall peace'. In 1951, at the teachers' national conference, peace education was taken up as a major topic in line with the conference theme 'Never Send Pupils to War Again'. In this way, the roots of peace education from the start have been intertwined with political action, for many teachers believe that, in order to teach freely about peace, an active peace education movement is essential in order to ensure the maintenance of a peaceful regime.[23]

In a wider societal context, grassroots action opposed to war and militarization has been carried out by a variety of mass-based movements from the early cold war onwards. Representative are the movement in support of the 'overall peace' in 1950–1, the anti-nuclear movement starting in the aftermath of the Bikini 'ashes of death' in 1954, the anti-security treaty revision movement of 1959–60, the anti-Vietnam War movement of the mid-1960s onwards and the Okinawan reversion movement mounted throughout the 1960s. In the cold war 1980s a powerful anti-nuclear (nuclear disarmament) movement burgeoned at the beginning of the decade. It developed in connection with the United Nations Second Special Session on Disarmament (SSDII). This is the last large-scale movement to gain the participation of ordinary citizens throughout Japan.

What is striking about the anti-nuclear movement at this time is the breadth and diversity of the participating groups. These included not only the communist-affiliated Gensuikyō, the socialist and Sōhyō-affiliated Gensuikin and other groups long at the centre of anti-nuclear activities, such as Nihon Hidankyō (The Japan Council of Hibakusha Organizations), but also the cooperative unions, women's associations and a whole range of professional and occupational groups that took action for the first time. Representative are the Japanese Writers against Nuclear Weapons, the Architects Association Demanding Abolition of Nuclear Weapons, the Association of Doctors and Dentists against Nuclear War, with poets, movie directors, cameramen, musicians and others also forming their own anti-nuclear groups.

Typically, such groups were formed in response to a mounting fear of nuclear war as well as in opposition to the increased pace of Japanese militarization. Thus, at the beginning of the 1980s, the Japanese Lawyers International Liaison Committee (Nihon Kokusai Hōritsuka Renraku Kyōkai) started an anti-nuclear signature collection campaign in February after a survey of the membership showed that 52 per cent feared an outbreak of nuclear war in the near future.[24] Nation-wide public opinion polls highlighted the extent of popular fear. In a June 1981 survey, for instance, 57 per cent of the respondents were concerned about the possible outbreak of an all-out nuclear war compared to 44 per cent in 1975 (35 per cent and 44 per cent respectively showed no concern).[25] Likewise, in an April 1982 survey, 63 per cent were concerned about the possibility of an all-out war using nuclear weapons.[26] Second, the increase in the percentage of the government's budget spent on the military, the improvements in the SDF's equipment, the expansion in their range of activities and so on, as discussed in Chapter 3, also served to convince ordinary citizens of the need to take action. Even before the advent of the Nakasone Cabinet, a March 1982 survey showed that 46 per cent of the respondents thought that right-wing attitudes were conspicuous on defence and constitutional questions, with only 18 per cent disagreeing.[27]

The strength of mass activity at this time can be seen from the following two examples. In the first place, anti-nuclear rallies held in 1982 in Hiroshima and Tokyo point to the strength of the broad-based support for promoting nuclear disarmament. Not only did the rallies attract the usual activists from the unions and peace groups, but many ordinary Japanese citizens who had maintained a distance from the anti-nuclear movement attended in large numbers. The size of the rallies indicates the strong support given at the grassroots level, with the organizers claiming that the Hiroshima rally drew 186,000 and the Tokyo rally 406,000, making them two of the largest rallies in the post-1945 period.[28] Second, a variety of groups were active in mass-based signature campaigns, including the above-mentioned newly established peace groups, religious organizations, the unions, students and so on. Over 80 million signatures in support of nuclear disarmament were delivered to the United Nations at the time of SSDII.[29] The number of telephone calls and letters from ordinary citizens requesting forms for signature collection is indicative of the widespread support for nuclear disarmament at the mass level.[30]

Shortly after the end of SSDII in 1982, however, anti-nuclear activities again dropped to a lull. In this way, large-scale movements opposed to nuclear weapons and militarization go through periodic cycles of intense activity and dormancy, often responding to immediate changes in the national and international political and security environments. The changed situation is symbolized by the fact that, after 1985, the communist and socialist anti-nuclear organizations abandoned the joint conferences that they had once again begun to hold from August 1977. These conflicts between different parts of the movement help to explain popular inactivity in the post cold-war era, and this is nothing unique to Japan.

At the same time, however, as the issues dominating the agenda in Japan in the 1980s focused on nuclear issues, disarmament and the 'hard side' aspects of Japanese militarization, the receding fear of nuclear war, especially after the end of the cold war, and the active steps for disarmament taken by the United States and Russia, as well as the decrease in Japanese military expenditures, the legitimization of the SDF's overseas despatches in terms of 'international contribution' and the advent of coalition governments, have all contributed to a lack of vitalization in the peace movement. Nevertheless we should note that, in the post cold-war era, the conception of 'peace action' may well have been broadened, with non-governmental organizations involved in a wide variety of 'international contribution', becoming an increasingly popular employment destination for young people, far beyond any interest expressed in the cold war 1980s.[31] In the post cold-war years of the early 1990s, therefore, apart from this change and the anti-nuclear and anti-militaristic attitudes of the people which, though strong, did not lead to mass action, the most significant aspect of peace activities has been as part of the proposals made to redefine security policy for a new Japanese identity in the post cold-war era.

THE UNFOLDING DEBATE ON SECURITY AND A ROLE IN THE WORLD

The cold war debate on militarization and demilitarization tended to unfold within parameters set by both internal and external pressures. Thus, the strength of mass opinion, as expressed through public opinion polls, mass action outside the Diet and the role of the Opposition within the Diet, interacted with the external pressure exerted by the United States and its domestic allies, creating a 'sandwiched state' where the ruling party would sometimes be forced to impose restrictions on the nation's military role.[32] In some cases, the policy enjoyed support within the ruling party, too, and was significant in restricting the role of Japan as a normal military state. This is the case, for instance, with the ban on the export of arms and military technology. True, on occasion the ban has been evaded and an exception was made of the United States in the 1980s. Nevertheless, despite such erosion of restraints, Japan certainly has not followed the United States in developing an enormous military–industrial complex, which sucks the 'best and the brightest' into the military rather than the civilian production process; nor has Japan joined in the scramble for arms markets, which is the hallmark of the present members of the UN Security Council. Japan's role in working to set up the United Nations Arms Register symbolizes the difference in approach.[33]

On the other hand, as in the case of the three non-nuclear principles, the third principle is more of an uncomfortable compromise between the internal demands of anti-nuclear attitudes and the external demands of US strategy, with the latter being given precedence over the former. So even though the opposition parties pushed for codification of the three non-nuclear principles, this was always resisted by the ruling LDP. Indeed, Japan's three non-nuclear principles were promulgated as one part of the Satō government's four nuclear principles, which included Japan's acceptance of nuclear deterrence: (1) adherence to the three non-nuclear principles; (2) promotion of nuclear disarmament; (3) dependence on the US nuclear deterrence in accordance with the US–Japan security treaty; and (4) giving highest priority to the peaceful use of nuclear energy.[34] From the outset, therefore, the third of the four nuclear principles directly undermined the value of the Japanese government's third non-nuclear principle.

It is in a sense against the background of this sort of political environment that the debate on Japan's defence and security policies and role in the world unfolded during the cold war era. The end of the cold war, the Gulf crisis and the following decisions to deploy Japanese forces in Cambodia and elsewhere have brought into sharp relief the changing nature of this debate. With the actual use of the SDF, for internationally sanctioned peace-keeping rather than for aggression, the contradictory interpretations of 'identity' and 'normality', as discussed in the Introduction, have lost their validity as markers in the present debate. In other words, the cold war division symbolized by the constitutional fault line of 'protect the Constitution' or 'revise the Constitution', with the political forces supporting the former, like the socialists, viewing the latter as 'reactionary', and the political forces supporting the latter, such as the LDP, viewing the former as 'utopian', no longer makes sense in the 'post cold-war' 'post-1955' era.

In the early 1990s, this changed situation led to a burst of intellectual activity reminiscent of the debate at the time of the Danwakai's proposal.[35] What role should Japan play in the post cold-war world? Should this be based on a military or a non-military international contribution? Of what significance is the Constitution in the post cold-war era? What security policy should Japan adopt? These were the kinds of question addressed in a variety of proposals that were put forward by political and intellectual groups.[36] Representative examples include the mid-term and final reports on Japan's role in international society issued by the then ruling LDP – the so-called Ozawa Committee reports of 1992 and 1993, which included a proposal for Japan's participation in UN peace-keeping forces; the proposal submitted in 1994 by the prime minister's defence advisory group, which called for the implementation of an active and constructive security policy; the proposal and final report of the Yomiuri Constitutional Investigation Committee, issued in 1992 and 1994, which aimed at a revision of the Constitution; and the proposal by a group of mainly politics and international relations specialists in the monthly journal *Sekai*, which in 1993 called for the introduction of a Fundamental Law on Peace, and in 1994 put forward a regional security proposal for Asia–Pacific.

Likewise politicians, political parties and political groups came forward with a variety of proposals during the period 1992–4, including the Japan New Party's policy outline; the Rengō Central Committee's view on state policy; the DSP's proposals on world peace and the constitutional problem; Yamahana Sadao's proposal on a new constitution; Eda Satsuki's proposal on peace and security; and the security proposal put forward by LDP politicians led by Mori Yoshirō. And, of course, the proposal by Ozawa Ichirō himself, as included in his book. As can be seen, a noteworthy characteristic of these recent proposals is their broad base, involving not only intellectuals, but a wide political spectrum of individuals, groups and parties.

With the formation of the Murayama coalition government in 1994, a socialist headed the government for the first time since the 1947 Katayama Cabinet. This again brought to the forefront of political debate the question of Japanese defence and security policies, as the socialists in opposition had regarded the SDF as unconstitutional and had opposed the US–Japan security treaty. Nevertheless, this did not lead to the implementation of the anti-militaristic policies pursued by the socialists as an opposition party. Indeed, the socialist prime minister was quick to abandon the party's longstanding opposition to the SDF as well as to the US–Japan security treaty: the party now accepts the constitutionality of the former and the necessity of the latter.[37] It is unclear at this time whether the party's about-face means that the socialists, as members of the governing coalition, will no longer act as an important brake on the expansion of the SDF, or whether they will try to push ahead with disarmament. Support for the latter policy certainly exists within the party.[38] At the least, the party seems to be committed to some reduction in military spending, even as a member of the government.[39]

It is in line with a perspective giving priority to disarmament and a renewal of Japan's demilitarized identity in the post cold-war era that, in both the April 1993 and December 1994 issues of *Sekai*, the above-mentioned intellectuals put forward two joint proposals (*kyōdō teigen*) to invigorate the principles of the Constitution, redefine the goal of disarmament and grapple with the existence and role of the SDF.[40] The March proposal was based on the following understanding of the international and domestic situation:[41]

1. The cold war has ended, and with it the era of world war and the danger of mutual destruction of the United States and the Soviet Union.
2. As a result of the cold war's end, the Warsaw Pact Treaty Organization has disappeared and the meaning of NATO has been transformed. Likewise, the environment surrounding the US–Japan security treaty has changed. At the same time, the outbreak of ethnic and regional conflicts has generated renewed interest in collective security under the United Nations.
3. In Japan the longstanding contradiction between the Constitution and the SDF, a product of the cold war, must be resolved.

On the basis of this understanding, the March proposal made the following recommendations:

1. Establishment of a Fundamental Peace Law (*Heiwa Kihonhō*) under Article 9 of the Constitution. This would be not only a way for Japan to contribute positively to world peace through non-military means, but on the domestic front would be also a way to give life to the formation of a national consensus on the reduction in the present size and establishment of the SDF to a military level permitted under the Constitution, namely, 'minimum necessary defence' (*saishogen bōgyoryoku*). This calls for a national effort and debate.
2. Reconciliation with former Asian victims of Japanese aggression. This is essential in order to move forward with creating a new security framework.
3. Implementation of minimum necessary defence based on a collective security system. However, minimum necessary defence is not based on a nation's right of self-defence, as an 'inherent right'; it derives from the collective security system and is subject to limitations.

In the December 1994 issue the co-proposers responded to a range of critics and developed their idea for a regional security framework in Asia–Pacific.[42] The main criticism centred on their proposal to make 'minimum necessary defence' constitutional. How was this concept different from the LDP's? As outlined in the December response:

> Our interpretation [of the Constitution] is that minimum necessary defence is not land, sea and air forces as renounced in the second clause of Article 9, nor war potential equivalent thereto. However, we do not deny that minimum necessary defence is armed power to be directed at external aggressors. Therefore, our interpretation is that under the Constitution the possession of 'special armed power', which is not the equivalent of [regular] military forces nor war potential, is possible.[43]

The crucial point of difference with the LDP's definition of 'minimum necessary defence' is that, as a result of the qualitative and quantitative build-up of the SDF, the expansion of their role, especially as seen in the patrolling of the SLOCs and their integration into US nuclear strategy, the SDF do not satisfy the criterion of 'minimum necessary defence', are unconstitutional and must therefore be cut back in terms of equipment and numbers under arms. The essential ingredients of 'minimum necessary defence' are to limit the SDF's duties to the protection of the life and property of the citizens within the geographic limits set by Japanese territory (land, sea, air) under democratic control and openness.[44]

Their understanding of the present SDF is as an 'auxiliary' of US forces. As such, the implementation of a policy of 'minimum necessary defence' cannot move forward without addressing the issue of the US–Japan security treaty. From their perspective, the treaty's military value to both Japan and the United States has decreased dramatically as a result of the collapse of the Soviet Union and the disappearance of the 'common enemy' at the base of the treaty. What with the reconciliation between Russia and the United States, as well as Russia and China; the joint entry of the two Koreas into the United Nations and the start of a process of reconciliation; the establishment of diplomatic relations between South Korea and Russia, and South Korea and China; the resolution of the Cambodian conflict, and other changes, the possibility now exists to move beyond the mainly 'hub and spokes' security system set in place by the United States during the cold war era. In this new international environment, the treaty thus should be demilitarized and transformed as part of a regional security system, where the 'promotion of economic cooperation', as stipulated in the treaty's Preamble and Article II, is strengthened and diversified. Giving life to this interpretation of the treaty also is seen to contribute to the goal of regaining the trust of the people of Asia.

The development of a multilateral regional collective security system incorporating a demilitarized US–Japan security treaty is the idea proposed. This would build on the ASEAN Regional Forum and would be based on the principle of equality between the participating members and the concept of 'common security'.[45] Given the different cold war and colonial experiences, as well as the diversity of history, politics, society, economy and culture in the region, the new collective security system must start from confidence-building measures aimed at creating a sense of common security. Japan should work through the ASEAN Regional Forum to strengthen the concept of common security as well as to promote the demilitarization of the sea where, as we have seen in Chapter 3, militarization was most conspicuous in the 1980s. As a first step, they propose developing regional cooperation for maritime safety in East and Southeast Asia by patrolling the Pacific and South China Sea.

CONCLUSION

In this way, intellectuals in the early 1990s followed the tradition of the Danwakai in putting forward concrete proposals on Japan's role in the world and the security policy to be pursued in line with the ideals of promoting demilitarization in the new environment of the post cold-war world. The goal of cutting back the SDF no doubt will meet resistance from those with a vested interest in the continued growth of the military, as witnessed by the purchase of advanced weaponry in line with cold war rather post cold-war strategies;[46] the transformation of the security treaty can only go ahead as a two-way process, with the United States still giving priority to Japan for US deployments and strategies;[47] the small step towards maritime cooperation is still on the horizon; and the ultimate goal of establishing a regional security system based on a concept of common security may never be realized. What is more, voices have been raised in favour of Japan developing a separate, non-military organization – a sort of Development and Environmental Protection PKO – as an alternative way to make an 'international contribution'.[48]

As we have seen, such ideas are just a part of the proposals made in the changing landscape of Japanese politics in the early 1990s. The choice will be made by the Japanese people. But that choice will influence the shape of the world in the twenty-first century. Whatever the result, the continuing influence of the war and the Constitution can be seen in this and other proposals, despite the passage of fifty years. The rejection of a normal military role and the creation of a new identity for Japan are at the heart of these efforts. The political battle may be lost. But the proposals have contributed to stimulating an important debate. Such debate is one of the essential ingredients in promoting democratic control and the preservation of a peaceful regime in Japan.

Appendix 1
Preamble and Article 9 of the Constitution of Japan

We, the Japanese people, acting through our duly elected represent-atives in the National Diet, determined that we shall secure for ourselves and our posterity the fruits of peaceful cooperation with all nations and the blessings of liberty throughout this land, and resolved that never again shall we be visited with the horrors of war through the action of government, do proclaim that sovereign power resides with the people and do firmly establish this Constitution. Government is a sacred trust of the people, the authority for which is derived from the people, the powers of which are exercised by the representatives of the people, and the benefit of which are enjoyed by the people. This is a universal principle of mankind upon which this Constitution is founded. We reject and revoke all constitutions, laws, ordinances, and rescripts in conflict herewith.

We, the Japanese people, desire peace for all time and are deeply conscious of the high ideals controlling human relationship, and we have determined to preserve our security and existence, trusting in the justice and faith of the peace-loving peoples of the world. We desire to occupy an honored place in an international society striving for the preservation of peace, and the banishment of tyranny and slavery, oppression and intolerance for all time from the earth. We recognize that all peoples of the world have the right to live in peace, free from fear and want.

We believe that no nation is responsible to itself alone, but that laws of political morality are universal; and that obedience to such laws is incumbent upon all nations who would sustain their own sovereignty and justify their sovereign relationship with other nations.

We, the Japanese people, pledge our national honor to accomplish these high ideals and purposes with all our resources.

Article 9. Aspiring sincerely to an international peace based on justice and order, the Japanese people forever renounce war as a sovereign right of the nation and the threat or use of force as means of settling international disputes.

In order to accomplish the aim of the preceding paragraph, land, sea, and air forces, as well as other war potential, will never be maintained. The right of belligerency of the state will not be recognized.

Appendix 2
Security treaty between the United States and Japan
September 8, 1951

Japan has this day signed a Treaty of Peace with the Allied Powers. On the coming into force of that Treaty, Japan will not have the effective means to exercise its inherent right of self-defence because it has been disarmed. There is danger to Japan in this situation because irresponsible militarism has not yet been driven from the world. Therefore, Japan desires a Security Treaty with the United States of America to come into force simultaneously with the Treaty of Peace between the United States of America and Japan. The Treaty of Peace recognizes that Japan as a sovereign nation has the right to enter into collective security arrangements, and further, the Charter of the United Nations recognizes that all nations possess an inherent right of individual and collective self-defence.

In exercise of these rights, Japan desires, as a provisional arrangement for its defense, that the United States of America should maintain armed forces of its own in and about Japan so as to deter armed attack upon Japan.

The United States of America, in the interest of peace and security, is presently willing to maintain certain of its armed forces in and about Japan, in the expectation, however, that Japan will itself increasingly assume responsibility for its own defense against direct and indirect aggression, always avoiding any armament which could be an offensive threat or serve other than to promote peace and security in accordance with the purposes and principles of the United Nations Charter.

Accordingly, the two countries have agreed as follows:

Article I. Japan grants, and the United States of America accepts the right, upon the coming into force of the Treaty of Peace and of this Treaty, to dispose United States land, air, and sea forces in and about Japan. Such forces may be utilized to contribute to the maintenance of the international peace and security in the Far East and to the security of Japan against attack from without, including assistance given at the express request of the Japanese Government to put down large-scale internal riots and disturbances in Japan, caused through instigation or intervention by an outside Power or Powers.

Article II. During the exercise of the right referred to in Article I, Japan will not grant, without the prior consent of the United States of America, any bases or any rights, power, or authority whatsoever, in or relating to bases or the right of garrison or of maneuver, or transit of ground, air, or naval forces to any third Power.

Article III. The conditions which shall govern the disposition of armed forces of the United States of America in and about Japan shall be determined by administrative agreements between the two Governments.

Article IV. This Treaty shall expire whenever in the opinion of the Governments of the United States of America and of Japan there shall have come into force such United Nations arrangements or such alternative individual or collective security dispositions as will satisfactorily provide for the maintenance by the United Nations or otherwise of international peace and security in the Japan Area.

Article V. This Treaty shall be ratified by the United States of America and Japan and will come into force when instruments of ratification thereof have been exchanged by them at Washington.

IN WITNESS WHEREOF the undersigned plenipotentiaries have signed this Treaty.

DONE in duplicate at the city of San Francisco, in the English and Japanese languages, this eighth day of September, 1951.

Appendix 3
Treaty of Mutual Cooperation and Security between the United States and Japan
Signed at Washington, D.C., January 19, 1960

The United States of America and Japan,

Desiring to strengthen the bonds of peace and friendship traditionally existing between them, and to uphold the principles of democracy, individual liberty, and the rule of law,

Desiring further to encourage closer economic cooperation between them and to promote conditions of economic stability and well-being in their countries,

Reaffirming their faith in the purposes and principles of the Charter of the United Nations, and their desire to live in peace with all peoples and all governments,

Recognizing that they have the inherent right of individual or collective self-defense as affirmed in the Charter of the United Nations,

Considering that they have a common concern in the maintenance of international peace and security in the Far East,

Having resolved to conclude a treaty of mutual cooperation and security,

Therefore agree as follows:

Article I. The Parties undertake, as set forth in the Charter of the United Nations, to settle any international disputes in which they may be involved by peaceful means in such a manner that international peace and security and justice are not endangered and to refrain in their international relations from the threat or use of force against the territorial integrity or political independence of any state, or in any other manner inconsistent with the purposes of the United Nations.

The Parties will endeavour in concert with other peace-loving countries to strengthen the United Nations so that its mission of maintaining international peace and security may be discharged more effectively.

Article II. The Parties will contribute toward the further development of peaceful and friendly international relations by strengthening their free institutions, by bringing about a better understanding of the principles upon which these institutions are founded, and by promoting conditions of stability and well-being. They seek to eliminate conflict in their international economic policies and will encourage economic collaboration between them.

Article III. The Parties, individually and in cooperation with each other, by means of continuous and effective self-help and mutual aid will maintain and develop, subject to their constitutional provisions, their capacities to resist armed attack.

Article IV. The Parties will consult together from time to time regarding the implementation of this Treaty, and, at the request of either Party, whenever the security of Japan or international peace and security in the Far East is threatened.

Article V. Each Party recognizes that an armed attack against either Party in the territories under the administration of Japan would be dangerous to its own peace and safety and declares that it would act to meet the common danger in accordance with its constitutional provisions and processes.

Any such armed attack and all measures taken as a result thereof shall be immediately reported to the Security Council of the United Nations in accordance with the provisions of Article 51 of the Charter. Such measures shall be terminated when the Security Council has taken the measures necessary to restore and maintain international peace and security.

Article VI. For the purpose of contributing to the security of Japan and the maintenance of international peace and security in the Far East, the United States of America is granted the use by its land, air, and naval forces of facilities and areas in Japan.

The use of these facilities and areas as well as the status of the United States armed forces in Japan shall be governed by a separate agreement, replacing the administrative Agreement under Article III of the Security Treaty between the United States of America and Japan, signed at Tokyo on February 28, 1952, as amended, and by such other arrangements as may be agreed upon.

Article VII. This Treaty does not affect and shall not be interpreted as affecting in any way the rights and obligations of the Parties under the Charter of the United Nations or the responsibility of the United Nations for the maintenance of international peace and security.

Article VIII. This Treaty shall be ratified by the United States of America and Japan in accordance with their respective constitutional processes and will enter into force on the date on which the instruments of ratification thereof have been exchanged by them in Tokyo.

Article IX. The Security Treaty between the United States of America and Japan signed at the city of San Francisco on September 8, 1951, shall expire upon the entering into force of this Treaty.

Article X. This Treaty shall remain in force until in the opinion of the Governments of the United States of America and Japan there shall have come into force such United Nations arrangements as will satisfactorily provide for the maintenance of international peace and security in the Japan area.

However, after the Treaty has been in force for ten years, either Party may give notice to the other Party of its intention to terminate the Treaty, in which case the Treaty shall terminate one year after such notice has been given.

IN WITNESS WHEREOF the undersigned plenipotentiaries have signed this Treaty.

DONE in duplicate at Washington in the English and Japanese languages, both equally authentic, this 19th day of January, 1960.

Glossary

ASDF	Air Self-Defence Forces
Danwakai	Heiwa Mondai Danwakai (Peace Issues Discussion Group)
DSP	Democratic Socialist Party
Gensuikin	Japan National Conference Against Atomic and Hydrogen Bombs
Gensuikyō	Japan Council Against Atomic and Hydrogen Bombs
GSDF	Ground Self-Defence Forces
hibakusha	victim of atomic bomb
JSP	Japan Socialist Party
LDP	Liberal-Democrat Party
MSDF	Maritime Self-Defence Forces
NGO	non-governmental organization
NHK	Nihon Hōsō Kyōkai (Japanese equivalent of the BBC)
PKF	peace-keeping forces
PKO	peace-keeping operations
PMO	Prime Minister's Office
SDF	Self-Defence Forces
SDI	Strategic Defence Initiative
SLOC	sea lines of communication
TMD	Theatre Missile Defence
UNTAC	United Nations Transitional Authority in Cambodia

Notes

INTRODUCTION

1. See Appendix 1 for a copy of the relevant sections of the Constitution.
2. The Japan Socialist Party (JSP) changed its English name in 1991 to the 'Social Democratic Party of Japan'. As the Japanese name (*Nihon Shakaitō*) remains unaltered, the convention throughout this book is to refer to the party as the Japan Socialist Party or JSP.
3. See Joseph P. Keddell, Jr., *The Politics of Defense in Japan: Managing Internal and External Pressures*, London, M.E. Sharpe, 1993.
4. See Thomas U. Berger, 'From sword to chrysanthemum: Japan's culture of anti-militarism', *International Security*, vol. 17, no. 4, 1993, pp. 119–50. With a particular emphasis on public opinion, see Tetsuya Umemoto, 'Arms and alliance in Japanese public opinion', PhD dissertation, Princeton, Princeton University, 1985.

CHAPTER 1

1. Max Weber, *Economy and Society*, edited by Guenther Roth and Claus Wittich, New York, Bedminster Press, 1968, pp. 56ff.
2. V.R. Berghahn, *Militarism: The History of an International Debate 1861–1979*, Cambridge, Cambridge University Press, 1981, p. 7. Berghahn's work is of particular value for understanding the German debate on militarism.
3. See Kjell Skjelsbaek, 'Militarism, its dimensions and corollaries: an attempt at conceptual clarification', *Journal of Peace Research*, vol. 16, no. 3, 1979, pp. 213–29; Marek Thee, 'Militarism and militarization in contemporary international relations', *Bulletin of Peace Proposals*, vol. 8, no. 4, 1977, pp. 296–309, also in Asbjorn Eide and Marek Thee, *Problems of Contemporary Militarism*, London, Croom Helm, 1980, pp. 15–35; Marek Thee, 'Militarism and militarization: their contemporary meaning', research paper, International Peace Research Institute, Oslo, 1984; Yoshikazu Sakamoto, 'Research on militarization', research paper, United Nations University, Tokyo, 1984.
4. Karl Liebknecht, *Militarism*, New York, B.W. Huebsch, 1917, especially chapter 2; Berghahn, *Militarism*, p. 21.

5. Vladimir I. Lenin, *Imperialism: The Highest Stage of Capitalism*, New York, International Publishers, 1939.

6. Rosa Luxemburg, *The Accumulation of Capital*, London, Routledge & Kegan Paul, 1951, especially pp. 454–67.

7. See Alfred Vagts, *A History of Militarism: Civilian and Military*, New York, Meridian Books, 1959 (revision of 1937 edition), especially the introduction.

8. Berghahn, *Militarism*, pp. 38–41.

9. On the abandonment of placing primary emphasis on demilitarization and democratization in Japan as a result of the intensification of the cold war in Asia–Pacific, see John W. Dower, *Empire and Aftermath: Yoshida Shigeru and the Japanese Experience, 1878–1954*, Cambridge, Harvard Council on East Asian Studies, 1979, pp. 305–68; and John W. Dower, 'Occupied Japan and the Cold War in Asia', in Michael J. Lacey (ed.), *The Truman Presidency*, Cambridge, Woodrow Wilson International Center for Scholars and Cambridge University, 1989, pp. 366–409.

10. According to Berghahn, the problem of militarism was not an important part of the post-war debate in Italy. Hence, our discussion is limited to Germany and Japan. Berghahn, *Militarism*, p. 48.

11. Berghahn, *Militarism*, pp. 55–6; G. Ritter, *The Sword and the Sceptre: The Problem of Militarism in Germany* (translation of the 1955 German edition, 4 vols), London, Allen Lane/Penguin Press, 1972, especially the introduction to volume 1.

12. Berghahn, *Militarism*, pp. 57–8ff.

13. For a study of his thought, see Rikki Kersten, *Japanese Democracy: Maruyama Masao and the Search for Autonomy 1945–1960*, London, Routledge, forthcoming.

14. Maruyama Masao, 'Gunkokushugi', *Seijigaku Jiten*, Tokyo, Heibonsha, 1954, pp. 303–5.

15. Even though the authors discussed here do not necessarily use the term 'militarization', we still consider their work as part of militarization research in the sense that the term is used here.

16. Harold D. Lasswell, 'The garrison-state hypothesis today' in Samuel Huntington (ed.), *Changing Patterns of Military Politics*, New York, Free Press of Glencoe, 1962, pp. 51–70. For an evaluation of Lasswell's research, see Samuel Huntington, *The Soldier and the State: The Theory and Politics of Civil–Military Relations*, Cambridge, Mass., Belknap Press of Harvard University, 1957, pp. 346–50.

17. Lasswell, 'The garrison-state hypothesis today', p. 51.

18. Dwight D. Eisenhower, *Public Papers of the Presidents of the United States, 1960–61*, Containing the Public Messages, Speeches and Statements of the President, Washington DC, US Government Printing Office, 1961, p. 1038.

19. Sakamoto, 'Research on militarization', p. 7. For early research on the military–industrial complex, see Fred Cook, *The Warfare State*, New York, Macmillan, 1962. For an interesting case study, see G. Adams, *The Iron Triangle:The Politics of Defense Contracting*, New York, Transaction Books, 1981; also see H. Schiller and J. Phillips (eds), *Super-State: Readings in the Military–Industrial Complex*, Urbana, University of Illinois, 1970.

20. John Kenneth Galbraith, *How to Control the Military*, New York, Doubleday, 1969.

21. Dieter Senghaas, 'Arms race by arms control?', *Bulletin of Peace Proposals*, vol. 4, no. 4, 1973, pp. 359–74.

22. V.V. Aspaturian, 'The Soviet military–industrial complex – does it exist?', *Journal of International Affairs*, vol. 26, no. 1, 1972, pp. 1–28. Also see David Holloway, 'War, militarism and the Soviet state', *Alternatives*, vol. 6, no. 1, 1980, pp. 59–92.

23. Egbert Jahn, 'The role of the armaments complex in Soviet society (is there a Soviet military–industrial complex?)', *Journal of Peace Research*, vol. 12, no. 3, 1975, pp. 179–94. Also see David Holloway, 'Technology and political decision in Soviet armaments policy', *Journal of Peace Research*, vol. 11, no. 4, 1974, pp. 257–79.

24. Egbert Jahn, 'Armaments and bureaucracy in the Soviet society', *Bulletin of Peace Proposals*, vol. 10, no. 1, 1979, pp. 108–15.

25. Mary Kaldor, *The Baroque Arsenal*, New York, Hill & Wang, 1981.

26. Eide and Thee, *Problems of Contemporary Militarism*, part IV.

27. Robin Luckham, 'Militarism and international dependence: a framework for analysis' in Jose J. Villamil (ed.), *Transnational Capitalism and National Development: New Perspectives on Dependence*, Atlantic Highlands, New Jersey, Humanities Press, 1979, pp. 145–81.

28. Kuno Osamu, *Heiwa no Ronri to Sensō no Ronri*, Tokyo, Iwanami Shoten, 1972.

29. See the 'Kagakusha Kyōto kaigi seimei' of August 1962 reproduced in *Sekai*, special issue, July 1985, pp. 209–12.

30. Miyata Mitsuo, *Kimitachi to Gendai*, Tokyo, Iwanami Shoten, 1980, pp. 73ff.

31. Dower, *Empire and Aftermath*, pp. 383ff.

32. Okauchi Kazuo, 'Densan, tanrō sōgi to saigunbi', *Sekai*, February 1953, p. 52.

33. See the Heiwa Mondai Danwakai's statement of February 1960, 'Futatabi anpo kaitei ni tsuite' reproduced in *Sekai* special issue, July 1985, esp. p. 177.

34. For a discussion of the end of the cold war and the theory of militarization, see Martin Shaw, *Post-Military Society: Militarism, Demilitarization and War at the End of the Twentieth Century*, Oxford, Polity Press, 1991, pp. 24–8.

CHAPTER 2

1. These statements were first published in the monthly magazine, *Sekai*: 'Sensō to heiwa ni kansuru Nihon no kagakusha no seimei' (March 1949); 'Kōwa mondai ni tsuite no heiwa mondai danwakai seimei' (March 1950); 'Mitabi heiwa ni tsuite' (December 1950). They were later appended to *Sekai* (September 1962), and then reproduced in a special issue of *Sekai* (July 1985). Quotations are from the July 1985 issue. For evaluation of the Group's statements and activities, see the discussions '"Heiwa mondai danwakai" ni tsuite', and 'Heiwa mondai danwakai to sono go', *Sekai* special issue, July 1985, pp. 2–53, 54–97; Masaru Tamamoto, 'Unwanted peace: Japanese intellectual thought in American

occupied Japan, 1948–1952', Baltimore, Johns Hopkins University, PhD dissertation, 1988; Seki Hiroharu, 'Heiwa no seijigaku' in Nihon Seiji Gakkai (ed.), Nenpō Seijigaku, *Kōdōron igo no Seijigaku*, Tokyo, Iwanami Shoten, 1977, pp. 91–120. A shortened English version, which was originally published as 'Politics of peace' in *Japan Quarterly*, vol. 24, no. 3, 1977, pp. 290–6, appears as chapter 9 in Seki's *The Asia–Pacific in the Global Formation: Bringing 'The Nation-State Japan' Back In*, Tokyo, Institute of Oriental Culture, University of Tokyo, 1986, pp. 139–46. Igarashi Takeshi, 'Sengo Nihon "gaikō taisei" no keisei: tainichi kōwa no teiketsu to seitōseiji', *Kokka Gakkai Zashi*, vol. 97, nos. 7–8, 1984, pp. 463–507; Takahashi Susumu and Nakamura Kenichi, 'Sengo Nihon no heiwaron: hitotsu no isō no bunseki', *Sekai*, June 1978, pp. 202–25. A revised English version of this article, 'Peace research in postwar Japan', can be found in The Japan Peace Research Group (ed.), *Peace Research in Japan 1978–79*, Tokyo, University of Tokyo Press, 1979, pp. 7–34. Sakamoto's introduction to an abridged version of 'On peace, for the third time' is also valuable. See Yoshikazu Sakamoto, 'Editor's introduction' in The Japan Peace Research Group (ed.), *Peace Research in Japan 1976*, Tokyo, University of Tokyo Press, 1977, pp. 1–4.

2. The UNESCO statement, 'Heiwa no tame ni shakai kagakusha wa kaku uttaeru', which first appeared in *Sekai*, January 1949, is reproduced in the July 1985 special issue, pp. 99–102.

3. The magazine's stance can be seen from the first volume, where the ideals of democracy, respect for the individual, freedom of thought and expression, and world peace are emphasized. For a discussion of post-1945 Japan taking account of the influence of the magazine, see John W. Dower, 'Nihon, kono hanseiki', *Sekai,* January 1995, pp. 59–67.

4. For further details, see '"Heiwa mondai danwakai" ni tsuite', and 'Heiwa mondai danwakai to sono go', pp. 6–9, 60–1. It should be noted that, by the 1980s, Shimizu had carried out an about-face and now supported Japan's possession of nuclear weapons. See his *Nippon yo Kokka tare, Kaku no Sentaku*, Tokyo, Bungei Shunjū, 1980.

5. See Igarashi, 'Sengo Nihon "gaikō taisei" no keisei', particularly on the Japan Socialist Party.

6. 'Heiwa mondai danwakai to sono go', p. 56.

7. Mori Kōichi (ed.), *Tetsugaku Jiten*, Tokyo, Aoki Shoten, 1971, p. 179.

8. Heibonsha (ed.), *Tetsugaku Jiten*, Tokyo, Heibonsha, 1971, p. 589.

9. Tsurumi Shunsuke, 'Kaisetsu' in Tsurumi Shunsuke (ed.), *Heiwa no Shisō*, sengo Nihon Shisō Taikei, vol. 4, Tokyo, Chikuma Shobō, 1968, p. 6.

10. Tsurumi, 'Kaisetsu' in Tsurumi (ed.), *Heiwa no Shisō*, pp. 15–16. Tsurumi considers that the effort to come to grips with the 'fifteen-year war' (*jūgonen sensō*) on the level of *shisō* is one of the origins of post-war peace thought.

> 'Postwar peace thought in Japan cannot be discussed separated from the fifteen years of war starting in 1931 and ending in 1945. This is because one of the sources giving life to postwar peace thought is the effort to deal with the fifteen-year war. (Tsurumi, 'Kaisetsu' in Tsurumi, ed., *Heiwa no Shisō*, p. 3)

11. Hence Tsurumi's approval of Yasuda Takeshi, who suggests the importance of the individual's feeling in the development of peace thought:

> If the type of peace theory which rests on an analysis of the current situation and future forecasts is not supported by personal commitment (*shijō*), then it cannot become peace thought, even though scholarship which balances war and peace is possible. (Tsurumi, 'Kaisetsu' in Tsurumi, ed, *Heiwa no Shisō*, p. 6)

Seki criticizes Tsurumi's division between thought, on the one hand, and scholarship, on the other:

> Once we accept the complete division between scholarship and thought, then even if peace thought is possible, it is totally impossible for peace research to exist as scholarship. This should not be so. It is only through a union with peace thought that true peace research can indicate the substance of theoretical structures as peace research. (Seki, 'Heiwa no seijigaku', p. 96)

12. 'Sensō to heiwa ni kansuru Nihon no kagakusha no seimei', p. 104. The relationship between intellectuals and the masses is tied to the problem of social change. See '"Heiwa mondai danwakai" ni tsuite', p. 38.
13. 'Sensō to heiwa ni kansuru Nihon no kagakusha no seimei', p. 103.
14. It should be noted that the sense of responsibility (*sekininkan*) pointed to here does not necessarily mean a sense of individual responsibility for being committed to the war. Maruyama Masao comments:

> That there were some points calling for self-examination (*hansei*) among intellectuals was of course recognised. In the law and politics section [of the Group] we were aware that, as a result of intellectuals not cooperating with each other, fascism could not be defeated. This kind of self-examination was self-criticism, but self-criticism as social scientists.

This lack of a sense of personal responsibility for the war is a point that Maruyama criticizes at this time. See '"Heiwa mondai danwakai" ni tsuite', pp. 37–8.
15. 'Heiwa no tame ni shakai kagakusha wa kaku uttaeru', p. 102. Nishina Yoshio strongly opposed the position taken in the UNESCO statement, and stressed the responsibility of scientists. 'Heiwa mondai danwakai to sono go', pp. 90–1. On scientists' war responsibility, also see '"Heiwa mondai danwakai" ni tsuite', p. 33.
16. This commitment to the people rather than the government is in marked contrast to the situation among US scientists. See Gregg Herken, 'American scientists and US nuclear weapons policy', *Peace and Change*, vol. 11, no. 1, 1985, pp. 19–30.
17. On Maruyama's contribution, see Rikki Kersten, *Japanese Democracy: Maruyama Masao and the Search For Autonomy 1945–1960*, London, Routledge, forthcoming.
18. Yoshida Shigeru, *The Yoshida Memoirs*, Boston, Houghton Mifflin, 1962, p. 8. Also see Koizumi Shinzō, *Heiwaron* (collected works), vol. 15, Tokyo, Bungei Shunjū, 1976.
19. 'Mitabi heiwa ni tsuite', pp. 123–5.

20. 'Mitabi heiwa ni tsuite', p. 124.
21. 'Kōwa mondai ni tsuite no heiwa mondai danwakai seimei', pp. 110–11. On the influence of these ideas on the left wing of the Japan Socialist Party, see 'Heiwa mondai danwakai to sono go', p. 63.
22. 'Sensō to heiwa ni kansuru Nihon no kagakusha no seimei', p. 106. Also see 'Mitabi heiwa ni tsuite', p. 121.
23. 'Kōwa mondai ni tsuite no heiwa mondai danwakai seimei', p. 110.
24. 'Sensō to heiwa ni kansuru Nihon no kagakusha no seimei', p. 103.
25. 'Kōwa mondai ni tsuite no heiwa mondai danwakai seimei', p. 110.
26. 'Mitabi heiwa ni tsuite', p. 122, original emphasis.
27. 'Mitabi heiwa ni tsuite', p. 123, original emphasis.
28. 'Mitabi heiwa ni tsuite', p. 122.
29. 'Mitabi heiwa ni tsuite', p. 122.
30. 'Mitabi heiwa ni tsuite', p. 129.
31. 'Mitabi heiwa ni tsuite', p. 143.
32. 'Mitabi heiwa ni tsuite', p. 123.
33. Miyazawa Ki'ichi and Sakamoto Yoshikazu (interview), 'Ajia ni okeru Nihon no shinrō' in Sakamoto Yoshikazu, *Heiwa: Sono Genjitsu to Ninshiki*, Tokyo, Mainichi Shimbunsha, 1976, p. 147.
34. Miyazawa and Sakamoto, 'Ajia ni okeru Nihon no shinrō', p. 148, my emphasis.
35. For the Group's thoughts on democracy, see Kersten, *Japanese Democracy*, chapter 7.
36. 'Mitabi heiwa ni tsuite', p. 122. On the redefinition of morality during the Second World War, making the bombing of non-combatants acceptable, see Barton J. Bernstein, 'The atomic bombings reconsidered', *Foreign Affairs*, vol. 74, no. 1, 1995, pp. 151–2.
37. Kuno Osamu, *Heiwa no Ronri to Sensō no Ronri*, Tokyo, Iwanami Shoten, 1972, p. 390.
38. For an evaluation, see Kuno Osamu, Rōyama Michio and Takabatake Michitoshi (roundtable), 'Heiwa undō no genten', *Asahi Jyānaru,* 24 March 1972, pp. 4–16, *Asāhi Jyānaru*, 31 March 1972, pp. 18–26. Igarashi, 'Sengo Nihon "gaikō taisei" no keisei', pp. 463–507.
39. Albert Camus, 'Neither victims nor executioners' in Peter Mayer (ed.), *The Pacifist Conscience: Classic Writings on Alternatives to Violent Conflict from Ancient Times to the Present*, New York, Holt Reinhart & Winston, 1966, p. 426.
40. For a full discussion, see A. Richard Konrad, 'Violence and the philosopher', *The Journal of Value Inquiry*, vol. 8, no. 1, 1974, pp. 37–45.
41. This tri-level approach to the problem of peace is one of the distinctive characteristics of 'peace theory' (*heiwaron*) as developed in post-1945 Japan. See Nakamura and Takahashi, 'Sengo Nihon no heiwaron'.
42. Masao Maruyama, 'Some reflections on article nine of the constitution', *Thought and Behaviour in Modern Japanese Politics*, Oxford, Oxford University Press, 1969, p. 301.

CHAPTER 3

1. For details, see *Bōei Handobukku*, Tokyo, Asagumo Shinbunsha, 1994, pp. 256–63.

2. See the interview with Yazaki Shinji, at the time Administrative Vice-Minister of Defence, 'Bōei kaikaku wa jidai no yōsei', *Kokubō*, January 1987, pp. 8–32, especially p. 13.

3. Unless otherwise stated, the data on the Self-Defence Forces were obtained directly from the Defence Agency or taken from the annual Defence Agency publication, *Bōei Hakusho* (Tokyo, Ōkurasho Insatsukyoku), or the annual *Bōei Handobukku* (Tokyo, Asagumo Shinbunsha). For regular updates on military affairs, see the monthly *Gunjiminron*.

4. The specific reasons why US strategy demanded closer cooperation with Japan and the details of the US and Soviet build-up in Asia-Pacific in the 1980s are not dealt with here. For a discussion, see Peter Hayes, Lyuba Zarsky and Waldon Bello, *American Lake: Nuclear Peril in the Pacific*, Harmondsworth, Penguin Books, 1986, especially part II.

5. For a detailed discussion of Japan's role in US maritime strategy, see the series by Fujishima Udai in the monthly *Gunshuku Mondai Shiryō*, which started in October 1984. In a December 1982 interview, even Admiral Sakonjo Naotoshi denied the likelihood of the Soviet Union actually attacking the sea lines of communication: 'It is totally inconceivable . . . that the Soviet Union's major surface ships will move into the Pacific and attack Japanese and American warships or cargo ships or sea lanes.' Cited in Hayes *et al.*, *American Lake*, p. 295.

6. *Asahi Jyānaru*, 24 February 1984, pp. 92–7.

7. US Department of Defense, *Report on Allied Contributions to the Common Defense*, Washington DC, US Government Printing Office, 1987. For a Japanese discussion, see Sekai Henshūbu, *Gunji Taikoku Nippon*, Tokyo, Iwanami Shoten, 1987, pp. 12–13.

8. It is beyond our discussion to deal with three other aspects of cooperation: communications, interoperability and joint arms production. For information on the role of Japan-based communication facilities in US nuclear strategy, see the journal *Sekai*, February 1985, pp. 103–119ff. On interoperability, see Fukuyoshi Shōji, 'Nichibei kyōdō enshū ga Nihon o sekken suru', *Gunjiminron*, July 1987, pp. 83–4. On joint arms production, see the studies by Kihara Masao, *Nihon no Gunji Sangyō*, Tokyo, Shin Nihon Shuppansha, 1994, especially chapter 9, and Michael W. Chinworth, *Inside Japan's Defense: Technology, Economics and Strategy*, London, Brassey, 1992, especially chapter 5.

9. For further details, see Fukuyoshi, 'Nichibei kyōdō enshū ga Nihon o sekken suru', pp. 77–83, and Sekai Henshūbu, *Gunji Taikoku Nippon*, pp. 20–7.

10. On the growing secrecy surrounding military affairs in the 1980s, as seen in the significant increase in the number of documents classified, see *Gunjiminron*, April 1987, pp. 23–4. In 1991 there were 1.9 million classified documents. Kyōdō Teigen, 'Ajia–Taiheiyō chīki anpo o kōsō suru', *Sekai*, December 1994, p. 40.

11. *Yomiuri Shinbun*, 6 January 1987.

12. Quoted in Fukuyoshi, 'Nichibei kyōdō enshū ga Nihon o sekken suru', p. 77.

13. The term 'combined exercises' is used to refer to exercises conducted on the basis of cooperation with other countries' armed forces. 'Joint

exercises' are conducted between the different arms of the military forces of one country. For details of the exercises, see *Gunjiminron*, April 1987, pp. 61–3.

14. On New Zealand's anti-nuclear policy, see Michael C. Pugh, *The ANZUS Crisis, Nuclear Visiting and Deterrence*, Cambridge, Cambridge University Press, 1989. Similarly, the Japanese port city of Kōbe, which from 1975 onwards has required all foreign naval vessels to submit a guarantee that they are not carrying nuclear weapons, has had some success in preventing nuclear-capable vessels from making port calls. See Ishiyama Toshihiko, 'Hikaku Kōbe-ko no jikken' in Nishida Masaru (ed.), *Hikaku Jichitai Undō no Riron to Jissai*, Tokyo, Orijin Shuppan Senta, 1985, pp. 192–200.

15. *Gunjiminron*, April 1987, p. 64. For details of Japan's earlier participation in RIMPAC exercises, see Chūma Kiyofuku, *Saigunbi no Seijigaku*, Tokyo, Chishikisha, 1985, pp. 136–40.

16. The details on the July 1980 exercise can be found in *Gunjiminron*, April 1987, pp. 68–70.

17. The details on the November 1983 exercise can be found in Fukuyoshi, 'Nichibei kyōdō enshū ga Nihon o sekken suru', p. 79.

18. A copy of the agreement, 'The exchange of technology agreement between Japan and the United States', 3 November 1983, appears as Appendix A of Reinhard Drifte, *Arms Production in Japan: The Military Applications of Civilian Technology*, Boulder, Westview Press, 1986.

19. A copy of the protocol, 'Detailed arrangements for the transfer of military technologies', 27 December 1985, appears as Appendix B in Drifte, *Arms Production in Japan*.

20. For a discussion, see Kihara, *Nihon no Gunji Sangyō*, especially chapters 8 and 14.

21. For details, see Drifte, *Arms Production in Japan*, chapter 6.

22. Daniel Sneider, 'Yes to Star Wars', *Far Eastern Economic Review*, 25 September 1986, pp. 28–9. For a full discussion, see Kihara, *Nihon no Gunji Sangyō*, especially chapters 13 and 14.

23. *Asahi Shinbun*, 8 December 1994.

24. A sense of what Nakasone had in mind can be gleaned from a bilingual edition of two speeches he made towards the end of his premiership. See Yasuhiro Nakasone, *My Political Philosophy*, Tokyo, Liberal Democratic Party, 1987. For a discussion of Nakasone's politics, see Watanabe Osamu, *Nihon Koku Kenpō 'Kaiseishi'*, Tokyo, Nippon Hyōronsha, 1987, chapter 4, and Osamu Watanabe, 'Nakasone Yasuhiro and post-war conservative politics: an historical interpretation', Oxford, Oxford University, Nissan Occasional Paper Series, No. 18, 1993.

25. For a discussion on the emergence of the debate on the Japanese state during the 1980s, see Ishida Takeshi, 'Sengo Nihon no kokka ishiki' in Sakamoto Yoshikazu (ed.), *Sekai Seiji no Kōzō Hendō* (vol. 2), Tokyo, Iwanami Shoten, 1995, pp. 269–333.

26. This law is often translated as 'anti-espionage law'. This suggests the control of foreign threats. As the name of the law in Japanese (*kokka himitsu hō*) makes clear, however, the law was intended as much for control of Japanese as of foreigners.

27. For a discussion, see K.V. Kesavan, *Japanese Defence Policy since 1976: Latest Trends*, Canberra Papers on Strategy and Defence, no. 31, The Strategic and Defence Studies Centre, Research School of Pacific Studies, Australia National University, 1984.
28. Itō Keiichi, '"1% waku" no rekishi to mondaiten: Sono yakuwari to kongo', *Seiron*, March 1987, p. 78.
29. The expression is Sakamoto's. See Yoshikazu Sakamoto, 'Introduction: Japan in global perspective', *Bulletin of Peace Proposals*, vol. 13, no. 1, 1982, p. 6.
30. Kaminishi Akio, *Bōei Seisaku no Kenshō: 1% Waku*, Tokyo, Kadokawa, 1986, p. 56.
31. This is one of the reasons for media criticism of the new measure. See *Asahi Shinbun*, 24 and 25 January 1987 and immediately thereafter.
32. For a discussion of the Ministry of Finance as a constraint on spending, see Joseph P. Keddell, Jr., *The Politics of Defense in Japan: Managing Internal and External Pressures*, London, M.E. Sharpe, 1993, pp. 18–21.
33. This is the amount minus expenses for national bonds and subsidies to local governments. See *Bōei Handobukku*, Tokyo, Asagumo Shinbunsha, 1986, pp. 212–14.
34. For an interesting discussion between a foreign office bureaucrat and a critic of Japan's 'strategic aid', see Hanabusa Masamichi and Murai Yoshinori, 'Enjo gyōsei o ronjiru', *Sekai*, December 1987, pp. 150–4.
35. On the different ways of calculating military expenditures, see Chūma Kiyofuku, *Gunjihi o Yomu*, Tokyo, Iwanami Shoten, 1986, esp. pp. 42–7, and more technically, Muroyama Yoshimasa, *Nichibei Anpo Taisei* (two volumes), Tokyo, Yūhikaku, 1992, especially pp. 247–58 (vol. 1), and chapter 4 (vol. 2).
36. *Asahi Shinbun*, 28 January 1987. *Mainichi Shinbun*, 3 March 1987.
37. Washimi Tomoyoshi, *Nihon no Gunjihi*, Tokyo, Gakushū no Tomosha, 1982, p. 132.
38. US Department of Defense, *Report on Allied Contributions to the Common Defense*, Washington, DC, Government Printing Office, 1987.
39. For a detailed discussion of the mechanisms of such 'hidden' military expenditures, see Yoshiike Kimichika, 'Kakusareta "boeihi": gonendo futan seido no shīkumi', *Shimin no Heiwa Hakusho*, Tokyo, Nippon Hyōronsha, 1983, pp. 246–58.
40. Sakai Akio, 'Nihon no gunjihi', *Shōgaku Ronshū*, vol. 31, no. 6, 1987, pp. 19–20.
41. Sekai Henshūbu, *Gunji Taikoku Nippon*, Tokyo, Iwanami Shoten, 1987, pp. 11–12.
42. Sekai Henshūbu, *Gunji Taikoku Nippon*, Tokyo, Iwanami Shoten, 1987, p. 12.
43. Sakai, 'Nihon no gunjihi', p. 10.
44. Sakai, 'Nihon no gunjihi', p. 15. For the wider implication of this change in priorities, see Maeda Tetsuo, 'Gunjihi "1%" waku toppa no kōzō', *Sekai*, November 1985, pp. 22–38. Sakai Akio, 'Gunji sangyō no tenkan', *Sekai*, February 1986, pp. 130–43.
45. The free-rider argument derives from the idea of the supply of public goods. See James M. Buchanan, *The Demand and Supply of Public Goods*, Chicago, Rand McNally, 1968, and Edward J. Mishan, 'The rela-

tionship between joint products, collective goods, and external effects',
Journal of Political Economy, vol. 77, no. 3, 1969, pp. 329–48.

46. The following is representative: 'Japan, freed by the American nuclear umbrella from the burden of funding a strong national defense, pioneers new technologies and grabs more markets from the U.S.', *US News and World Report*, 5 August 1985, p. 43.

47. Cited in Hayes *et al.*, *American Lake*, p. 412. Also see their discussion of the 'Soviet threat' (pp. 291–320), where they conclude: 'Thus encircled, the Soviets must find the Far East more of a defensive liability than an offensive asset' (p. 320).

48. A major new study contends that 'the strategies of deterrence and compellance were generally more provocative than restraining and that they prolonged rather than ended the cold war'. See Richard N. Lebow and Janice G. Stein, *We All Lost the Cold War*, Princeton, Princeton University Press, 1994, p. ix.

49. The figures in this paragraph are from Muroyama, *Nichibei Anpo Taisei* (vol. 1), pp. 212–19.

50. Hideki Kan, 'The significance of the US–Japan security system to the United States: a Japanese perspective', *Peace and Change*, vol. 12, no. 3/4, 1987, p. 18.

51. Cited in Hayes *et al.*, *American Lake*, p. 65. For the role of Japanese bases, see pp. 68ff.

52. The statement is by Morton Halperin, who served as Under-Secretary of Defence in the Johnson administration, as cited in Kan, 'The significance of the US–Japan security system to the United States', p. 21.

53. It should be remembered that, before the revision of the treaty in 1960, the United States incurred much less obligation to defend Japan. For details see Yoshihisa Hara, 'The significance of the US–Japan security system to Japan: the historical background', *Peace and Change*, vol. 12, no. 3/4, 1987, pp. 29–38.

54. For an interesting Japanese perspective on the changes at the international level connected with the decline of the United States as a hegemonic power, see Shindō Eiichi, 'Gaikō no honryō: ima nani o nasubeki ka', *Sekai*, December 1987, pp. 54–7, and Shindō Eiichi, *Gendai Funsō no Kōzō. Hikyoku Moderu no Kōchiku no tame ni*, Tokyo, Iwanami Shoten, 1987.

55. *Asahi Shinbun*, 31 December 1987.

56. The figures in this paragraph are from the Ministry of Foreign Affairs, North American Bureau, as well as the Defence Agency. By the time of the 1988 budget Japan's contribution to maintaining American forces deployed overseas had become the highest in the world. *Asahi Shinbun*, 9 January 1988.

57. Sakai, 'Nihon no gunjihi', pp. 25–6.

58. 'Introduction' of 'nuclear weapons' includes the problem of planes, such as the nuclear-capable F-16s deployed at Misawa, as well as vessels, although as the build-up in the 1980s was mainly naval, we here focus on the latter.

59. A summary of the evidence appears in Nīhara Shōji, *Abakareta Nichibei Kaku Mitsuyaku*, Tokyo, Shin Nihon Shuppansha, 1987, ch. 1.

60. This was the interpretation given by former Ambassador Edwin O. Reischauer in an interview in 1981. See *Mainichi Shinbun*, 18 May 1981.

For the full interview and other details on 'introduction', see Komori Yoshihisa, *Kaku wa Mochikomareta ka*, Tokyo, Bungei Shunjū, 1982.

61. On the Notes, see John Welfield, *An Empire in Eclipse: Japan in the Postwar American Alliance System*, London, Athlone, 1988, pp. 61ff.
62. For a discussion, see Daniel Okimoto, 'Chrysanthemum without the sword: Japan's nonnuclear policy' in Martin E. Weinstein (ed.), *Northeast Asian Security after Vietnam*, Urbana, University of Illinois Press, 1982, p. 136. As far as 'prior consultation' is concerned, in February 1986 Foreign Minister Abe Shintarō clarified that, under the US–Japan security treaty, Japan did not have the right to request prior consultation. See *Asahi Shinbun*, 9 February 1986.
63. Hayes *et al.*, *American Lake*, p. 85, original emphasis. Also see the tables on pp. 86–7.
64. Hayes *et al.*, *American Lake*, p. 76.
65. Hayes *et al.*, *American Lake*, p. 98. They also add: 'Although undocumented, confidential sources informed the authors that the Navy also kept anti-submarine depth bombs offshore Japan's coast for aircraft at Atsugi after 1960' (p. 98).
66. Cited in Hayes *et al.*, *American Lake*, p. 98.
67. Edwin O. Reischauer, *My Life between Japan and America*, New York, Harper & Row, 1986, p. 299.
68. Nīhara, *Abakareta Nichibei Kaku Mitsuyaku*, p. 3, my emphasis. The original English and a Japanese translation of the telegram appear on pp. 1–9.
69. Nīhara, *Abakareta Nichibei Kaku Mitsuyaku*, p. 7, my emphasis.
70. *Akahata*, 11 April 1987.
71. Hayes *et al.*, *American Lake*, p. 91.
72. The story broke in the *Mainichi Shinbun*, 18 May 1981.
73. Reischauer, *My Life between Japan and America*, p. 347.
74. For details on the Tomahawk, see Sekai Henshūbu. *Tomahōku to wa*, Tokyo, Iwanami Shoten, 1984.
75. LaRocque declared before a Congressional committee:

    My experience has been that any ship that is capable of carrying nuclear weapons carries them. They do not off-load them when they go into foreign ports such as Japan or other countries. If they are capable of carrying them they normally keep them aboard ship at all times except when the ship is in overhaul or in for major repairs. (Joint Committee on Atomic Energy, US Congress Subcommittee on Military Applications, *Proliferation of Nuclear Weapons*, 10 September 1974, p. 18)

76. *Gunjiminron*, April 1987, p. 80.
77. *Asahi Shinbun*, 12 June, 12 July 1985.
78. *Asahi Shinbun*, 20 June 1987.
79. *Sekai Nippō*, 1 January 1982.
80. Bōeicho Chōkan Kanbō Kōhōka, *Anpo, bōei mondai nado ni kansuru kokumin ishiki chōsa*, February 1983–April 1985, p. 103.
81. Bōeicho Chōkan Kanbō Kōhōka, *Anpo, bōei mondai nado ni kansuru kokumin ishiki chōsa*, p. 102.
82. Prime Minister Nakasone played a lead role in stressing the compat-

ibility between 'internationalism' and 'nationalism'. See Nakasone, *My Political Philosophy*, esp. pp. 9–10. For the ideological role of 'internationalization' in Japan in the 1980s, see Befu Harumi, *Ideorogī toshite no Nihon Bunkaron*, Tokyo, Shisō no Kagakusha, 1987, part 3.

83. Mitsuo Miyata, 'The politico-religion of Japan: the revival of militarist mentality', *Bulletin of Peace Proposals*, vol. 13, no. 1, 1982, p. 25.

84. Concern over Japan's military build-up started to be expressed again as the Nakasone administration came closer to breaking through the 1 per cent ceiling, and soon thereafter. See, for example, *Asahi Shinbun*, 13 January, 30 May, 5 June 1987. It should be noted, however, that Chinese criticism of the US–Japan security treaty, a constant theme in the 1960s, was not raised in the 1980s. The residual fear of militarism in other parts of Asia can be seen from a 1987 poll of members of ASEAN (excluding Brunei) commissioned by Japan's Ministry of Foreign Affairs which shows that other Asians still fear a revival of Japanese militarism (figures in parentheses are for 1983): Indonesia 21 per cent (19 per cent), Malaysia 34 per cent (37 per cent), the Philippines 47 per cent (28 per cent), Singapore 29 per cent (35 per cent), Thailand 54 per cent (53 per cent) (*Asahi Shinbun*, 13 July 1987).

85. For further details on the change in Opposition party policies see Kurokawa Shūji, *Nihon no Bōeihi o Kangaeru: Gunkaku Rosen no Mekanizumu*, Tokyo, Daiyamondosha, 1983.

CHAPTER 4

1 Figures are taken from the annual *Bōei Handobukku*, Tokyo, Asagumo Shinbunsha.

2. For a discussion on the legacy of the cold war in this region, and the implications for future security, see Nakanishi Terumasa, 'Introduction' and chapter 8, 'Ajia no mirai ni' in Nakanishi Terumasa (ed.) *Ajia dō Kawaru ka? 90 nendai no Ajia no Sōgō Anzen Hoshō*, Tokyo, Nihon Keizai Shinbunsha, 1993. Also see Andrew Mack, 'Key issues in the Asia–Pacific' in Richard Leaver and James L. Richardson (eds), *The Post-Cold War Order: Diagnoses and Prognoses*, Saint Leonards, New South Wales, Allen & Unwin, 1993, pp. 147–59.

3. The '1955 system' (*gojūgo-nen taisei*) takes its name from the year that the LDP was formed and the two wings of the socialists reunited as the JSP. The system finally collapsed in 1993 with the end of single-handed LDP rule. In essence, the *gojūgo-nen taisei* implied a stand-off between the conservatives and socialists over a wide range of issues, as in that between 'capitalism' and 'socialism' at the international level. It also implied fundamental disagreement over 'peace–war issues', such as the constitutionality of the SDF. As time passed, however, this public face of confrontation went hand in hand with close cooperation in Diet management and policy-making. Despite the LDP enjoying an overwhelming majority of seats in the Diet, therefore, the opposition often cooperated in behind-the-scene deals with the ruling party. For a discussion, see Nihon Seiji Gakkai (ed.), 'Gojūgo-nen taisei no keisei to hōkai', *Seijigaku Nenpō 1977*, Tokyo, Nihon Seiji Gakkai, 1979, and Junnosuke Masumi, 'The 1955 system in Japan and its subsequent development',

Asian Survey, vol. 28, no. 3, 1988, pp. 286–306.

4. For current details, see *Asahi Shinbun*, 28 November 1994.

5. On the United States' use of the United Nations in promoting its own interests, see Maurice Bertrand, 'The role of the United Nations in the context of the changing world order' in Yoshikazu Sakamoto (ed.), *Global Transformation: Challenges to the State System'*, Tokyo, United Nations University Press, 1994, pp. 462–74. For a study of the Gulf War, see Lawrence Freedman and Efraim Karsh, *The Gulf Conflict, 1990–1991: Diplomacy and War in the New World Order*, London, Faber & Faber, 1993.

6. Chapter IX, Article 96, states:

> Amendments to this Constitution shall be initiated by the Diet, through a concurring vote of two-thirds or more of all the members of each House and shall thereupon be submitted to the people for ratification, which shall require the affirmative vote of a majority of all votes cast thereon, at a special referendum or at such election as the Diet shall specify.
>
> Amendments when so ratified shall immediately be promulgated by the Emperor in the name of the people, as an integral part of this Constitution.

7. See the intra-party division on the revision of the section of the LDP party platform referring to the Constitution (*Asahi Shinbun*, 17 December 1994, 24 December 1994).

8. Kyōdō Teigen, 'Ajia–Taiheiyō chīki anpo o kōsō suru', *Sekai*, December 1994, p. 25. Also see Bernard K. Gordon, 'Japan: searching once again' in James C. Hsiung (ed.), *Asia Pacific in the New World Order*, London, Lynne Rienner Publishers, 1993, p. 58.

9. For these and other political statements supporting the constitutionality of nuclear weapons for defensive purposes, see Hattori Manabu, 'Nihon no kaku seisaku to konnichi no kadai', *Shakaishugi* (special edition), October 1994, pp. 67–74.

10. A copy of the ban can be found in Kenmochi Kazumi, *PKO Hahei: Bunseki to Shiryō*, Tokyo, Rokufu Shuppan, 1992, p. 234.

11. As Satō stated: 'The provisions of the Constitution make overseas service impossible' (John Welfield, *An Empire in Eclipse: Japan in the Postwar American Alliance System*, London, Athlone, 1988, p. 250).

12. Fujī Haruo, *Jieitai ni Aka Shingō*, Tokyo, Orijinaru Shuppansha, 1990, p. 98.

13. *Mainichi Shinbun* (evening edition), 28 October 1980.

14. For details, see James E. Auer, *The Postwar Rearmament of Japanese Maritime Forces, 1945–1971*, New York, Praeger, 1973.

15. Cited in Welfield, *An Empire in Eclipse*, p. 243.

16. Kyōdō Teigen, 'Ajia-Taiheiyō chīki anpo o kōsō suru', pp. 31–2.

17. On 'prior consultation', see Chapter 3.

18. Cited in Sasaki Yoshitaka, *Kaigai o Wataru Jieitai: PKO Rippō to Seiji Kenryoku*, Tokyo, Iwanami Shoten, 1992, p. 56.

19. For a discussion of this sense of vulnerability, see Takehiko Kamo, 'The internationalization of the state: the case of Japan' in Yoshikazu Sakamoto (ed.), *Global Transformation: Challenges to the State System*,

Tokyo, United Nations University Press, 1994, esp. pp. 118ff. For a more general discussion of the psychological aspects of the relationship, see Masaru Tamamoto, 'The Japan that wants to be liked: society and international participation' in Danny Hunger and Paul Blackburn (eds), *Japan's Emerging Global Role*, London, Lynne Rienner, 1993, pp. 37–54.

20. These telephone calls are discussed in Kunimasa Takeshige and Takabatake Michitoshi, '"Hahei Kokkai" no butaiura', *Sekai*, December 1990, pp. 24ff.

21. Kunimasa and Takabatake, '"Hahei Kokkai" no butaiura', p. 23.

22. See, for example, *Japan Times*, 27 December 1990.

23. Cited in Satō Seisaburō, '"Sengo ishiki" no dasei o tatsu aki', *Chūō Kōron*, November 1990, p. 106.

24. *Far Eastern Economic Review*, 31 January 1991, p. 47.

25. *Far Eastern Economic Review*, 20 June 1991, p. 50.

26. *Economist*, 19 January 1991, p. 27.

27. *Newsweek*, 1 October 1990, p. 4.

28. *Far Eastern Economic Review*, 7 February 1991, p. 10.

29. For a detailed discussion of Ozawa Ichirō's role, see Sasaki, *Kaigai o Wataru Jieitai*. For the role played by *zoku giin* in policy-making in general, see Inoguchi Takashi and Iwai Tomoaki, *Zokugiin no Kenkyū: Jimintō Seiken o Gyūjiru Shuyakutachi*, Tokyo, Nihon Keizai Shinbunsha, 1987.

30. Ozawa Ichirō's bestseller in Japan, which provides an insight into his political goals, has been translated as *Blueprint for a New Japan: The Rethinking of a Nation*, Tokyo, Kōdansha International, 1994. The cover reads: 'The Political Bombshell Privately Translated by the CIA'. See especially ch. 3, 'Defining the national interest', in Book I, pp. 36–45, and Book II, 'Becoming a "normal nation"', pp. 91–150.

31. The full details of Japan's response can be found in Bōei Nenkan Hakkōkai, *Bōei Nenkan (1992 Nenban)*, Tokyo, Bōei Nenkan Hakkōkai, 1992, pp. 42–82. Also see Courtney Purrington and A.K., 'Tokyo's policy responses during the Gulf crisis', *Asian Survey*, vol. 31, March 1991, pp. 307–23; and Takashi Inoguchi, 'Japan's response to the Gulf crisis: an analytical overview', *Journal of Japanese Studies*, vol. 17, no. 2, 1991, pp. 257–73.

32. Sasaki, *Kaigai o Wataru Jieitai*, p. 70.

33. Takesada Hideshi, 'Mada "kaku" no kirifuda o tebasanai Kita Chōsen', *Sekai Shūhō*, 15 November 1994, pp. 10–15.

34. Cited in Sasaki, *Kaigai o Wataru Jieitai*, p. 32.

35. Sasaki, *Kaigai o Wataru Jieitai*, p. 32.

36. For the bill, see *Asahi Shinbun*, 9 October 1990.

37. For the support and opposition to Japan's entry into the UN Security Council, see *Asahi Shinbun*, 4, 6, 10 and 25 October 1994. For a fuller discussion of the reasons, see the special section on Japan's bid for a seat on the UN Security Council in *Hōgaku Seminā*, no. 482, February 1995, pp. 14–29.

38. Sasaki, *Kaigai o Wataru Jieitai*, p. 48.

39. *Kenpō Undō*, December 1990, p. 196.

40. *Asahi Shinbun* (evening edition), 16 October 1990.

41. *Kenpō Undō*, December 1990, p. 196.
42. The agreement between the LDP, DSP and Kōmei Party can be found in the annual, *Bōei Handobukku*, Tokyo, Asagumo Shinbunsha, 1994, p. 464.
43. See *Bōei Handobukku*, 1994, pp. 461–2.
44. Shida Masamichi, 'Kaigai hōjin no kyūshutsu wa minkanki de', *Sekai*, May 1994, p. 96. These were originally under the Prime Minister's Office, but were transferred to the Defence Agency in 1992.
45. *Asahi Shinbun*, 19 and 22 January 1991.
46. Murata Hisanori, 'Jieitai kaigai hahei to gikaisei minshushugi', *Kumamoto Hōgaku*, vol. 76, June 1993, pp. 2–29.
47. Cited in Sasaki, *Kaigai o Wataru Jieitai*, pp. 123–4.
48. Gotōda Masaru, *Naikaku Kanbōcho Chōkan*, Tokyo, Kōdansha, 1989, pp. 104–8.
49. *Asahi Shinbun*, 25 April 1991.
50. Kazuyoshi Abe, 'The Japanese business community: response to the Gulf war', *Japanese Review of International Affairs*, vol. 5, fall/winter 1991, p. 197.
51. Abe, 'The Japanese business community', p. 198.
52. *Nihon Keizai Shinbun* (evening edition), 20 August 1991.
53. Fujishima Udai, 'PKO hōan (jieitai kaigai hahei hōan) 3 nen kōshite tsui ni "seiritsu"', *Gunshuku Mondai Shiryō*, August 1992, p. 83.
54. For a copy of the law, see Kenmochi, *PKO Hahei*, pp. 199–220.
55. For a copy of the revision, see Kenmochi, *PKO Hahei*, pp. 221–4.
56. On reactions, see Kenmochi, *PKO Hahei*, pp. 7–17.
57. See Kenmochi, *PKO Hahei*, pp. 199–206.
58. Sasaki, *Kaigai o Wataru Jieitai*, p. 145.
59. In order to circumvent this problem, the government introduced a distinction in Japanese between *shiki* (command) and *sashizu* (orders). For the government's distinction, see *Bōei Handobukku*, 1994, pp. 475–7.
60. *Yomiuri Shinbun*, 1 June 1992.
61. *Asahi Shinbun* (evening edition), 19 November 1994.
62. Itō Hideko, 'Jieikan no hanashi o kīte', *Sekai*, March 1994, p. 119.
63. Critic Katō Shūichi, for instance, takes this line. See Shūichi Katō, 'The internationalization of Japan' in Glenn D. Hook and Michael A. Weiner (eds), *The Internationalization of Japan*, London, Routledge, 1992, p. 310.
64. See Satō Seisaburō, '"Sengo ishiki" no dasei o tatsu aki', p. 112.
65. *Asahi Shinbun*, 15 July 1992.
66. Maeda Tetsuo (ed.), *Jieitai o do Suru ka*, Tokyo, Iwanami Shoten, 1992, p. ii.
67. Mori Hideki, 'Kenpō no heiwashugi o dō tori atsukau beki ka: kyūjō no kihansei o kenji suru koto no jūyōsei', *Zenei*, November 1994, p. 28.
68. Kenmochi, *PKO Hahei*, especially the introduction.
69. On Japan's role, see K.V. Kesavan, 'Japan's role in the resolution of the Cambodian conflict', paper presented at the International Peace Research Association, Kyōto Conference, 1992.
70. *Nihon Keizai Shinbun*, 22 March 1992.
71. *Asahi Shinbun*, 14 April 1992.
72. *Ajia Jihō*, August 1992, p. 27. For details of Akashi's activities, see Akashi Yasushi, 'Kanbojia nikki', *Chūō Kōron*, March 1994, pp. 163–83, and

following journal issues.

73. For full details on the SDF deployments in Cambodia, see the unattributed chapter, 'Jieitai PKO haken no kōdō gaiyō to kongo no kadai' in *Bōei Nenkan* (1994 edition), Tokyo, Bōei Nenkan Hakkōkai, 1994, pp. 51–79. For a critical appraisal, see Ryokufū Shuppan (ed.), *Kanbojia PKO: Bunseki to Shiryō*, Tokyo, Ryokufū Shuppan, 1992.

74. For a discussion, see Arizawa Naoaki, 'Jieitai PKO haken no ichinen', *Sekai*, November 1993, pp. 61–2; interviews, 'Kanbojia PKO o furikaette', *Sekai*, March 1994, p. 114.

75. Murata, 'Jieitai kaigai hahei to gikaisei minshushugi'.

76. *Asahi Shinbun*, 25 November 1994.

CHAPTER 5

1. Karel van Wolferen, 'Japan's non-revolution', *Foreign Affairs*, vol. 72, no. 4, 1993, p. 62. Also see Donald R. Hellmann, *Japanese Foreign Policy and Domestic Politics*, Berkeley, University of California Press, 1969; George Packard, *Protest in Tokyo: The Security Treaty Crisis of 1960*, Princeton, Princeton University Press, 1966.

2. Martin Weinstein, *Japan's Postwar Defense Policy, 1947–1968*, New York, Columbia University Press, 1971; Tetsuya Umemoto, 'Arms and alliance in Japanese public opinion', PhD dissertation, Princeton, Princeton University, 1985; Thomas U. Berger, 'From sword to chrysanthemum: Japan's culture of anti-militarism', *International Security*, vol. 17, no. 4, 1993, pp. 119–50.

3. See, for instance, Sakamoto Yoshikazu, 'Heiwashugi no gyakusetsu to kōsō', *Sekai*, July 1994, pp. 22–40.

4. This chapter focuses on 'mass opinion', as seen in nation-wide opinion polls, not 'attentive opinion', as expressed by the 'attentive public'. See Gabriel A. Almond, *The American People and Foreign Policy*, New York, Fredrick A. Praeger, 1960 [1950].

5. Unless otherwise noted, the public opinion polls utilized in this chapter are drawn from the following sources. The newspaper polls are as published in the Tokyo editions of the *Asahi Shinbun*, *Yomiuri Shinbun* and *Mainichi Shinbun*. The exact dates of publication can be found by consulting the newspapers' almanacs (e.g. *Asahi Nenkan*). The Nikkei database can be used for polls from 1985 onwards. The Prime Minister's Office polls are as published in the monthly issues of *Gekkan Yoron Chōsa*. These polls are also available in the annual, *Bōei Handobukku* (Tokyo, Asagumo Shinbunsha), and the *Bōei Hakusho* (Tokyo, Ōkurasho Insatsukyoku). The Nihon Hōsō Kyōkai (NHK) data are drawn from *Hōsō Kenkyū to Chōsa*, the quarterly journal of the NHK *Hōsō Yoron Chōsasho*. A useful source for public opinion data is the *Yoron Chōsa Nenkan*, which is published by the Minister's Secretariat, Public Relations Department (Naikaku Sōridaijin Kanbō Kōhōshitsu). The abbreviations used in the figures are as follows:

　　A = *Asahi Shinbun*
　　J = *Jiji Tsūshinsha*
　　K = *Kyōdō Tsūshinsha*

M = *Mainichi Shinbun*
N = *Nihon Hōsō Kyōkai* (NHK)
P = Prime Minister's Office
Y = *Yomiuri Shinbun*

The month in which the survey was carried out is listed before the pollster, with the year followed by the month. For instance, an *Asahi* poll carried out in March 1994 appears as 9403A.

6. See the *Yomiuri Shinbun*, 3 November 1994. For a discussion, see the monthly journal, *This is Yomiuri*, December 1994. For a critique, see *Zenei*, January 1995, especially Izumi Shigeyuki, '"Gunji taikokuka" e no kōdō to sakubō: Yomiuri Shinbunsha no "kenpō kaisei shian" o hihan suru', pp. 64–77. Also see the Conclusion.

7. Watanabe Yōzō, *Gendai Nihon Shakai to Minshushugi*, Tokyo, Iwanami Shoten, 1982, p. 86.

8. John Mueller, 'Review: American public opinion and the Gulf war: some polling issues', *Public Opinion Quarterly*, vol. 57, no. 1, 1993, p. 86.

9. Polls over the years show that over two-thirds of Americans have consistently approved of the use of the atomic bombs against Hiroshima and Nagasaki. See Bernard M. Kramer, S. Michael Kalick and Michael A. Milburn, 'Attitudes toward nuclear weapons and nuclear war: 1945–1982', *Journal of Social Issues*, vol. 39, no. 1, 1983, p. 13. On the source for the change in morality that these attitudes indicate, see Barton J. Bernstein, 'The atomic bombings reconsidered', *Foreign Affairs*, vol. 74, no. 1, 1995, pp. 135–52.

10. Nagasaki Hōsō, *Chūgoku Hōsō Hibakusha 30 Nen Genbaku to Heiwa ni kansuru Yoron Chōsa: Nagasaki, Hiroshima Ryōshimin no Hibaku Ishiki*, May 1975.

CHAPTER 6

1. On this perspective, see Michael J. Shapiro, *Language and Political Understanding: The Politics of Discursive Practices*, New Haven, Yale University Press, 1981.

2. Shapiro, *Language and Political Understanding*, p. 5.

3. For representative research on the political role of language, see Murray Edelman, *The Symbolic Uses of Politics*, Urbana, University of Illinois Press, 1964; Murray Edelman, *Politics as Symbolic Action*, Chicago, Markham Publishing, 1971; Murray Edelman, *Political Language: Words that Succeed and Policies that Fail*, New York, Academic Press, 1977; Harold Lasswell and Nathan Leites (eds), *Language of Politics: Studies in Quantitative Semantics*, Cambridge, Mass., MIT Press, 1965; Doris A. Graber, *Verbal Behavior and Politics*, Urbana, University of Illinois Press, 1976; Michael Shapiro (ed.), *Language and Politics*, Oxford, Blackwells, 1984.

For case studies on the role of language, see Ian Slater, 'Orwell, Marcuse and the language of politics', *Political Studies*, vol. 23, no. 4, 1975, pp. 459–74; Alex Carey, 'Word-power in politics: "terror", "aggression", and "refugees" in the semantics of violence and repression', *Et*

Cetera, vol. 37, no. 1, 1980, pp. 53–64; Walter Laqueur, 'Foreign policy and the English language', *The Washington Quarterly*, vol. 4, no. 1, 1981, pp. 3–12.

For work on language and security, particularly nuclear issues, see Paul Chilton, 'Nukespeak: nuclear language, culture and propaganda' in Crispin Aubrey (ed.), *Nukespeak: The Media and the Bomb*, London, Comedia Publishing Group, 1982, pp. 94–112; Stephen Hilgartner, Richard Bell and Rory O'Connor, *Nukespeak: Nuclear Language, Visions, and Mindset*, San Francisco, Sierra Club, 1982; Robin Luckham, 'Of arms and culture', *Current Research on Peace and Violence*, vol. 7, no. 1, 1984, pp. 1–64; R.B.J. Walker, 'Contemporary militarism and the discourse of dissent' in R.B.J. Walker (ed.), *Culture, Ideology, and World Order*, Boulder, Westview Press, 1984, pp. 302–22; Paul Chilton (ed.), *Language and the Nuclear Arms Debate: Nukespeak Today*, London, Frances Pinter, 1985; David Campbell, *Writing Security: United States Foreign Policy and the Politics of Identity*, Manchester, Manchester University Press, 1992.

4. For an overview of Japanese work on language and politics, see Kurihara Akira, 'Gengo no seijigaku – kiso ronri no tame no tankyū nōto', *Nihon Seiji Gakkai Nenpō 1976*, Tokyo, Iwanami Shoten, 1977, pp. 63–90. For the current state, with specific reference to issues of war and peace, see the proceedings of the panel of the Heiwa Gakkai organized by the author, in *Heiwa Kenkyū*, vol. 14, November 1989, pp. 5–34. For other work, see Ishida Takeshi, *Nihon no Seiji to Kotoba* (2 volumes), Tokyo, University of Tokyo Press, 1989, especially the second volume on 'peace' and the 'state', and Yamamoto Mitsuru, *Fumō no Gensetsu: Kokkai Tōben no naka no Nichibei Kankei*, Tokyo, Japan Times, 1992. For a politician's own view on the use of language in Japanese politics, see Kunihiro Masao, 'Kotoba ga shisō o suiraku saseru', *Sekai*, April 1994, pp. 50–8.

5. On the importance of perspective in communication, see R.M. Blakar, 'Language as a means of social power' in J.L. Mey (ed.), *Pragmalinguistics: Theory and Practice, Series Janua Linguarum*, The Hague, Mouton, 1979, pp. 131–69; R. Rommetveit and R.M. Blakar, *Studies of Language, Thought and Verbal Communication*, New York, Academic Press, 1979.

6. Honda Katsuichi, *Korosu Gawa no Ronri*, Tokyo, Asahi Shinbunsha, 1984; Honda Katsuichi, *Korosareru Gawa no Ronri*, Tokyo, Asahi Shinbunsha, 1982.

7. Adolf Hitler, *Mein Kampf*, trans. Ralph Manheim, Boston, Houghton & Mifflin, 1943.

8. Cited in Robert Jay Lifton, *The Nazi Doctors: A Study of the Psychology of Evil*, London, Macmillan, 1986, p. 16.

9. John W. Dower, *War Without Mercy: Race and Power in the Pacific War*, New York, Pantheon Books, 1986.

10. For a general discussion of discourse, see Shapiro, *Language and Political Understanding*, pp. 65–94; William E. Connolly, *The Terms of Political Discourse*, 2nd edn, Oxford, Robertson, 1983; Anthony Wilden, *System and Structure: Essays in Communication and Exchange*, 2nd edn, London, Tavistock, 1980, esp. pp. 491, 502–3.

11. As in Herman Kahn, *On Thermonuclear War*, Princeton, Princeton University Press, 1960, p. 19.
12. See Carol Cohn, 'Sex and death in the rational world of defense intellectuals', *Signs*, vol. 12, no. 4, 1987, pp. 687–718. The US navy, prior to 'going nuclear', was highly critical of the immorality of Air Force-style strategic bombing. As Rear-Admiral Ralph Ofstie stated before Congress in 1949, strategic bombing was 'ruthless and barbaric ... random mass slaughter of men, women and children ... militarily unsound ... morally wrong ... contrary to our fundamental ideals' (cited in Fred Kaplan, *The Wizards of Armageddon*, New York, Simon & Schuster, 1983, p. 232).
13. For the early response to the bomb by the media in the United States, see Robert K. Manoff, 'Covering the bomb: press and state in the shadow of nuclear war' in Department of Journalism and Mass Communication (ed.), *War, Peace and the News Media*, New York, New York University, 1983, pp. 197–237. For the situation in Japan, see my 'Censorship and reportage of atomic damage and casualties in Hiroshima and Nagasaki', *Bulletin of Concerned Asian Scholars*, vol. 23, no. 1, 1991, pp. 13–25.
14. For a brief but excellent discussion of this dual role of euphemism, see William Lutz, 'Notes toward a description of doublespeak', *Quarterly Review of Doublespeak*, vol. 10, no. 4, 1984, pp. 1–2.
15. George Orwell, *Nineteen Eighty-Four*, Harmondsworth, Penguin, 1954.
16. Paul Chilton, 'Nukespeak', p. 107.
17. George Orwell, 'Politics and the English language', *The Orwell Reader*, New York, Harcourt Brace, 1956, p. 363.
18. *Asahi Shinbun*, 26, 27 June 1982. For the background to such types of change, see Katō Shūichi, 'Kyōkasho ken'etsu no byōri', *Sekai*, October 1982, pp. 36–7.
19. Ishimaki Yasuhiro, 'Hajimatta arata na "kyōkasho kōgeki"', *Sekai*, November 1982, pp. 26–9.
20. See the Conclusion and note 11 thereof.
21. Fujio Masayuki, 'Hōgen daijin ōi ni hoeru', *Bungei Shunjū*, October 1986, pp. 122–33.
22. A public opinion survey carried out by the *Yomiuri* indicates that, although 46.9 per cent of those polled agreed that a problem existed in the Ministry of Education's request to substitute 'advance' for 'aggression', 22.2 per cent thought it natural and 30.9 per cent gave no answer (*Yomiuri Shinbun*, 13 February 1982).
23. *Asahi Shinbun*, 29, 30 July 1982.
24. *Asahi Shinbun* (evening edition), 29 July 1982.
25. *Asahi Shinbun*, 24 August 1982; *Asahi Jyanaru*, 10 September 1982, p. 7.
26. *Asahi Shinbun*, 24 July 1982.
27. *Asahi Shinbun*, 27, 28, 29 July 1982.
28. Ienaga Saburō in *Asahi Jyanaru*, 10 September 1982, p. 7.
29. For representative critical comments, see Yamanaka Hisashi, 'Hakkiri shita Monbushō no "Shīna haken gun, Chōsen sōtokufu" teki kankaku', *Asahi Jyānaru*, 10 September 1982, p. 11; Yano Tōru, 'Towareteiru no wa Nihon no kokka imēji', *Chūō Kōron*, October 1982, p. 109; Nagahara Keiji, 'Heiwa kyōiku to kyōkasho mondai' in *Shimin no Heiwa Hakusho '83*, Tokyo, Nippon Hyōronsha, 1983, p. 123; Katō, 'Kyōkasho ken'etsu

no byōri', pp. 38–40.

30 *Akahata*, 29 July 1982. Prime Minister Satō commented as follows: 'I don't think it is useful to say such things as that this country is an aggressive country [*shinryaku kuni*] or pacifistic.' More forthright apologies have occurred in the interim, especially after the end of the cold war and the start of coalition governments. Prime Minister Kaifu was the first prime minister during the LDP era to make a more forthright apology when he declared: 'I express our sincere contrition at Japanese past actions which inflicted unbearable suffering and sorrow upon a great many people of the Asia–Pacific region' (*Far Eastern Economic Review*, 20 June 1991, p. 44).

31. *Asahi Shinbun*, 28 July 1982.

32. *Mainichi Shinbun*, 3 August 1982.

33. Although this was the first time that the expression appeared in the joint communiqué, the previous prime minister, Ōhira Masayoshi, had also started to talk about the US–Japan relationship as an 'alliance'.

34. *Asahi Shinbun* (evening edition), 9 May 1981.

35. For the roots of Japanese anti-Soviet sentiment in historical and contemporary perspective, see Nakamura Kenichi, 'Soren kyōiron kara no dakkyaku', *Sekai*, April 1985, pp. 56–73.

36. On the connection between euphemism and metaphor see Paul Chilton, 'Metaphor, euphemism and the militarization of language', *Current Research on Peace and Violence*, vol. 10, no. 1, 1987, pp. 7–19.

37. F. Haynes, 'Metaphor as interactive', *Educational Theory*, vol. 25, no. 3, 1975, p. 272, original emphasis.

38. Max Black, *Models and Metaphors: Studies in Language and Philosophy*, Ithaca, Cornell University Press, 1962, especially ch. 3.

39. Black, *Models and Metaphors*, p. 39, emphasis added. For two other important works on how metaphor creates new meaning, see Ernst Cassirer, *Language and Myth*, New York, Dover, 1946; Philip Wheelwright, *Metaphor and Reality*, Bloomington, Indiana University Press, 1962.

40. Black, *Models and Metaphors*, p. 37 (emphasis added). Also see Max Black, 'More about metaphor' in Andrew Ortony (ed.), *Metaphor and Thought*, Cambridge, Cambridge University Press, 1979, p. 37.

41. For a discussion of the disease–cure metaphor, see John Horton, 'Order and conflict theories of social problems as competing ideologies', *American Journal of Sociology*, vol. 71, no. 6, 1966, pp. 701–13

42. Cited in Edwin Black, 'The second persona', *The Quarterly Journal of Speech*, vol. 56, no. 2, 1970, p. 114.

43. Susan Sontag, *Illness as Metaphor*, New York, Farrar, Straus & Giroux, 1978, p. 69, emphasis added.

44. Cited in John Halverson, 'The psycho-pathology of style: the case of right-wing rhetoric', *The Antioch Review*, vol. 31, no. 1, 1971, pp. 101–3.

45. Cited in Donald Schön, 'Generative metaphor: a perspective on problem-setting in social policy' in Andrew Ortony (ed.), *Metaphor and Thought*, Cambridge, Cambridge University Press, 1979, p. 262, original emphasis.

46. Cited in Robert J. Sternberg, Roger Tourangeau and Georgia Nigro, 'Metaphor, induction and social policy: the convergence of macroscopic and microscopic views', in Andrew Ortony (ed.), *Metaphor and Thought*,

Cambridge, Cambridge University Press, 1979, p. 349.
47. *Newsweek*, 15 April 1985, p. 26B.
48. *Time*, 31 March 1986, pp. 6, 8.
49. *Asahi Shinbun*, (evening edition) 12 May 1981.
50. *Asahi Shinbun*, 9 May 1981.
51. For a review of Nakasone's rhetoric more generally, see *Asahi Shinbun*, 26 February 1983.
52. *Washington Post*, 21 January 1983. *Asahi Shinbun*, 22 January 1983.
53. Of course, as a metaphor, the meaning is open to interpretation. In the case of Britain, it appears that Soviet propagandists used the phrase in the 1950–1 period to describe Britain's role as host to US forces. Winston Churchill similarly used the phrase to characterize Britain as an island carrier of planes, hence 'unsinkable'. His warning to the House of Commons on 9 December 1951 'that by creating the American atomic base in East Anglia, we have made ourselves the target, and perhaps the bull's eye, of a Soviet attack' is the line of criticism that opposition forces have used against the presence of US bases in Japan, too. I am indebted to Duncan Campbell of the *New Statesman* for information on the use of 'unsinkable aircraft carrier' in Britain.
54. There appears to be some confusion in the English literature as to whether Nakasone actually used 'unsinkable' or whether he was misquoted, and actually said 'a giant aircraft carrier'. Although he seems at first to have denied that he used this expression, and the fault lay with his interpreter, the prime minister did admit that he used this expression on return to Japan. Front-page newspaper headlines declared: 'The Prime Minister admits "unsinkable aircraft carrier" statement' (*Asahi Shinbun*, 22 January 1983). The attempts he made to defend his use of the expression in the Diet debates suggest that he first denied using the expression as a result of the political storm he had stirred up.
55. *Yosan Iinkai Kaigiroku Dai San Gō*, 3 February 1983, p. 21.
56. 'Kokumu daijin no enzetsu ni taisuru Asukata Ichio kun shitsugi', *Shūgiin Kaigiroku San Gō*, 27 January 1983, p. 34.
57. Oe Kenzaburō comments in Iwanami Shoten Henshūbu (ed.), *Nihon no Ikikata to Heiwa no Mondai*, Tokyo, Iwanami Shoten, 1983, pp. 208–9.
58. *Washington Post*, 23 January 1983.
59. An *Asahi* survey showed that 61 per cent of those questioned were against the prime minister's use of 'unsinkable aircraft carrier' and other such expressions (*Asahi Shinbun*, 21 February 1983).
60. *Yosan Iinkai Kaigiroku Dai San Gō*, 3 February 1983, p. 2.
61. *Asahi Shinbun* (evening edition), 29 August 1964.
62. *Asahi Shinbun* (evening edition), 29 August 1964.
63. *Asahi Shinbun*, 1 February 1968.
64. *Asahi Shinbun*, 1 February 1968.
65. *Asahi Shinbun*, 28 October 1967.
66. Arase and Okayasu interviewed the *Asahi Shinbun*'s Washington correspondent regarding the nuclear-allergy metaphor. Although the correspondent was not certain that he was the originator of the metaphor, it seems clear that he did not think he was influenced by US

government officials in his use of the metaphor. He replied in part:

> In regard to your questions about nuclear allergy, it is something that happened a long time ago and I cannot remember exactly, but I think I can generally say what follows: 1) At the time I wrote the article in question, I had not heard any US officials use the expression 'nuclear-weapons allergy'. I feel the word certainly smacks of being 'Japanese-made English', and I have at least no recollection of the American side using expressions like 'nuclear allergy' or 'allergic to nuclear weapons'. I think when we discussed these types of issues we both used expressions such as 'nervous about', 'sensitive to' and 'susceptible'. (Arase Yutaka and Okayasu Shigehiro, 'Kaku arerugī to anpo kōgai', *Sekai*, March 1968, pp. 76–7).

However, US officials had used the 'nuclear allergy' metaphor, at least in official documents. See US Department of State, Division of Research for Far East, Office of Intelligence Research, *The Relationship of Japan to Nuclear Weapons and Warfare* (top secret), Washington, DC, 1957, declassified, p. 1. I thank Peter Hayes for this information.

67. On countermetaphors, see Edelman, *Politics as Symbolic Action*, p. 69; Kenneth J. Gergen, *Toward Transformation in Social Knowledge*, New York, Springer Verlag, 1982, pp. 143–5.
68. *Asahi Shinbun*, 4 December 1967.
69. T.J. Pempel, 'Japan's nuclear allergy', *Current History*, vol. 68, no. 404, 1975, pp. 169–73, 183.
70. L. Tuft, *Allergy Management in Clinical Practice*, Saint Louis, Mosby, 1973, p. 2, emphasis added.
71. On the importance of ambiguity for the political functioning of metaphor, see Nels Johnson, 'Palestinian refugee ideology: an enquiry into key metaphors', *Journal of Sociological Research*, vol. 34, no. 4, 1978, p. 536.
72. Cited in George Lackoff and M. Johnson, *Metaphors We Live By*, Chicago, University of Chicago Press, 1980, p. 157.
73. *Dai 22 bu Okinawa Mondai nado ni kansuru Tokubetsu Īinkai Kaigiroku Dai Ichi Gō*, 4 December 1967, p. 6.
74. *Dai 22 bu Okinawa Mondai nado ni kansuru Tokubetsu Īinkai Kaigiroku Dai Ichi Gō*, 4 December 1967, p. 6.
75. *Asahi Shinbun*, 13 November 1994. The research group was led by Rōyama Michio, presently Professor at Sophia University in Tokyo.
76. Kusuda Minoru, *Shuseki Hishokan: Satō Sōri to no 10 nen kan*, Tokyo, Bungei Shunjū, 1975, p. 167.
77. The word 'nuclear', which young Japanese commonly associated with the 'dark image' of Hiroshima and Nagasaki in the late 1960s, was associated with the 'bright image' of peaceful use by the late 1970s. See *Asahi Shinbun*, 30 October 1978.
78. Political leaders in Japan have often referred to constitutional, defence and nuclear issues as 'taboo'. The reason for this is suggested by Hertzler, who notes how words are tabooed in order to try to manipulate reality. Anderson points to the possible relationship between metaphors and taboos by suggesting that metaphors may arise to replace words or phrases expressing taboos. See Joyce Hertzler, *A Sociology of*

Language, New York, Random House, 1965, pp. 24–6; C.C. Anderson, 'The psychology of the metaphor', *The Journal of Genetic Psychology*, vol. 105, no. 1, 1964, p. 56.
79. See letters to the editor, *Asahi Shinbun*, 23 July 1968.
80. *Asahi Shinbun*, 1 February 1968.
81. *Asahi Shinbun*, 16 July 1968.

CHAPTER 7

1. On macro discourse, see Paul Chilton, 'Introduction' in Paul Chilton (ed.), *Language and the Nuclear Arms Debate: Nukespeak Today*, London, Frances Pinter, 1985, p. xiv.
2. The link between being atom-bombed and the right to possess nuclear weapons was proposed by Shimizu Ikutarō, who argued: 'if we gain any privilege from being the first country to be atom bombed, isn't it the privilege to be the first, before others, to produce and possess nuclear weapons?' See his *Nippon yo Kokka tare, Kaku no Sentaku*, Tokyo, Bungei Shunjū, 1980, p. 90.
3. The meaning of *hibakusha* is discussed in detail below. In a legal sense, however, *hibakusha* can be considered to be those exposed to the atomic bombs: (1) directly, i.e. residents of Hiroshima, Nagasaki, and certain nearby areas; (2) indirectly, such as rescue workers; (3) *in utero*. See the Committee for the Compilation of Materials on Damage Caused by the Atomic Bombs in Hiroshima and Nagasaki, *Hiroshima and Nagasaki: The Physical, Medical, and Social Effects of the Atomic Bombings*, Tokyo, Iwanami Shoten, 1981, p. 394.
4. Murakami Shigeyoshi, *Yasukuni Jinja*, Tokyo, Iwanami Shoten, 1985, p. 22.
5. Mitsuo Miyata, 'The politico-religion of Japan: the revival of militarist mentality', *Bulletin of Peace Proposals*, vol. 13, no. 1, 1982, p. 25.
6. Miyata, 'The politico-religion of Japan', p. 26.
7. As Bernstein states: 'In the spring and summer of 1945, no American leader believed – as some later falsely claimed – that they planned to use the A-bomb to save half a million lives.' See Barton J. Bernstein, 'The atomic bombings reconsidered', *Foreign Affairs*, vol. 74, no. 1, 1995, p. 149.
8. This is not to imply that the *hibakusha* are a homogeneous group. Two points should be made: first, Ishida Tadashi has divided the *hibakusha* into two types: 'drifters' and 'resisters'. Our main concern is with the 'resisters' who have played the major role in the *hibakusha* movement. See Ishida Tadashi, *Hangenbaku: Nagasaki Hibakusha no Seikatsu*, Tokyo, Miraisha, 1973. Second, a study by Hatsuse Ryūhei and Matsuo Masatsugu shows that what determines attitudes towards nuclear issues is party affiliation; in other words, the experience of being atom-bombed does not appear to be correlated with nuclear attitudes. See their 'Nihonjin no kaku ishiki kōzō – hibaku taiken oyobi seitō shiji', Hiroshima University, Institute for Peace Science, Kenkyū Hōkoku, no. 1 (undated).
9. This is the position taken by the *hibakusha* organization, Hidankyō. See *Asahi Shinbun*, 9 December 1994. Also see the *hibakusha* intellectual, Itō Takeshi, *Hiroshima, Nagasaki kara Sekai to Mirai e*, Tokyo, Keisō Shobō, 1985, pp. 82–3.

10. Rufus E. Miles Jr., 'Hiroshima: the strange myth of half a million lives saved', *International Security*, vol. 10, no. 2, 1985, pp. 121–3. Others have estimated a larger number, but still nothing like the number later used by President Truman to justify the bombings. See Bernstein, 'The atomic bombings reconsidered', p. 149.

11. Miles mentions, for instance, that the figure of half a million lives saved and other figures of similar magnitude appear in history textbooks used in US secondary schools. Miles, 'Hiroshima: the strange myth of half a million lives saved', p. 121. The depth of US support for the role of the bomb in speeding the war's end came up in 1994, when the US Post Office announced that, as part of the fiftieth anniversary celebrations of the war's end, it planned to issue a commemorative stamp in 1995 with the mushroom cloud and the caption 'Atomic bombs hasten war's end. August 1945'. It was only as a result of Japanese pressure and the intervention of President Clinton that the issue did not go ahead. This is nevertheless the common view of US politicians. See *Asahi Shinbun*, 3 December 1994, 9 December 1994. For a full discussion, see Sodei Rinjirō, 'Genbaku tōka no rekishi to seiji', *Sekai*, February 1995, pp. 131–41.

12. The Committee for the Compilation of Materials on Damage Caused by the Atomic Bombs in Hiroshima and Nagasaki, *Hiroshima and Nagasaki*, p. 335.

13. Maruyama Masateru, 'Hiroshima, Nagasaki, Bikini' in Okakura Koshirō, Maruyama Maseratu and Seki Hiroharu (eds), *Heiwa no Tankyū*, Tokyo, Jiji Tsūshin, 1975, p. 89.

14. From 1948 to 1952, too, radioactivity was deliberately released into the atmosphere in the state of Utah as part of an experiment. On the Soviet side, according to a documentary film belonging to the military uncovered in 1993, 45,000 military personnel and several thousand civilians were deliberately exposed to an atmospheric nuclear explosion in the Urals in September 1954 as part of a military exercise.

15. Itō, *Hiroshima, Nagasaki kara Sekai to Mirai e*, pp. 82–3.

16. Itō, *Hiroshima, Nagasaki kara Sekai to Mirai e*, pp. 133–4.

17. Despite the change to a socialist coalition government in 1994, the government still has been reluctant to take an active role in promoting nuclear disarmament, as seen in its opposition to supporting a motion on the illegality of nuclear weapons at the United Nations. See *Asahi Shinbun*, 16 December 1994. Also see *Asahi Shinbun*, 3 November 1994.

18. From the *hibakusha*'s point of view, a crucial flaw in this legislation is the failure to admit clearly the state's responsibility, as encapsulated in the term 'state compensation' (*kokka hoshō*). See *Asahi Shinbun*, 27 October, 9 December 1994.

19. According to a 1985 survey by the Ministry of Health and Welfare, which was published in May 1990, the total number of confirmed deaths from the atomic bombing is 295,956. In addition, 25,190 persons could not be confirmed. There are approximately 340,000 *hibakusha* still alive.

20. The case appears in *Japanese Annual of International Law*, vol. 8, 1964, pp. 212–52.

21. See note 18 above. The position of not making 'state compensation' was also taken in 1994 in respect of aid for the mainly Korean women

used as sex-slaves during the war. See the 1995 budget allocation, *Asahi Shinbun*, 26 December 1994.

22. See the concluding chapter for further discussion.

23. On the controversy, see *Asahi Shinbun*, 8, 14, 17, 22 and 24 December 1994. For a fuller discussion, see Sodei, 'Genbaku tōka no rekishi to seiji'.

24. For details on Occupation censorship, see Monica Braw, *The Atomic Bomb Suppressed: American Censorship in Japan 1945–1949*, Lund, Liber Forlag, 1986. Also see Monica Braw, *The Atomic Bomb Suppressed: American Censorship in Occupied Japan*, New York, M.E. Sharpe, 1991. The effect of the censorship can be seen to have gone beyond the official end in 1949, as in the case of the delay in publishing the full report of *Genshi Bakudan Higai Chōsa*, an extensive survey carried out by Japanese scientists of the Special Committee for the Investigation of Atomic Bomb Damages between 14 September 1945 and December 1946. It was not released in full until May 1953. I thank David Swain for this information.

25. For details see Braw, *The Atomic Bomb Suppressed. American Censorship in Japan 1945–1949*, 1986, and my 'Censorship and reportage of atomic damage and casualties in Hiroshima and Nagasaki', *Bulletin of Concerned Asian Scholars*, vol. 23, no. 1, 1991, pp. 13–25.

26. Braw, *The Atomic Bomb Suppressed*, 1986, p. 99.

27. Braw, *The Atomic Bomb Suppressed*, 1986, p. 139.

28. For details see Braw, *The Atomic Bomb Suppressed*, 1986, pp. 99–104.

29. For details see Wilfred Burchett, *Shadows of Hiroshima*, London, Verso, 1983, pp. 18–23.

30. The *Asahi* was no doubt aware of the existence of the full report by the Special Committee for the Investigation of Atomic Bomb Damages (see note 24). A summary report of the group's work was issued on 1 August 1951.

31. Kasugai Kunio, 'Kaku arerugi no keisei katei' in Kokumin Kōza, *Nihon no Anzen Hoshō: Okinawa Fukki e no Michi*, Tokyo, Hara Shobō, 1968, p. 128.

32. The Committee for the Compilation of Materials on Damage Caused by the Atomic Bombs in Hiroshima and Nagasaki, *Hiroshima and Nagasaki*, p. 575.

33. The Committee for the Compilation of Materials on Damage Caused by the Atomic Bombs in Hiroshima and Nagasaki, *Hiroshima and Nagasaki*, p. 576.

34. The Committee for the Compilation of Materials on Damage Caused by the Atomic Bombs in Hiroshima and Nagasaki, *Hiroshima and Nagasaki*, p. 577.

35. *Asahi Shinbun*, 18 March 1954.

36. *Asahi Shinbun*, 18 March 1954.

37. For some reason confusion still exists on the number of cranes. An interview with Sadako's family on 13 October 1984 put the figure at 645, with this additional comment: 'there are others she started but did not finish' (account of brother Masahiro). See Robert Del Tredici, *At Work in the Fields of the Bomb*, New York, Harper & Row, 1987, p. 154.

38. Betty Lifton, 'The girl of the paper cranes', *New York Times Magazine*, 1 August 1965.
39. Tredici, *At Work in the Fields of the Bomb*, p. 155.
40. Itō, *Hiroshima, Nagasaki kara Sekai to Mirai e*, p. 67. In Japanese another Chinese character with the same sound is used to distinguish those exposed to radiation, as in bomb tests, from those exposed to the atomic explosions. This expands the embrace of '*hibakusha*' as discussed below.
41. These are the 'resisters' in Ishida's use of the term. See note 8.
42. For information on the Korean *hibakusha*, see the Committee for the Compilation of Materials on Damage Caused by the Atomic Bombs in Hiroshima and Nagasaki, *Hiroshima and Nagasaki*, pp. 462–75.
43. The Committee for the Compilation of Materials on Damage Caused by the Atomic Bombs in Hiroshima and Nagasaki, *Hiroshima and Nagasaki*, p. 465. It should also be noted that, from 1991, the annual peace declaration of Nagasaki city mentioned for the first time the prisoners-of-war from over twenty countries also exposed to the atomic bombings.
44. Itō, *Hiroshima, Nagasaki kara Sekai to Mirai e*, p. 68, original emphasis.
45. Cited in Itō, *Hiroshima, Nagasaki kara Sekai to Mirai e*, p. 42.
46. Itō, *Hiroshima, Nagasaki kara Sekai to Mirai e*, pp. 72–3.
47. The estimate is from the conference, as cited in *Imidasu*, Tokyo, Shūeisha, 1994, p. 320.

CONCLUSION

1. For the Gaullist approach to an independent role for Japan, which has been overshadowed by a policy centring on the United Nations, see Shintarō Ishihara, *The Japan That Can Say No*, London, Simon & Schuster, 1991.
2. Nakasone and Ozawa no doubt embrace this ultimate goal.
3. Representative of the Japanese scholars who stress the importance of maintaining the US–Japan security treaty is Satō Seisaburō. See, for instance, 'Reisengo no Ajia Taiheiyō ni okeru Nichibei dōmei', *Kokusai Mondai*, no. 401, August 1993, pp. 2–8. This also is used by Ozawa Ichirō as a reason for cooperating with the United States through the United Nations. See Ichirō Ozawa, *Blueprint for a New Japan: The Rethinking of a Nation*, Tokyo, Kōdansha International, 1994, especially pp. 104–7. It should also be noted that support for the treaty in East Asia is often phrased in terms of restraining Japan. See the comments by Singapore's Lee Kuan Yew, *Far Eastern Economic Review*, 20 June 1991, p. 45.
4. Watanabe Osamu, '90 nendai Nihon kokka to tennōsei', *Bunka Hyōron*, special issue, October 1990, p. 30.
5. Thomas U. Berger, 'From sword to chrysanthemum: Japan's culture of anti-militarism', *International Security*, vol. 17, no. 4, 1993, pp. 148–9.
6. For a discussion of the type of conservative criticism, as in the so-called 1955 *ureubeki* textbook campaign and the 1980s *henkō* textbook campaign, see Takahashi Shin'ichi and Hoshino Yasusaburō (ed. supervisors), *Kyōkasho ga Nerawarete iru: Futatabi Kuru ka Kokutaika no Jidai*, Tokyo, Ayumi Shuppan, 1981, pp. 30–48; Katsuno Naoyuki, *Kyōiku Kihon Hōsei to Kyōkasho Mondai*, Kyōtō, Hōritsu Bunka, 1982, esp. ch. 2; Takashima Nobuyoshi, *80 Nendai no Kyōkasho Mondai*, Tokyo, Shin

Nihon Shuppansha, 1984, pp. 57–114; Kyōkasho Kentei Soshō o Shien suru Zenkoku Renraku kai Kyōkasho Kentei Seido Kentō Iinkai (Daihyō, Nagai Kenichi) (ed.), *Minna de Kangaeyo: Nihon no Kyōkasho Seido*, Kyōkasho Kentei Soshō o Shien suru Zenkoku Renraku kai Kyōkasho Kentei Seido Kentō Iinkai Tokyo, 1982, pp. 195–217.

7. Ienaga has brought three cases against the state in 1965, 1967 and 1984. To summarize, Ienaga lost the 1965 and the 1967 cases, but in the 1984 case the Tokyo High Court ruled in 1993 that, in regard to the ministry's certification of his sections on the Nanjing massacre, it had overstepped its 'discretionary powers', and this was illegal. Nevertheless, none of the rulings accepted Ienaga's fundamental point that his texts had been censored as a result of the certification system. As the state did not appeal the 1993 ruling by May 1994, this ruling stands. It is significant in that, for the first time, the courts did accept that the ministry had overstepped its powers. For an early discussion of this case, see Saburō Ienaga, 'The historical significance of the Japanese textbook lawsuit', *Bulletin of Concerned Asian Scholars*, vol. 2, no. 4, 1970, pp. 2–12; R.P. Dore, 'Textbook censorship in Japan: the Ienaga case', *Pacific Affairs*, vol. 43, no. 4 (1970–1), pp. 548–56. For a critical discussion of the recent ruling in the context of the others, see Nihon Shuppan Rōdō Kumiai (ed.), *Kyōkasho Repōtō '94*, Tokyo, Nihon Shuppan Rōdō Kumiai, 1994, pp. 18–21. For a comparison of Japanese and German texts, see Ian Buruma, *The Wages of Guilt: Memories of War in Germany and Japan*, London, Jonathan Cape, 1994.

8. Ienaga, 'The historical significance of the Japanese textbook lawsuit', p. 9.

9. Nihon Kyōshoku Kumiaiin (ed.), *Kōtō Gakkō Kyōkasho no Kenkyū: 82 Nenpan Kokugo, Shakai no Hikaku Bunseki*, Tokyo, Nihon Kyōshoku Kumiai, 1981.

10. Nihon Kyōshoku Kumiaiin (ed.), *Kōtō Gakkō Kyōkasho no Kenkyū*.

11. For the controversial certification of this text, see *Asahi Shinbun*, 28 May, 30 May, 4 June, 5 June, 2 July 1986. For a detailed discussion, see the various articles in Nihon Shuppan Rōdō Kumiai (ed.), *Kyōkasho Repōtō '87*, Tokyo, Nihon Shuppan Rōdō Kumiai, 1987, pp. 2–29.

12. Nihon Shuppan Rōdō Kumiai (ed.), *Kyōkasho Repōtō '87*, p. 1.

13. On Chinese criticism, see Laura Newby, *Sino-Japanese Relations: China's Perspective*, London, Routledge, 1988, pp. 50–3. On Korean criticism, see Chong-Sik Lee, *Japan and Korea: The Political Dimension*, Stanford, Hoover Institute Press (Stanford University), 1985, ch. 6.

14. For details, see Leonard J. Schoppa, *Education Reform in Japan: Immobilist Politics*, London, Routledge, 1991.

15. For a discussion of the new system, see Nihon Shuppan Rōdō Kumiai (ed.), *Kyōkasho Repōtō '90*, Tokyo, Nihon Shuppan Rōdō Kumiai, 1990, pp. 1–34.

16. Nihon Shuppan Rōdō Kumiai (ed.), *Kyōkasho Repōtō '94*, p. 22.

17. The six subjects taught under social studies have been divided into two main subject areas, history and geography, on the one hand, and civics, on the other.

18. Nihon Shuppan Rōdō Kumiai (ed.), *Kyōkasho Repōtō '94*, pp. 31–63.

19. For comparison of all of the pre-inspection and post-inspection sections

of the textbooks dealing with PKO activities, see Nihon Shuppan Rōdō Kumiai (ed.), *Kyōkasho Repōtō '94*, pp. 64–78.

20. Monbushō, *Atarashī Kenpō no Hanashi*, Tokyo, Monbushō, 1947, pp. 18, 20.

21. Hisako Ukita, 'A preliminary introduction to the peace education movement in Japan' in The Japan Peace Research Group (ed.), *Peace Research in Japan 1974–75*, Tokyo, Tokyo University Press, 1976, p. 83.

22. For details, see Hiroshima Heiwa Kyōiku Kenkyūjo (ed.), *Heiwa Kyōiku Kenkyū*, no. 2, 1975, pp. 6–14.

23. Nihon Kyōshokuin Kumiai (ed.), *Heiwa Kyōiku Undōshi: Nikyōsō Kyōken 30 nen no Ayumi*, Tokyo, Nihon Kyōshokuin Kumiai, 1982, pp. 53–7.

24. *Asahi Shinbun*, 19 February 1982.

25. *Asahi Shinbun*, 14 June 1981, 23 July 1975.

26. *Asahi Shinbun*, 13 April 1982.

27. NHK survey, March 1982.

28. The exact numbers differ according to source, with the numbers given by the police authorities tending to play down the size of the gatherings. The numbers quoted here are the ones used in newspaper headlines and magazines. On the Hiroshima rally, see *Asahi Jyanaru*, 2 April 1982, pp. 6–9. On the Tokyo rally, see *Asahi Jyanaru*, 24 May 1982.

29. Although this number is accepted, significant duplications and triplications are said to have meant that the actual number of Japanese who signed the petition was only 28 million – still an enormous number. See Sunao Suzuki, 'Public attitudes towards peace', *Bulletin of the Atomic Scientists*, vol. 40, no. 2, 1984, p. 29.

30. For a full discussion of the growth of the movement at this time, and the involvement of ordinary citizens, see Onishi Hitoshi, 'Nihon no hankaku undō: 1982 nen zenhan no SSDII kokumin undō suishin renraku kaigi no undō o chūshin ni'jo, *Hōgaku* (Tōhoku University), vol. 49, no. 2, June 1985, pp. 167–200; Onishi Hitoshi, 'Nihon no hankaku undō: 1982 nen zenhan no SSDII kokumin undō suishin renraku kaigi no undō o chūshin ni'ge, *Hōgaku* (Tōhoku University), vol. 49, no. 3, August 1985, pp. 392–424.

31. *Nihon Keizai Shinbun* (evening edition), 3 December 1994.

32. Information is only starting to emerge on the CIA's role in providing financial backing to the LDP as a 'domestic ally' during the late 1950s early 1960s. See *The New York Times*, 9 November 1994, and the discussion in the Japanese press at that time. Fuller details are available on the Soviet support of the socialist party. See Nagoshi Kenrō, *Kuremurin Himitsu Bunsho wa Kataru*, Tokyo, Chūō Kōronsha, 1994.

33. Malcolm Chalmers, Owen Greene, Edward J. Laurance and Herbert Wulf (eds), *Developing the UN Register of Conventional Arms*, Bradford, University of Bradford, 1994.

34. In a Diet session in January 1968 the prime minister expanded on the meaning of the four principles:

> 1. Japan will not produce, possess or permit the introduction into its territory of nuclear weapons; 2. A complete and general ban on nuclear arms is the ardent wish of the Japanese people, but as an

immediate measure Japan will make efforts to promote nuclear dis-

armament; 3. Japan maintains defence forces under the Constitution only against attacks by conventional weapons and relies on America's nuclear capability against nuclear attacks; 4. Japan will tackle the peaceful utilization of nuclear energy by making the utmost efforts in that direction. (*Japan Times*, 31 January 1968)

35. For a discussion, see Kimura Shinsuke, 'Heiwa ni tsuite motto giron shiyō', *Sekai*, March 1994, p. 125.

36. For a discussion on representative proposals, see Kimura, 'Heiwa ni tsuite motto giron shiyō', pp. 125–34; *Asahi Shinbun*, 23 November 1994. The Ozawa Committee Report and the Yomiuri proposal to revise the Constitution have stirred most interest. For a discussion of the former, see Nishi Osamu, 'Nihon no kokusai kōken o meguru giron: Ozawa chōsakai hōkoku nado ni tsuite', *Shin Bōei Ronshū*, vol. 20, no. 2, 1992, pp. 68–81. On the latter, see the monthly journal *This is Yomiuri*, December 1994. For a critique, see the monthly journal *Zenei*, January 1995.

37. For a discussion of socialist opposition to this about-face, see Kantō Shikyoku Seijiundō Kenkyūbukai, 'Jieitai gōken, hibusō chūritsu hōki o yurusanu Shakaitō kūgatsu rinji taikai', *Shakaishugi*, no. 370, September 1994, pp. 10–15.

38. *Asahi Shinbun*, 29 November 1994.

39. *Asahi Shinbun*, 19 November 1994. Also see the discussion on the 1995 financial year budget, *Asahi Shinbun*, 21 December 1994, 26 December 1994. It should also be noted, however, that the budget that the coalition approved included an item for research on the Theatre Missile Defence (TMD). On the TMD, see Yamashita Masamitsu, Takai Susumu and Iwata Shūichirō, *TMD Senīki Dandō Misairu Bōei*, Tokyo, TBS Britannica, 1994.

40. The *kyōdō teigen* were put forward by Koseki Shōichi (Rikkyō University), Suzuki Yūji (Hōsei University), Takahashi Susumu (Tokyo University), Takayanagi Sakio (Chūō University), Tsuboi Yoshiaki (Hokkaido University), Maeda Tetsuo (military specialist), Yamaguchi Jirō (Hokkaidō University), Yamaguchi Sadao (Rikkyō University) and Wada Haruki (Tokyo University).

41. Kyōdō Teigen, 'Heiwa kihonhō', *Sekai*, April 1993, pp. 52–67. A summary of the main points can also be found in *Sekai*, December 1994, p. 22.

42. Kyōdō Teigen, 'Ajia–Taiheiyō chīki anpo o kōsō suru', *Sekai*, December 1994, pp. 22–40.

43. Kyōdō Teigen, 'Ajia–Taiheiyō chīki anpo o kōsō suru', p. 25.

44. Kyōdō Teigen, 'Ajia–Taiheiyō chīki anpo o kōsō suru', p. 27.

45. On the ASEAN Regional Forum, see Furukawa Eiichi, 'Higashi Ajia no chīki anpo de tōwaku ga zureru: Nishigawa to ASEAN', *Sekai Shūhō*, 30 August 1994, pp. 16–19. On 'common security', see the report of the Independent Commission on Disarmament and Security Issues, *Common Security: A Programme for Disarmament*, London, Pan Books, 1982.

46. This is the case with the purchase of planes for air warning and control

(AWACS). See Gregg Rubinstein, 'Nihon wa kōgeki no ryōku o takamete iru ka', *Sekai*, May 1994, especially pp. 103–5. On the function of AWACS, see Ebata Kensuke, 'AWACS to wa nani ka', *Sekai Shūhō*, 20 October 1992, pp. 40–5.

47. This can be seen, for instance, in the strengthening of US bases in Japan, especially Okinawa, despite the reduction of facilities elswhere in the region.

48. Sakamoto Yoshikazu, 'Heiwashugi no gyakusetsu to kōsō', *Sekai*, July 1994, pp. 38ff.

References

ENGLISH

Newspapers and magazines

Economist
Far Eastern Economic Review
Japan Times
New York Times Magazine
Newsweek
Time
US News and World Report
Washington Post

Books, book chapters and articles

Abe, K., 'The Japanese business community: response to the Gulf war', *Japanese Review of International Affairs*, vol. 5, fall/winter 1991.

Adams, G. *The Iron Triangle: The Politics of Defense Contracting*, New York, Transaction Books, 1981.

Almond, G.A., *The American People and Foreign Policy*, New York, Praeger, 1960 [1950].

Anderson, C.C., 'The psychology of the metaphor', *The Journal of Genetic Psychology*, vol. 105, no. 1, 1964.

Aspaturian, V.V., 'The Soviet military–industrial complex – does it exist?' *Journal of International Affairs*, vol. 26, no. 1, 1972.

Auer, J.E., *The Postwar Rearmament of Japanese Maritime Forces, 1945–1971*, New York, Praeger, 1973.

Berger, T.U., 'From sword to chrysanthemum: Japan's culture of anti-militarism', *International Security*, vol. 17, no. 4, 1993.

Berghahn, V.R., *Militarism: The History of an International Debate 1861–1979*, Cambridge, Cambridge University Press, 1981.

Bernstein, B.J., 'The atomic bombings reconsidered', *Foreign Affairs*, vol. 74, no. 1, 1995.

Bertrand, M., 'The role of the United Nations in the context of the changing world order' in Yoshikazu Sakamoto (ed.), *Global Transformation:*

Challenges to the State System, Tokyo, United Nations University Press, 1994, pp. 462–74.

Black, E., 'The second persona', *The Quarterly Journal of Speech*, vol. 56, no. 2, 1970.

Black, M., *Models and Metaphors: Studies in Language and Philosophy*, Ithaca, Cornell University Press, 1962.

Black, M., 'More about metaphor' in Andrew Ortony (ed.), *Metaphor and Thought*, Cambridge, Cambridge University Press, 1979, pp. 19–43.

Blakar, R.M., 'Language as a means of social power' in J.L. Mey (ed.), *Pragmalinguistics: Theory and Practice, Series Janua Linguarum*, The Hague, Mouton, 1979, pp. 131–69.

Braw, M., *The Atomic Bomb Suppressed: American Censorship in Japan 1945–1949*, Lund, Liber Forlag, 1986.

Braw, M., *The Atomic Bomb Suppressed: American Censorship in Occupied Japan*, New York, M.E. Sharpe, 1991.

Buchanan, J.M., *The Demand and Supply of Public Goods*, Chicago, Rand McNally, 1968.

Burchett, W., *Shadows of Hiroshima*, London, Verso, 1983.

Buruma, I., *The Wages of Guilt: Memories of War in Germany and Japan*, London, Jonathan Cape, 1994.

Campbell, D., *Writing Security: United States Foreign Policy and the Politics of Identity*, Manchester, Manchester University Press, 1992.

Camus, A., 'Neither victims nor executioners' in Peter Mayer (ed.), *The Pacifist Conscience: Classic Writings on Alternatives to Violent Conflict from Ancient Times to the Present*, New York, Holt Reinhart & Winston, 1966.

Carey, A., 'Word-power in politics: "terror", "aggression", and "refugees" in the semantics of violence and repression', *Et Cetera*, vol. 37, no. 1, 1980.

Cassirer, E., *Language and Myth*, New York, Dover, 1946.

Chalmers M., O. Greene, E.J. Laurance and H. Wulf (eds), *Developing the UN Register of Conventional Arms*, Bradford, University of Bradford, 1994.

Chilton, P., 'Nukespeak: nuclear language, culture and propaganda' in C. Aubrey (ed.), *Nukespeak: The Media and the Bomb*, London, Comedia Publishing Group, 1982, pp. 94–112.

Chilton, P. (ed.), *Language and the Nuclear Arms Debate: Nukespeak Today*, London, Frances Pinter, 1985.

Chilton, P., 'Metaphor, euphemism and the militarization of language', *Current Research on Peace and Violence*, vol. 10, no. 1, 1987.

Chinworth, M.W., *Inside Japan's Defense: Technology, Economics and Strategy*, London, Brassey, 1992.

Cohn, C., 'Sex and death in the rational world of defense intellectuals', *Signs*, vol. 12, no. 4, 1987.

Committee for the Compilation of Materials on Damage Caused by the Atomic Bombs in Hiroshima and Nagasaki, *Hiroshima and Nagasaki: The Physical, Medical, and Social Effects of the Atomic Bombings*, Tokyo, Iwanami Shoten, 1981.

Connolly, W.E., *The Terms of Political Discourse*, 2nd edn, Oxford, Robertson, 1983.

Cook, F., *The Warfare State*, New York, Macmillan, 1962.

Dore, R.P., 'Textbook censorship in Japan: the Ienaga case', *Pacific Affairs*, vol. 43, no. 4, 1970–1.

Dower, J.W., *Empire and Aftermath: Yoshida Shigeru and the Japanese Experience, 1878–1954*, Cambridge, Harvard Council on East Asian Studies, 1979.

Dower, J.W., *War Without Mercy: Race and Power in the Pacific War*, New York, Pantheon Books, 1986.

Dower, J.W., 'Occupied Japan and the Cold War in Asia' in M.J. Lacey (ed.), *The Truman Presidency*, Cambridge, Woodrow Wilson International Center for Scholars and Cambridge University, 1989, pp. 366–409.

Drifte, R., *Arms Production in Japan: The Military Applications of Civilian Technology*, Boulder, Westview Press, 1986.

Edelman, M., *The Symbolic Uses of Politics*, Urbana, University of Illinois Press, 1964.

Edelman, M., *Politics as Symbolic Action*, Chicago, Markham Publishing, 1971.

Edelman, M., *Political Language: Words that Succeed and Policies that Fail*, New York, Academic Press, 1977.

Eide, A. and M. Thee, *Problems of Contemporary Militarism*, London, Croom Helm, 1980.

Eisenhower, D.D., *Public Papers of the Presidents of the United States, 1960–61, Containing the Public Messages, Speeches and Statements of the President*, Washington DC, US Government Printing Office, 1961.

Freedman, L. and E. Karsh, *The Gulf Conflict, 1990–1991: Diplomacy and War in the New World Order*, London, Faber & Faber, 1993.

Galbraith, J.K., *How to Control the Military*, New York, Doubleday, 1969.

Gergen, K.J., *Toward Transformation in Social Knowledge*, New York, Springer Verlag, 1982.

Gordon, B.K., 'Japan searching once again' in J.C. Hsiung (ed.), *Asia Pacific in the New World Order*, London, Lynne Rienner Publishers, 1993, pp. 49–70.

Graber, D.A., *Verbal Behavior and Politics*, Urbana, University of Illinois Press, 1976.

Halverson, J., 'The psycho-pathology of style: the case of right-wing rhetoric', *The Antioch Review*, vol. 31, no. 1, 1971.

Hara, Y., 'The significance of the US–Japan security system to Japan: the historical background', *Peace and Change*, vol. 12, no. 3/4, 1987.

Hayes, P., L. Zarsky and W. Bello, *American Lake: Nuclear Peril in the Pacific*, Harmondsworth, Penguin Books, 1986.

Haynes, F., 'Metaphor as interactive', *Educational Theory*, vol. 25, no. 3, 1975.

Hellmann, D.R., *Japanese Foreign Policy and Domestic Politics*, Berkeley, University of California Press, 1969.

Herken, G., 'American scientists and US nuclear weapons policy', *Peace and Change*, vol. 11, no. 1, 1985.

Hertzler, J., *A Sociology of Language*, New York, Random House, 1965.

Hilgartner S., R. Bell and R. O'Connor, *Nukespeak: Nuclear Language, Visions, and Mindset*, San Francisco, Sierra Club, 1982.

Hitler, A., *Mein Kampf*, trans., Ralph Manheim, Boston, Houghton & Mifflin, 1943.

Holloway, D., 'Technology and political decision in Soviet armaments policy', *Journal of Peace Research*, vol. 11, no. 4, 1974.

Holloway, D., 'War, militarism and the Soviet state', *Alternatives*, vol. 6, no. 1, 1980.

Hook, G.D., 'Censorship and reportage of atomic damage and casualties in Hiroshima and Nagasaki', *Bulletin of Concerned Asian Scholars*, vol. 23, no. 1, 1991.

Horton, J., 'Order and conflict theories of social problems as competing ideologies', *American Journal of Sociology*, vol. 71, no. 6, 1966.

Huntington, S., *The Soldier and the State: The Theory and Politics of Civil–Military Relations*, Cambridge, Mass., Belknap Press of Harvard University, 1957.

Ienaga, S., 'The historical significance of the Japanese textbook lawsuit', *Bulletin of Concerned Asian Scholars*, vol. 2, no. 4, 1970.

Independent Commission on Disarmament and Security Issues, *Common Security: A Programme for Disarmament*, London, Pan Books, 1982.

Inoguchi, T., 'Japan's response to the Gulf crisis: an analytical overview', *Journal of Japanese Studies*, vol. 17, no. 2, 1991.

Ishihara, S., *The Japan That Can Say No*, London, Simon and Schuster, 1991.

Jahn, E., 'The role of the armaments complex in Soviet society (is there a Soviet military–industrial complex?)', *Journal of Peace Research*, vol. 12, no. 3, 1975.

Jahn, E., 'Armaments and bureaucracy in the Soviet society', *Bulletin of Peace Proposals*, vol. 10, no. 1, 1979.

Joint Committee on Atomic Energy, US Congress Subcommittee on Military Applications, *Proliferation of Nuclear Weapons*, 10 September 1974.

Johnson, N., 'Palestinian refugee ideology: an enquiry into key metaphors', *Journal of Sociological Research*, vol. 34, no. 4, 1978.

Kahn, H., *On Thermonuclear War*, Princeton, Princeton University Press, 1960.

Kaldor, M., *The Baroque Arsenal*, New York, Hill & Wang, 1981.

Kamo, T., 'The internationalization of the state: the case of Japan' in Yoshikazu Sakamoto (ed.), *Global Transformation: Challenges to the State System*, Tokyo, United Nations University Press, 1994, pp. 107–33.

Kan, H., 'The significance of the US–Japan security system to the United States: a Japanese perspective', *Peace and Change*, vol. 12, no. 3/4, 1987.

Kaplan, F., *The Wizards of Armageddon*, New York, Simon & Schuster, 1983.

Kato, S., 'The internationalization of Japan' in G.D. Hook and M.A. Weiner (eds), *The Internationalization of Japan*, London, Routledge, 1992, pp. 310–16.

Keddell, J.P. Jr., *The Politics of Defense in Japan: Managing Internal and External Pressures*, London, M.E. Sharpe, 1993.

Kersten, R., *Japanese Democracy: Maruyama Masao and the Search for Autonomy 1945–1960*, London, Routledge, forthcoming.

Konrad, A.R, 'Violence and the philosopher', *The Journal of Value Inquiry*, vol. 8, no. 1, 1974.

Kramer, B.M., S.M. Kalick and M.A. Milburn, 'Attitudes toward nuclear weapons and nuclear war: 1945–1982', *Journal of Social Issues*, vol. 39, no. 1, 1983.

Lackoff, G. and M. Johnson, *Metaphors We Live By*, Chicago, University of Chicago Press, 1980.

Laqueur, W., 'Foreign policy and the English language', *The Washington Quarterly*, vol. 4, no. 1, 1981.

Lasswell, H.D., 'The garrison-state hypothesis today' in S. Huntington (ed.), *Changing Patterns of Military Politics*, New York, Free Press of Glenco, 1962, pp. 51–70.

Lasswell, H. and N. Leites (eds), *Language of Politics: Studies in Quantitative Semantics*, Cambridge, Mass., MIT Press, 1965.

Lebow, R.N., and J.G. Stein, *We All Lost the Cold War*, Princeton, Princeton University Press, 1994.

Lee, C.-S., *Japan and Korea: The Political Dimension*, Stanford, Hoover Institute Press (Stanford University), 1985.

Lenin, V.I, *Imperialism: The Highest Stage of Capitalism*, New York, International Publishers, 1939.

Liebknecht, K., *Militarism*, New York, B.W. Huebsch, 1917.

Lifton, R.J., *The Nazi Doctors: A Study of the Psychology of Evil*, London, Macmillan, 1986.

Luckham, R., 'Militarism and international dependence: a framework for analysis' in J.J. Villamil (ed.), *Transnational Capitalism and National Development: New Perspectives on Dependence*, Atlantic Highlands, New Jersey, Humanities Press, 1979, pp. 145–81.

Luckham, R., 'Of arms and culture', *Current Research on Peace and Violence*, vol. 7, no. 1, 1984.

Lutz, W., 'Notes toward a description of doublespeak', *Quarterly Review of Doublespeak*, vol. 10, no. 4, 1984.

Luxemburg, R., *The Accumulation of Capital*, London, Routledge & Kegan Paul, 1951.

Mack, A., 'Key issues in the Asia–Pacific' in R. Leaver and J. L. Richardson (eds), *The Post-Cold War Order: Diagnoses and Prognoses*, Saint Leonards, New South Wales, Allen & Unwin, 1993, pp. 147–59.

Manoff, R.K., 'Covering the bomb: press and state in the shadow of nuclear war' in Department of Journalism and Mass Communication (ed.), *War, Peace and the News Media*, New York, New York University, 1983, pp. 197–237.

Maruyama, M., *Thought and Behaviour in Modern Japanese Politics*, Oxford, Oxford University Press, 1969.

Masumi, J., 'The 1955 system in Japan and its subsequent development', *Asian Survey*, vol. 28, no. 3, 1988.

Miles, R.E., Jr., 'Hiroshima: the strange myth of half a million lives saved', *International Security*, vol. 10, no. 2, 1985.

Mishan, E.J., 'The relationship between joint products, collective goods, and external effects', *Journal of Political Economy*, vol. 77, no. 3, 1969.

Miyata, M., 'The politico-religion of Japan: the revival of militarist mentality', *Bulletin of Peace Proposals*, vol. 13, no. 1, 1982.

Mueller, J., 'Review: American public opinion and the Gulf war: some polling issues', *Public Opinion Quarterly*, vol. 57, no. 1, 1993.

Nakasone, Y., *My Political Philosophy*, Tokyo, Liberal Democratic Party, 1987.

Newby, L., *Sino-Japanese Relations: China's Perspective*, London, Routledge, 1988.

Okimoto, D., 'Chrysanthemum without the sword: Japan's nonnuclear policy' in Martin E. Weinstein (ed.), *Northeast Asian Security after Vietnam*, Urbana, University of Illinois Press, 1982, pp. 128–56.

Orwell, G., *Nineteen Eighty-Four*, Harmondsworth, Penguin, 1954.

Orwell, G., 'Politics and the English language', *The Orwell Reader*, New York, Harcourt Brace, 1956.

Ozawa, I., *Blueprint for a New Japan: The Rethinking of a Nation*, Tokyo, Kōdansha International, 1994.

Packard, G., *Protest in Tokyo: The Security Treaty Crisis of 1960*, Princeton, Princeton University Press, 1966.

Pempel, T.J., 'Japan's nuclear allergy', *Current History*, vol. 68, no. 404, 1975.

Pugh, M.C., *The ANZUS Crisis, Nuclear Visiting and Deterrence*, Cambridge, Cambridge University Press, 1989.

Purrington, C. and A.K. 'Tokyo's policy responses during the Gulf crisis', *Asian Survey*, vol. 31, March 1991.

Reischauer, E.O., *My Life between Japan and America*, New York, Harper & Row, 1986.

Ritter, G., *The Sword and the Sceptre: The Problem of Militarism in Germany* (translation of the 1955 German edition, 4 vols), London, Allen Lane/Penguin Press, 1972.

Rommetveit, R. and R.M. Blakar, *Studies of Language, Thought and Verbal Communication*, New York, Academic Press, 1979.

Sakamoto, Y., 'Editor's introduction' in The Japan Peace Research Group (ed.), *Peace Research in Japan 1976*, Tokyo, University of Tokyo Press, 1977.

Sakamoto, Y., 'Introduction: Japan in global perspective', *Bulletin of Peace Proposals*, vol. 13, no. 1, 1982.

Schiller, H. and J. Phillips (eds), *Super-State: Readings in the Military –Industrial Complex*, Urbana, University of Illinois, 1970.

Schön, D., 'Generative metaphor: a perspective on problem-setting in social policy' in Andrew Ortony (ed.), *Metaphor and Thought*, Cambridge, Cambridge University Press, 1979, pp. 254–83.

Schoppa, L.J., *Education Reform in Japan: Immobilist Politics*, London, Routledge, 1991.

Seki, H., 'Politics of peace', *Japan Quarterly*, vol. 24, no. 3, 1977.

Seki, H., *The Asia–Pacific in the Global Formation: Bringing 'The Nation-State Japan' Back In*, Tokyo, Institute of Oriental Culture, University of Tokyo, 1986.

Senghaas, D., 'Arms race by arms control?' *Bulletin of Peace Proposals*, vol. 4, no. 4, 1973.

Shapiro, M.J., *Language and Political Understanding: The Politics of Discursive Practices*, New Haven, Yale University Press, 1981.

Shapiro, M.J. (ed.), *Language and Politics*, Oxford, Blackwells, 1984.

Shaw, M., *Post-Military Society: Militarism, Demilitarization and War at the End of the Twentieth Century*, Oxford, Polity Press, 1991.

Skjelsbaek, K., 'Militarism, its dimensions and corollaries: an attempt at conceptual clarification', *Journal of Peace Research*, vol. 16, no. 3, 1979.

Slater, I., 'Orwell, Marcuse and the language of politics', *Political Studies*, vol. 23, no. 4, 1975.

Sontag, S., *Illness as Metaphor*, New York, Farrar, Straus & Giroux, 1978.

Sternberg, R.J., R. Tourangeau and G. Nigro, 'Metaphor, induction and social policy: the convergence of macroscopic and microscopic views' in Andrew Ortony (ed.), *Metaphor and Thought*, Cambridge, Cambridge University Press, 1979, pp. 325–53.

Suzuki, S., 'Public attitudes towards peace', *Bulletin of the Atomic Scientists*, vol. 40, no. 2, 1984.

Takahashi, S. and K. Nakamura 'Peace research in postwar Japan' in The Japan Peace Research Group (ed.), *Peace Research in Japan 1978–79*, Tokyo, University of Tokyo Press, 1979.

Tamamoto, M., 'The Japan that wants to be liked: society and international participation' in D. Hunger and P. Blackburn (eds), *Japan's Emerging Global Role*, London, Lynne Rienner, 1993, pp. 37–54.

Thee, M., 'Militarism and militarization in contemporary international relations', *Bulletin of Peace Proposals*, vol. 8, no. 4, 1977.

Tredici R.D., *At Work in the Fields of the Bomb*, New York, Harper & Row, 1987.

Tuft, L., *Allergy Management in Clinical Practice*, Saint Louis, Mosby, 1973.

Ukita, H., 'A preliminary introduction to the peace education movement in Japan' in The Japan Peace Research Group (ed.), *Peace Research in Japan 1974–75*, Tokyo, University of Tokyo Press, 1976.

US Department of Defense, *Report on Allied Contributions to the Common Defense*, Washington DC, US Government Printing Office, 1987.

US Department of State, Division of Research for Far East, Office of Intelligence Research, *The Relationship of Japan to Nuclear Weapons and Warfare* (top secret), Washington DC, 1957, declassified.

Vagts, A., *A History of Militarism: Civilian and Military*, New York, Meridian Books, 1959 (revision of 1937 edition).

van Wolferen, K., 'Japan's non-revolution', *Foreign Affairs*, vol. 72, no. 4, 1993.

Walker, R.B.J., 'Contemporary militarism and the discourse of dissent' in R.B.J. Walker (ed.), *Culture, Ideology, and World Order*, Boulder, Westview Press, 1984, pp. 302–22.

Weber, M., *Economy and Society*, ed. Guenther Roth and Claus Wittich, New York, Bedminster Press, 1968.

Weinstein, M., *Japan's Postwar Defense Policy, 1947–1968*, New York, Columbia University Press, 1971.

Welfield, J., *An Empire in Eclipse: Japan in the Postwar American Alliance System*, London, Athlone, 1988.

Wheelwright, P., *Metaphor and Reality*, Bloomington, Indiana University Press, 1962.

Wilden, A., *System and Structure: Essays in Communication and Exchange*, 2nd edn, London, Tavistock, 1980.

Yoshida, S., *The Yoshida Memoirs*, Boston, Houghton Mifflin, 1962.

Unpublished doctoral dissertations; research, occasional and conference papers

Kesavan, K.V., *Japanese Defence Policy since 1976: Latest Trends*, Canberra Papers on Strategy and Defence, no. 31, The Strategic and Defence Studies Centre, Research School of Pacific Studies, Australia National University, 1984.

Kesavan, K.V., 'Japan's role in the resolution of the Cambodian conflict', paper presented at the International Peace Research Association, Kyōto Conference, 1992.

Sakamoto, Y., 'Research on militarization', research paper, United Nations University, Tokyo, 1984.

Tamamoto, M., 'Unwanted peace: Japanese intellectual thought in American occupied Japan, 1948–1952', Baltimore, Johns Hopkins University, PhD dissertation, 1988.

Thee, M., 'Militarism and militarization: their contemporary meaning', research paper, International Peace Research Institute, Oslo, 1984.

Umemoto, T., 'Arms and alliance in Japanese public opinion', PhD dissertation, Princeton, Princeton University, 1985.

Watanabe, O,. 'Nakasone Yasuhiro and post-war conservative politics: an historical interpretation', Oxford, Oxford University, Nissan Occasional Paper Series, no. 18, 1993.

Other (English)

Japanese Annual of International Law, vol. 8, 1964.

JAPANESE

Newspapers and selected serials

Akahata
Asahi Shinbun
Mainichi Shinbun
Nihon Keizai Shinbun
Yomiuri Shinbun

Ajia Jihō
Asahi Jyānaru
Chūō Kōron
Gekkan Yoron Chōsa
Gunjiminron
Gunshuku Mondai Shiryō
Heiwa Kenkyū
Hōgaku Seminā
Hōsō Kenkyū to Chōsa
Kenpō Undō
Sekai
Sekai Nippō

This is Yomiuri
Zenei

Books, book chapters, and articles

Akashi, Y., 'Kanbojia nikki', *Chūō Kōron*, March 1994.

Arase, Y. and S. Okayasu,'Kaku arerugī to anpo kōgai', *Sekai*, March 1968.

Arizawa, N., 'Jieitai PKO haken no ichinen', *Sekai*, November 1993.

Befu, H., *Ideorogī toshite no Nihon Bunkaron*, Tokyo, Shisō no Kagakusha, 1987.

Bōeicho Chōkan Kanbō Kōhōka, *Anpo, bōei mondai nado ni kansuru kokumin ishiki chōsa*, February 1983–April 1985.

Chūma, K., *Saigunbi no Seijigaku*, Tokyo, Chishikisha, 1985.

Chūma, K., *Gunjihi o Yomu*, Tokyo, Iwanami Shoten, 1986.

Dower, J.W., 'Nihon, kono hanseiki', *Sekai*, January 1995.

Ebata, K., 'AWACS to wa nani ka', *Sekai Shūhō*, 20 October 1992.

Fujī, H., *Jieitai ni Aka Shingō*, Tokyo, Orijinaru Shuppansha, 1990.

Fujio, M., 'Hōgen daijin ōi ni hoeru', *Bungei Shunjū*, October 1986.

Fujishima, U., 'PKO hōan (jieitai kaigai hahei hōan) 3 nen kōshite tsui ni "seiritsu"', *Gunshuku Mondai Shiryō*, August 1992.

Fukuyoshi, S., 'Nichibei kyōdō enshū ga Nihon o sekken suru', *Gunjiminron*, July 1987.

Furukawa, E., 'Higashi Ajia no chīki anpo de tōwaku ga zureru: Nishigawa to ASEAN', *Sekai Shūhō*, 30 August 1994.

Gotōda, M., *Naikaku Kanbōcho Chōkan*, Tokyo, Kōdansha, 1989.

Hanabusa, M. and Y. Murai, 'Enjo gyōsei o ronjiru', *Sekai*, December 1987.

Hatsuse, R., and Matsuo, M., 'Nihonjin no kaku ishiki kōzō – hibaku taiken oyobi seitō shiji', Hiroshima University, Institute for Peace Science, Kenkyū Hōkoku, no. 1. (undated)

Hattori, M., 'Nihon no kaku seisaku to konnichi no kadai', *Shakaishugi* (special edition), October 1994.

Heiwa Mondai Danwakai, 'Sensō to heiwa ni kansuru Nihon no kagakusha no seimei', *Sekai*, March 1949.

Heiwa Mondai Danwakai, 'Kōwa mondai ni tsuite no heiwa mondai danwakai seimei', *Sekai*, March 1950.

Heiwa Mondai Danwakai, 'Mitabi heiwa ni tsuite', *Sekai*, December 1950.

Heiwa Mondai Danwakai, *Sekai*, September 1962, appended statements.

Heiwa Mondai Danwakai, 'Futatabi anpo kaitei ni tsuite', *Sekai*, special issue, July 1985.

Heiwa Mondai Danwakai, *Sekai*, special issue, July 1985.

Hiroshima Heiwa Kyōiku Kenkyūjo (ed.), *Heiwa Kyōiku Kenkyū*, no. 2, 1975.

Honda, K., *Korosareru Gawa no Ronri*, Tokyo, Asahi Shinbunsha, 1982.

Honda, K., *Korosu Gawa no Ronri*, Tokyo, Asahi Shinbunsha, 1984.

Igarashi, T., 'Sengo Nihon "gaikō taisei" no keisei: tainichi kōwa no teiketsu to seitōseiji', *Kokka Gakkai Zashi*, vol. 97, nos. 7–8, 1984.

Inoguchi, T. and Iwai, T., *Zokugiin no Kenkyū: Jimintō Seiken o Gyūjiru Shuyakutachi*, Tokyo, Nihon Keizai Shinbunsha, 1987.

Ishida, T., *Hangenbaku: Nagasaki Hibakusha no Seikatsu*, Miraisha, Tokyo, 1973.

Ishida, T., *Nihon no Seiji to Kotoba* (2 volumes), Tokyo, University of Tokyo Press, 1989.

Ishida, T., 'Sengo Nihon no kokka ishiki' in Y. Sakamoto, *Sekai Seiji no Kōzō Hendō* (vol. 2), Tokyo, Iwanami Shoten, 1995, pp. 269–333.

Ishimaki, Y., 'Hajimatta arata na "kyōkasho kōgeki"', *Sekai*, November 1982.

Ishiyama, T., 'Hikaku Kōbe-ko no jikken' in Nishida Masaru (ed.), *Hikaku Jichitai Undō no Riron to Jissai*, Tokyo, Orijin Shuppan Senta, 1985.

Itō, H., 'Jieikan no hanashi o kīte', *Sekai*, March 1994.

Itō, K., '"1% waku" no rekishi to mondaiten: Sono yakuwari to kongo', *Seiron*, March 1987.

Itō, T., *Hiroshima, Nagasaki kara Sekai to Mirai e*, Tokyo, Keisō Shobō, 1985.

Iwanami Shoten Henshūbu (ed.), *Nihon no Ikikata to Heiwa no Mondai*, Tokyo, Iwanami Shoten, 1983.

Izumi, S., '"Gunji taikokuka" e no kōdō to sakubō: Yomiuri Shinbunsha no "kenpō kaisei shian" o hihan suru', *Zenei*, January 1995.

'Jieitai PKO haken no kōdō gaiyō to kongo no kadai' in *Bōei Nenkan* (1994 edition), Tokyo, Bōei Nenkan Hakkōkai, 1994, pp. 51–79.

Kagakusha Kyōtō Kaigi, 'Kagakusha Kyōtō Kaigi seimei', *Sekai*, Special Issue, July 1985.

Kaminishi, A., *Bōei Seisaku no Kenshō: 1% Waku*, Tokyo, Kadokawa, 1986.

'Kanbojia PKO o furikaette', *Sekai*, March 1994.

Kantō Shikyoku Seijiundō Kenkyūbukai, 'Jieitai gōken, hibusō chūritsu hōki o yurusanu Shakaitō kūgatsu rinji taikai', *Shakaishugi*, no. 370, September 1994.

Kasugai, K., 'Kaku arerugi no keisei katei' in Kokumin Kōza, *Nihon no Anzen Hoshō: Okinawa Fukki e no Michi*, Tokyo, Hara Shobō, 1968.

Katō, S., 'Kyōkasho ken'etsu no byōri', *Sekai*, October 1982.

Katsuno, N., *Kyōiku Kihon Hōsei to Kyōkasho Mondai*, Kyōtō, Hōritsu Bunka, 1982.

Kenmochi, K., *PKO Hahei: Bunseki to Shiryō*, Tokyo, Rokufu Shuppan, 1992.

Kihara, M., *Nihon no Gunji Sangyō*, Tokyo, Shin Nihon Shuppansha, 1994.

Kimura, S., 'Heiwa ni tsuite motto giron shiyō', *Sekai*, March 1994.

Koizumi, S., *Heiwaron* (collected works), vol. 15, Tokyo, Bungei Shunjū, 1976.

Komori, Y., *Kaku wa Mochikomareta ka*, Tokyo, Bungei Shunjū, 1982.

Kunihiro, M., 'Kotoba ga shisō o suiraku saseru', *Sekai*, April 1994.

Kunimasa, T. and Takabatake, M., '"Hahei Kokkai" no butaiura', *Sekai*, December 1990.

Kuno, O., *Heiwa no Ronri to Sensō no Ronri*, Tokyo, Iwanami Shoten, 1972.

Kurihara, A., 'Gengo no seijigaku – kiso ronri no tame no tankyū nōto', *Nihon Seiji Gakkai Nenpō 1976*, Tokyo, Iwanami Shoten, 1977, pp. 63–90.

Kurokawa, S., *Nihon no Bōeihi o Kangaeru: Gunkaku Rosen no Mekanizumu*, Tokyo, Daiyamondosha, 1983.

Kusuda, M., *Shuseki Hishokan: Satō Sōri to no 10 nen kan*, Tokyo, Bungei Shunjū, 1975.

Kyōdō Teigen, 'Heiwa kihonhō', *Sekai*, April 1993.

Kyōdō Teigen, 'Ajia–Taiheiyō chīki anpo o kōsō suru', *Sekai*, December 1994.

Kyōkasho Kentei Soshō o Shien suru Zenkoku Renraku kai Kyōkasho Kentei Seido Kentō Iinkai (Daihyō, Nagai Kenichi) (ed.), *Minna de Kangaeyo: Nihon no Kyōkasho Seido*, Kyōkasho Kentei Soshō o Shien suru Zenkoku

Renraku kai Kyōkasho Kentei Seido Kentō Iinkai Tokyo, 1982.

Maeda, T., 'Gunjihi "1%" waku toppa no kōzō', *Sekai*, November 1985, pp. 22–38.

Maeda, T., (ed.), *Jieitai o dō Suru ka*, Tokyo, Iwanami Shoten, 1992.

Maruyama, M., 'Hiroshima, Nagasaki, Bikini' in K. Okakura, M.Maruyama and H. Seki (eds), *Heiwa no Tankyū*, Tokyo, Jiji Tsūshin, 1975.

Miyata, M., *Kimitachi to Gendai*, Tokyo, Iwanami Shoten, 1980.

Miyazawa, K., and Y. Sakamoto, (interview), 'Ajia ni okeru Nihon no shinrō' in Sakamoto Yoshikazu, *Heiwa: Sono Genjitsu to Ninshiki*, Tokyo, Mainichi Shinbunsha, 1976.

Monbushō, *Atarashī Kenpō no Hanashi*, Tokyo, Monbushō, 1947.

Mori, H., 'Kenpō no heiwashugi o dō toriatsukau beki ka: kyūjō no kihansei o kenji suru koto no jūyōsei', *Zenei*, November 1994.

Murakami, S., *Yasukuni Jinja*, Tokyo, Iwanami Shoten, 1985.

Murata, H., 'Jieitai kaigai hahei to gikaisei minshushugi', *Kumamoto Hōgaku*, vol. 76, June 1993.

Muroyama, Y., *Nichibei Anpo Taisei* (two volumes), Tokyo, Yūhikaku, 1992.

Nagahara, K., 'Heiwa kyōiku to kyōkasho mondai' in *Shimin no Heiwa Hakusho '83*, Tokyo, Nippon Hyōronsha, 1983.

Nagasaki Hōsō, *Chūgoku Hōsō Hibakusha 30 Nen Genbaku to Heiwa ni kansuru Yoron Chōsa: Nagasaki, Hiroshima Ryōshimin no Hibaku Ishiki*, May 1975.

Nagoshi, K., *Kuremurin Himitsu Bunsho wa Kataru*, Tokyo, Chūō Kōronsha, 1994.

Nakamura, K., 'Soren kyōi ron kara no dakkyaku', *Sekai*, April 1985.

Nakanishi, T., (ed.), *Ajia do Kawaru ka? 90 nendai no Ajia no Sōgō Anzen Hoshō*, Tokyo, Nihon Keizai Shinbunsha, 1993.

Nihon Kyōshoku, Kumiaiin (ed.), *Kōtō Gakkō Kyōkasho no Kenkyū: 82 Nenpan Kokugo, Shakai no Hikaku Bunseki*, Tokyo, Nihon Kyōshoku Kumiai, 1981.

Nihon Kyōshokuin Kumiai (ed.), *Heiwa Kyōiku Undōshi: Nikyōsō Kyōken 30 nen no Ayumi*, Tokyo, Nihon Kyōshokuin Kumiai, 1982.

Nihon Seiji Gakkai (ed.), 'Gojūgo-nen taisei no keisei to hōkai', *Seijigaku Nenpō 1977*, Tokyo, Nihon Seiji Gakkai, 1979.

Nīhara, S., *Abakareta Nichibei Kaku Mitsuyaku*, Tokyo, Shin Nihon Shuppansha, 1987.

Nishi, O., 'Nihon no kokusai kōken o meguru giron: Ozawa chōsakai hōkoku nado ni tsuite', *Shin Bōei Ronshū*, vol. 20, no. 2, 1992.

Okauchi, K., 'Densan, tanrō sōgi to saigunbi', *Sekai*, February 1953.

Ōnishi, H., 'Nihon no hankaku undō: 1982 nen zenhan no SSDII kokumin undō suishin renraku kaigi no undō o chūshin ni jo', *Hōgaku* (Tōhoku University), vol. 49, no. 2, June 1985.

Ōnishi, H., 'Nihon no hankaku undō: 1982 nen zenhan no SSDII kokumin undō suishin renraku kaigi no undō o chūshin ni ge', *Hōgaku* (Tōhoku University), vol. 49, no. 3, August 1985.

Rubinstein, G., 'Nihon wa kōgeki no ryōku o takamete iru ka', *Sekai*, May 1994.

Ryokufū Shuppan (ed.), *Kanbojia PKO: Bunseki to Shiryō*, Tokyo, Ryokufū Shuppan, 1992.

Sakai, A., 'Gunji sangyō no tenkan', *Sekai*, February 1986.

Sakai, A., 'Nihon no gunjihi', *Shōgaku Ronshū*, vol. 31, no. 6, 1987.

Sakamoto, Y., 'Heiwashugi no gyakusetsu to kōsō', *Sekai*, July 1994.

Sasaki, Y., *Kaigai o Wataru Jieitai: PKO Rippō to Seiji Kenryoku*, Tokyo, Iwanami Shoten, 1992.

Satō, S., '"Sengo ishiki" no dasei o tatsu aki', *Chūō Kōron*, November 1990.

Satō, S., 'Reisengo no Ajia Taiheiyō ni okeru Nichibei dōmei', *Kokusai Mondai*, no. 401, August 1993.

Sekai Henshūbu, *Tomahōku to wa*, Tokyo, Iwanami Shoten, 1984.

Sekai Henshūbu, *Gunji Taikoku Nippon*, Tokyo, Iwanami Shoten, 1987.

Seki, H., 'Heiwa no seijigaku' in Nihon Seiji Gakkai (ed.), Nenpō Seijigaku, *Kōdōron igo no Seijigaku*, Tokyo, Iwanami Shoten, 1977.

Shida, M., 'Kaigai hōjin no kyūshutsu wa minkanki de', *Sekai*, May 1994.

Shimizu, I., *Nippon yo Kokka tare, Kaku no Sentaku*, Tokyo, Bungei Shunjū, 1980.

Shindō, E., *Gendai Funsō no Kōzō: Hikyoku Moderu no Kōchiku no tame ni*, Tokyo, Iwanami Shoten, 1987.

Shindō, E., 'Gaikō no honryō: ima nani o nasubeki ka', *Sekai*, December 1987.

Sodei, R., 'Genbaku tōka no rekishi to seiji', *Sekai*, February 1995.

Takahashi, S. and Y. Hoshino (ed. supervisors), *Kyōkasho ga Nerawarete iru: Futatabi Kuru ka Kokutaika no Jidai*, Tokyo, Ayumi Shuppan, 1981.

Takahashi, S., and K. Nakamura, 'Sengo Nihon no heiwaron: hitotsu no isō no bunseki', *Sekai*, June 1978.

Takashima, N., *80 Nendai no Kyōkasho Mondai*, Tokyo, Shin Nihon Shuppansha, 1984.

Takesada, H., 'Mada "kaku" no kirifuda o tebasanai Kita Chōsen', *Sekai Shūhō*, 15 November 1994.

Tsurumi, S., (ed.) *Heiwa no Shisō*, Sengo Nihon Shisō Taikei, vol. 4, Tokyo, Chikuma Shobō, 1968.

UNESCO statement, 'Heiwa no tame ni shakai kagakusha wa kaku uttaeru', *Sekai*, January 1949, July 1985, special issue.

Washimi, T., *Nihon no Gunjihi*, Tokyo, Gakushū no Tomosha, 1982.

Watanabe, O., *Nihon Koku Kenpō 'Kaiseishi'*, Tokyo, Nippon Hyōronsha, 1987.

Watanabe, O., '90 nendai Nihon kokka to tennōsei', *Bunka Hyōron*, special issue, October 1990.

Watanabe, Y., *Gendai Nihon Shakai to Minshushugi*, Tokyo, Iwanami Shoten, 1982.

Yamamoto, M., *Fumō no Gensetsu: Kokkai Tōben no naka no Nichibei Kankei*, Tokyo, Japan Times, 1992.

Yamashita, M., S. Takai and S. Iwata, *TMD Senīki Dandō Misairu Bōei*, Tokyo, TBS Britannica, 1994.

Yano, T., 'Towareteiru no wa Nihon no kokka imēji', *Chūō Kōron*, October 1982.

Yazaki, S. (interview), 'Bōei kaikaku wa jidai no yōsei', *Kokubō*, January 1987.

Yoshiike, K., 'Kakusareta "bōeihi": gonendo futan seido no shikumi', *Shimin no Heiwa Hakusho*, Tokyo, Nippon Hyōronsha, 1983.

Diet proceedings

Dai 22 bu Okinawa Mondai nado ni kansuru Tokubetsu Īinkai
Kaigiroku Dai Ichi Gō, December, 1967
Shūgiin Kaigiroku San Gō, January 1983
Yosan Īinkai Kaigiroku Dai San Gō, February 1983

Annuals

Asahi Nenkan
Bōei Handobukku
Bōei Hakusho
Bōei Nenkan
Kyōkasho Repōtō
Mainichi Nenkan
Nihon Seijigaku Nenpō
Yomiuri Nenkan
Yoron Chōsa Nenkan

Reference books

Imidasu, Tokyo, Shūeisha, 1994.
Seijigaku Jiten, Tokyo, Heibonsha, 1954.
Mori, K. (ed.) *Tetsugaku Jiten*, Tokyo, Aoki Shoten, 1971
Heibonsha (ed.) *Tetsugaku Jiten*, Tokyo, Heibonsha, 1971

Index